ALLEN GUTTMANN

A WHOLE NEW BALL GAME

AN INTERPRETATION OF AMERICAN SPORTS

The University of North Carolina Press
Chapel Hill & London

Manufactured in the United States of America

Library of Congress Cataloging-in-Publication Data

Guttmann, Allen.
A whole new ball game: an interpretation of American sports /
Allen Guttmann.
p. cm.
Bibliography: p.
Includes index.
ISBN 0-8078-1786-4
1. Sports—United States—History. 2. Sports—Social aspects—
United States. I. Title.
GV583.G87 1988 87-26131
796'.0973—dc19 CIP

The paper in this book meets the guidelines
for permanence and durability of the
Committee on Production Guidelines for
Book Longevity of the Council on Library Resources.
92 91 90 89 88 5 4 3 2 1

An earlier version of several paragraphs of Chapter 5 appeared in the *Yale Review* (Summer 1985). Chapter 8 is extensively revised from "The Tiger Devours the Literary Magazine," in *The Governance of Intercollegiate Athletics*, edited by James Frey, pp. 70–79 (Champaign, Ill.: Leisure Press, 1982).

A Whole New Ball Game

To Milton and His Friends

Contents

Contents

Preface

Nearly as certain as death and taxes, and more agreeable, is the fact that almost every American has participated in sports at some level, talked about sports, attended sports events, and followed sports in the daily press and the electronic media. Pollsters have learned that the vast majority of Americans, women as well as men, are fans. Everyone is more or less an expert. On the other hand, hardly anyone bothers to consult the books, articles, and scholarly papers produced by the historians, anthropologists, sociologists, and psychologists who have staked out "sports studies" as their field of specialization. I hope to alter, however slightly, this great imbalance between popular fascination and critical investigation. I hope to bridge the gap between those who simply care about sports and those who care about them in a disciplined, reflective way.

I have *not* written a comprehensive history of American sports. Such histories exist and some of them are admirable works of acumen and diligence. I have not attempted to do what I have done in previous work, i.e., to offer a theoretical statement about the nature of modern sports. The present study is an *interpretation*, a selective history of American sports which seeks to set sports within a larger social framework and, simultaneously, to use sports for what they reveal about the larger culture. As the English historian Joseph Strutt realized nearly two centuries ago, the relative freedom of the sphere of sports enables us to see what men and women truly value when they are least constrained by circumstance:

> In order to form a just estimation of the character of any particular people, it is absolutely necessary to investigate the Sports and Pastimes most generally prevalent among them. War, policy [politics], and other contingent circumstances, may effectually place men, at different times, in different points of view, but, when we follow them into their retirements, where no disguise is necessary, we are most likely to see them in their true state, and may best judge of their natural dispositions.[1]

While I am reasonably confident that specialists in sports studies will find this study something more than a textbook restatement of what is already widely known, I have written primarily for nonspecialists, for historians and sociologists who are ready to admit that sports are an important part of popular culture and, as such, an appropriate matter for social history. I have also cherished the notion that "common readers" still exist, men and women impelled to read not by the threats of their teachers nor by the imperatives of their profession but simply because they are curious about human behavior.

Acknowledgments are rather a problem. Since I began to specialize in sports studies, some fifteen years ago, scores of scholars have generously helped me in all the many ways that scholars help each other, but I find it hard to single out a group of them to thank for help with this particular project. I offer my collective gratitude. And I wish specifically to thank President Peter Pouncey and Dean Richard Fink of Amherst College for moral and financial support, Alan Trachtenberg and Iris Tillman Hill for detailed criticisms of the manuscript, and Doris Bargen for fifteen years of constant encouragement and emotional support.

ONE

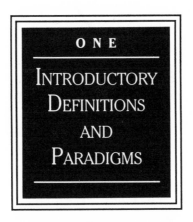

Introductory Definitions and Paradigms

A German specialist exasperated by the terminological confusion that beclouds the field of sports studies recently published a short book entitled *What Is Sport Anyway?* (1983). Much as one might prefer simply to "get on with it," ignoring the problem of definition, Egon Steinkamp's question is a necessary one. Despite the hundreds of definitions that have been suggested, there is no consensus on terminology.

One response to the problem of definition, a response somewhat different from Steinkamp's, begins with the attempt to sort out such key terms as *play*, *games*, *contests*, and *sports*. Sports can reasonably be defined as a category of *play* to the degree that they are done for their own sake and not for some utilitarian purpose. One becomes involved in a sport—in theory—not for extrinsic rewards (parental approval, academic credit, cardiovascular fitness, or take-home pay) but for the intrinsic pleasures of the activity. More precisely, sports must be classified as *games* because sports are regulated, rather than spontaneous play. One intrinsic pleasure of sports activity is that it occurs as all games do within a set of rules that simultaneously enable and constrain. It may seem quirky to refer to gymnastic meets and track-and-field events as games, but we do, after all, speak of the Olympic Games, ancient and modern. This much linguistic latitude is not too much to ask.

Although many games, like Pig Latin and leapfrog, are played noncompetitively, other games, such as Scrabble and rugby, are *contests* with winners and losers. The obsessive desire to win at all costs, regardless of the rules of the game, can endanger and destroy the spirit of cooperative competition, but the satisfactions of victory and the consolations of defeat are not in themselves extraneous to sports contests as autotelic activities; they are a legitimate part of the process. Finally, if one distinguishes between play and utilitarian effort, between games and spontaneous play, and between contests and noncompetitive games, a fourth distinction follows. The differences between Scrabble and rugby are many, but the most relevant for our purpose is clearly that rugby requires much more physical skill. This physical component is what distinguishes some contests as *sports*. There is no a priori way to decide how much of a physical component is necessary. Nonetheless, the animal joy of human movement and the opportunity to test one's physical skills against another person's are certainly among any sport's intrinsic pleasures.

This conception of the relationships among play, games, contests, and sports can be expressed in the form of a simple diagram.

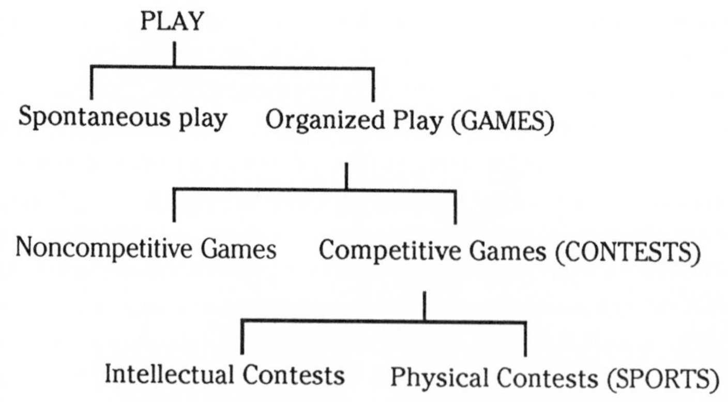

PLAY, GAMES, CONTESTS, SPORTS

3

Introductory Definitions and Paradigms

All definitions of sports are somewhat arbitrary because sports are aspects of culture. Some scholars, influenced by a remark in Ludwig Wittgenstein's *Philosophical Investigations*, opt for a more nominalistic approach that conceptualizes sports as a family of activities too loosely related for precise definition. But Wittgenstein never had to make sense of the jumble of miscellaneous activities that someone somewhere sometime has referred to as sports. As a practical matter, it seems reasonable to adopt a paradigmatic definition that enables the scholar to distinguish clearly between sports (i.e., autotelic physical contests) and all those other activities that can be gathered together under the ample rubric "Pastimes and Recreations."

Most scholars agree that a paradigmatic definition is useful and that it makes sense to consider sports as rule-bound autotelic activities. The most common skirmishes take place around the stipulation that all sports are, by definition, contests. Philosophers such as Egon Steinkamp, anthropologists such as Brian Sutton-Smith, and sociologists such as John Loy have all contributed greatly to the development of sports studies without this emphasis on the distinction between competitive and noncompetitive games. Steinkamp argues, for instance, that sports are frequently but not invariably characterized by competition. Popular speech bears him out: recreational cycling, jogging, hiking, and swimming are commonly referred to as sports. The counterargument to such expansiveness is pragmatic: the best definition of sports is the one that enables the definer to reap the greatest harvest of insights. I have found it useful to stipulate competition as a necessary element in my definition.

Whether or not it is true in all cultures, it is certainly true that in ours there is a powerful tendency to transform noncompetitive games into contests. The mild excitements of solitaire are widely preferred to the insipid pastime of randomly arraying cards on a table. In traditional Indonesian culture, antagonisms tend to be concealed and competition tends to be downplayed; when young men are engaged in a soccer game, care is taken that the contest end in a tie. In American culture, however, the gently noncompetitive game of frisbee, invented in 1948 by Walter Frederick Morrison, quickly led to "Ultimate Frisbee" and the Rose Bowl World Frisbee Championships of 1974.

4

A Whole New Ball Game

The agonistic interaction of a contest seems to mobilize Americans' energies beyond what is possible in noncompetitive situations. Provided that the situation is not excessively stressful, subjects in psychological experiments do better when the task to be performed is made into a contest. Beyond that, psychologists discovered, nearly a century ago, that the physical presence of a human competitor stimulated subjects to higher levels of achievement than they were able to attain when measured only by a stopwatch or a speedometer. If the exercise and development of physical skills and the attainment of a sense of mastery over one's own body are among the intrinsic pleasures associated with sports, which seems to be the case, then it follows that the challenge of the contest enhances these skills and heightens this sense of mastery. The quest for the highest possible level of performance requires competition. In other words, we need each other as opponents if we hope to achieve what the philosopher Paul Weiss refers to as "the excellence of the body."

This need is integrally related to the concept of fair play. The relationship requires a word of clarification. Where there is no contest, the concept of fair play is meaningless. Civility and a host of other virtues may be called upon when people hike or jog together, but fair play is not involved. Fair play involves more than simply abiding by the rules of the game; it also requires that participants seek out opponents who can challenge them to rise to their highest level of achievement. Athletes who cheat and otherwise play unfairly deprive themselves of the opportunity to excel in reality rather than in appearance. Fair play also means that athletes experience more pleasure from a well-played narrow loss than from a lop-sided triumph over an inferior opponent. For this reason, many observers felt that the gold medals won at the boycott-diminished Olympic Games of 1980 and 1984 were tarnished by the absence of many of the strongest challengers. Easy victory is of little value.

Admittedly, this paradigmatic conception of sports and this interpretation of fair play utilize "ideal types" of the sort that Max Weber sought to justify in *Economy and Society*. In reality, people become involved in sports for prestige, economic advantage, course credit, and therapy as well as simply for the intrinsic pleasure of the physical contest. It is impossible to say whether players in the National Football League still experience satisfactions intrinsic to the game, or whether they are motivated entirely by the pursuit of fame and fortune. In reality, athletes do not always search for worthy opponents, and fair play is jeopardized at all levels, from Little League to the Olympics, by a win-at-all-costs attitude. Nonetheless, the impossibility of wholly unambiguous empirical determinations is not a valid argument against an "ideal-type" definition. Conceptual clarity, after all, is what enables us to assess the differences between the ideal and the actual. Weber stated his methodological convictions defiantly: "The more precisely and unambiguously constructed the ideal types are, indeed, the more distant from the real world [je welt*fremder*], the better they fulfill their terminological and classificatory as well as their heuristic functions." In further support of the usefulness of the "ideal-type" approach, one might invoke the example of the natural sciences. Nature has neither prime numbers nor perfect circles, but physicists and engineers use mathematics to overcome Earth's gravity and land men on the moon.[1]

The intent of my considerably more mundane effort has been to apply my paradigm historically in order to analyze the nature of modern sports, specifically in American variants that are fundamentally different from primitive, ancient, medieval, and Renaissance sports. For the study of European and American sports, a historical perspective reveals differences more important than those detected by a synchronic cross-cultural approach. For instance, American baseball is different from cricket and very different from soccer, but these three games are all quite similar when compared to the popular Afghan game of *buzkashi*, which traditionally consisted of hundreds of horsemen seeking to make off with the headless carcass of a goat. When the formal-structural properties of modern sports are contrasted with those of previous ages, one discovers certain characteristics of modern sports:

secularism: despite their tendency to become ritualized and to arouse the deepest passions, modern sports are not related—as primitive and ancient sports were—to some transcendent realm of the sacred;

equality: modern sports require, at least in theory, that everyone be admitted to the game on the basis of his or her personal ability and that the rules be the same for all contestants;

bureaucratization: local, regional, national, and international bureaucracies now administer every level of modern sports from the Little Leagues to the Olympic Games;

specialization: many modern sports (rugby, soccer, and American football) have evolved from earlier, less differentiated games, and many (baseball, cricket, and football) have a gamut of specialized roles and playing positions;

rationalization: the rules of modern sports are constantly scrutinized and frequently revised from a means-ends point of view; athletes train scientifically, employ technologically advanced equipment, and strive for the most efficient use of their skills;

quantification: in modern sports, as in almost every other aspect of our lives, we live in a world of numbers;

the obsession with records: the unsurpassed quantified achievement, which is what we mean by "record" in this uniquely modern usage, is a constant challenge to all who hope to surpass it.

In response to this selection of characteristics, one might reasonably ask, What of professionalization and commercialization? If one defines the first concept by the commitment of time and energy, rather than by the receipt of the income which makes possible the commitment of such time and energy, then professionalization can best be understood as an aspect of specialization. In this sense of the concept, many "student-athletes" in the United States and most members of the Soviet Union's sports elite are professionals, i.e., men and women specializing in sports achievements. Commercialization is absent from my list of characteristics because modern sports have been fully institutionalized in societies where markets are narrowly circumscribed as well as in societies where markets are thought to be divinely ordained. Where capitalism dominates the economic sphere, which is certainly the case in the United States, modern sports tend to be commercialized; where capitalism has been supplanted, more or less, by a state-controlled economic system, the commercialization of sports has been minimized (but not entirely eliminated; consider the Soviet Union's sale of television rights to the 1980 Olympic Games).

In considering this proposed set of characteristics, one must bear in mind that they are not a random collection. They interact systematically. One might even invent a (false) teleology and maintain that, in order to achieve records, the first six characteristics are necessary preconditions. The modern quest for records is certainly unthinkable without quantification. The 3:30 mile may well be a will o' the wisp, but the unclocked 3:30 mile is an impossibility. It is also impossible, after a certain point reached by the untrained body, to set records without specialization and rationalization (which include scientific facilities, equipment, and training). But specialization and rationalization usually imply bureaucratic organization, without which world championships cannot be staged nor rules established nor equipment standardized nor records duly certified. The quest for records also assumes certain kinds of equality. There must be equality within the rules of the game. In fact, equality can only be approximated. For instance, when baseball's regular season was lengthened from 154 to 162 games, Roger Maris hit more home runs in a single season than Babe Ruth had. Whether or not he broke the Babe's record is debatable. If we add another ten or twenty games, someone is sure to outslug Maris and be credited with another dubious record. There must also be—in the "ideal type" of modern sports—equal opportunity to enter the contest. If the fastest runners or swimmers are barred from competition because of religion, nationality, occupation, or skin color, then the alleged record is devalued, if not rendered farcical. Who wants to jump farther than any other white married Episcopalian lawyer?

Finally, the very notion of a record is probably more compatible with the standards of a secular society than with one closely oriented to the transcendent realm of the sacred.

> This is a difficult notion to grasp and perhaps even an unpalatable one, but it may be that the dynamics of modern athletic achievement commence with the secularization of society. When qualitative distinctions fade and lose their force, we turn to quantitative ones. When we can no longer distin-

> guish the sacred from the profane or even the good from the bad, we content ourselves with minute discriminations between the batting averages of the .308 hitter and .307 hitter. Once the gods have vanished from Mount Olympus or from Dante's Paradise, we can no longer run to appease them or to save our souls, but we can set a new record. It is a uniquely modern form of immortality.[2]

To these speculations should be added the observation that the seven above-mentioned traits refer to logical relationships and not to a chronological sequence. No one of these characteristics is unique to the modern world; taken together, however, they have clearly distinguished modern sports from those of the past. The history of American sports can be conceptualized as the transition from premodern to modern forms. Whether the abuses of the present system and the efforts to avoid them presage a further transition to postmodern sports is a question that must be addressed.

Modernization theories have fallen into disfavor because of their allegedly simplistic assumptions about the inevitability, ubiquity, and desirability of modernization. Michel Foucault has been especially critical of such assumptions in his many influential studies of historical discontinuity. Since I remain committed to modernization as a heuristic concept, I feel obliged to offer clarifications and caveats. The history of nineteenth-century and early twentieth-century sociology is, to a remarkable degree, the history of successive attempts to describe sociocultural differences across time and space. The contrast between medieval rule by divine right and modern legitimation by appeals to popular sovereignty is, like the contrast between the kinship systems of preliterate tribes and the bureaucratic organization of the modern corporation, too immense to be ignored or dismissed with pieties about "the family of man." Various terms have been used to analyze these contrasts. Karl Marx wrote of feudalism and capitalism, Ferdinand Toennies of community and society, Emile Durkheim of mechanical and organic solidarity, Max Weber of traditional and modern society, and Talcott Parsons of particularistic and universalistic forms of social organization. Their efforts were, of course, only the most famous conceptualizations (and they were, obviously, far more subtle and complex than my reduction to single phrases can possibly imply). In more recent years, scholars have employed an array of more or less sophisticated empirical measurements to plot the processes that have transformed traditional communities into modern societies. For the American scene generally, Richard D. Brown's *Modernization* (1976) is an exemplary essay. For American sports, specifically, Melvin L. Adelman's *A Sporting Time: New York City and the Rise of Modern Athletics, 1820–1870* (1986) can be taken as a model.

Although I cannot imagine a more useful approach to the fundamental transformation that every historian recognizes, the paradigm of modernization has undeniable drawbacks. It is too abstract to account for every detail in history's vast panorama. It can easily be misinterpreted to mean that the observed changes occurred as part of some uniform and inevitable process that must of necessity and by some preordained schedule transform each and every aspect of each and every society in precisely the same way. Most importantly, modernization theory can be misused as a facile instrument of ethical judgment—as if modern ways were somehow a *moral* as well as a technological advance beyond traditional customs. Brown has wisely cautioned against this arrogant assumption:

> As an organizing theme "modernization" bears some resemblance to the old idea of progress as the major process in Western society. It also resembles the dialectical materialism of Marx, and from a historiographical perspective it may indeed be descended from both interpretations. But unlike its predecessors, the idea of modernization does not imply inevitability or even necessarily improvement. Technical development, complexity, specialization, and rationality do not necessarily generate a better, more just, more humane, or more satisfactory society.[3]

While nineteenth-century observers may have felt optimism about the future, those of us who have experienced the twentieth century have reason to ponder the adverse effects as well as the benefits of modernization. Toxic wastes and nuclear catastrophes are as much a part of modernity as are laser surgery and telecommunications.

Finally, if such qualifications and caveats seem an inadequate response to the criticisms of modernization theory as a descriptive framework, one may ask, Is there a better way to conceptualize the differences between New York and New Guinea? Is there a better way, in the domain of sports, to understand the contrast between the medieval free-for-all known as folk-football and the globally televised spectacle of the World Cup? As Peter N. Stearns remarks in a perceptive discussion of the historiographical advantages and disadvantages of the concept of modernization, "There is more sense of dissatisfaction with the approach than coherent comment or presentation of alternatives."[4] Stearns concludes that some version of the concept is inescapable.

If one accepts this conclusion, as I do, one can scarcely avoid a comment on the relationship of modernization theory to what Stearns refers to as "the related but less flexible causal framework of Marxism."[5] Since Marx and Engels conceptualized the transition from feudalism to capitalism as an inevitable stage in human progress, Marxism has been committed to its own notion of modernization theory. The quarrel between Marxists and non-Marxists is over the attempt to explain the factors involved in a process that everyone seems to recognize. The "dialectical materialism" of the Marxist tradition differs importantly from the "idealism" of Max Weber in that Marx and Engels emphasized the mode of material production, while Weber's multivolume historical investigation of the sociology of religion sought to demonstrate that the religions of mankind have influenced economic behavior even as they have themselves been influenced by economic institutions. Weber's other great work, *Economy and Society*, can be read as an argument for the realm of politics as something other than Marxist "superstructure." Ideas matter.

Ideas certainly matter in the history of sports, a domain where men and women are relatively free from the constraints of material necessity. The constellation of ideas that Alfred North Whitehead referred to as the scientific revolution of the seventeenth century influenced the formal-structural characteristics of modern sports. It is, for instance, difficult to imagine the pervasive quantification of modern sports apart from the scientific-technological mania for numerical measurement. Whether this scientific influence was more or less important than capitalism, Marxism's familiar candidate for causal determination, has been and doubtless will continue to be the occasion for heated debate among sports historians and sociologists. While I do not conceive of this present study as a direct contribution to that debate, I do hope to demonstrate that a modernization theory inspired by Weber can successfully come to terms with the particularities of sports history and can also do justice to the historical moment—to the relations of production as well as to the commitments of religious faith. I have attempted here to write social as well as cultural history and to emphasize the historical circumstances and contexts within which instances of premodern, modern, and postmodern sports have occurred. I have sought to be attentive to the interactions of such sociologically relevant factors as ideology, class, ethnicity, race, and gender as they have impeded, furthered, modified, and distorted American sports. At the same time, I have clung to my paradigm in an effort to avoid the quagmire of unstructured data into which more than one unwary sports historian has tumbled.

Historiography is inevitably a process of selection. Interpretation begins with the historian's exclusions and inclusions. Since I have not endeavored to produce a "complete" or even a comprehensive history of American sports, I feel obliged to indicate my reasons for writing the twelve chapters that follow.

A brief discussion of pre-Columbian sports is useful because the sports of the American Indians were most emphatically *not* modern. In fact, there is reason to ask if they were sports at all, in the sense of my heuristic paradigm. The Puritans appear next, not because they determined the subsequent contours of American history (although Sacvan Bercovitch and numerous other historians apparently believe that they did), but because their ambivalence about sports provides some interesting insights into what Perry Miller grandly referred to as "the Puritan mind." The chapter on the South discusses the obsessions that prevented the "sportsmen" of the region, aristocrats as well as backwoodsmen, from contributing very much to the emergence of modern sports. The fifth and sixth chapters focus on two popular sports: baseball, whose fascination depended on the paradoxical combination of premodern and modern characteristics; and basketball, the archetypical modern sport. In both chapters I am concerned not only with the development of the typically modern but also with the social forces and demographic factors that have distorted and degraded both games. The next two chapters form another pair in that they concern the controversial intrusion of modern sports into the domain of childhood and the sphere of higher education. Chapters 9 and 10 examine the gradual entry of blacks and women into the world of modern sports and the ethical questions raised by this belated inclusion of previously excluded groups. Chapter 11 analyzes the ironic destruction of the human body by activities that allegedly contribute to its perfection. Since many Americans have been horrified by the reality of modern sport, it is useful to devote a chapter to their search for alternatives distant in time and space. The last chapter offers some predictions about the future course of American sports.

Throughout the study, I have kept my footnotes to a minimum. More detailed information on my sources appears in the bibliographical essay.

And now it is indeed time to "get on with it."

TWO

Pre-Columbian Sports

Why Indian Sports?

Does a consideration of pre-Columbian sports properly fall within the scope of a book on American sports? I have obviously answered the question affirmatively, but a few words of justification are called for. Pre-Columbian cultures existed in the geographical area now known as the United States, and representatives of these cultures still survive on lands reserved for them. The Europeans and Africans who came or were brought to the New World in the sixteenth and seventeenth centuries entered into a still unfinished cultural interaction with the peoples whom they "discovered." The predominantly European culture of the colonists has developed into a new mix of European, African, Asian, and "native American" characteristics. The game of lacrosse is the best-known example from the realm of sports. Played in many parts of North America by many different tribes, it was borrowed by Europeans and eventually adapted into a modern sport.

The survival of aspects of pre-Columbian cultures in relative isolation or as a part of modern American culture is reason enough to study their sports in the present context. A further justification is that the contrast between pre-Columbian and modern American sports is, in itself, an important anthropological lesson. To consider, however briefly, the stickball game of the Mississippi Choctaws and the "relay race" of the Jicarilla Apaches is to realize that *Homo ludens* wears many different guises.

Inclusion of pre-Columbian sports raises the problem of nomenclature. The term "pre-Columbian" is not only awkward but also misleading—most of our knowledge of pre-Columbian culture consists of inferences from post-Columbian evidence. Some scholars and many polemicists opt for the term "native American" in order to avoid using the term "Indian," which they consider a Eurocentric misnomer. While references to "native Americans" do remind the reader that someone was here to welcome, instruct, learn from, resist, and be killed by the European latecomers, I prefer the less polemical conventional term "Indian." After all, the newer usage does *not* eliminate the problem of naming from a European point of view. The best reason to stay with older usage is that the term "Indian" need not imply any ethical judgment whatsoever on the course of American history.

The Sacred and the Secular

Modern sports are secular. In their most intensely ritualized organizational form, the Olympic Games, they take on some of the attributes of a secular religion, but modern sports are not ordinarily perceived by athletes or by spectators as religious ceremonies in the obvious ways that a Roman Catholic mass or an African Methodist Episcopal Zionist funeral are. No matter how important they seem to their players and spectators, modern sports do not provide encounters with what theologians refer to as "the numinous."

The games played by adult members of the Indian tribes, however, were normally occasions for interaction with the mysterious realm of the sacred. The qualifications ("adult," "normally") are essential. In every known culture children run races, throw stones, wrestle, and play games, some of which clearly prepare them for culturally approved male and female roles, others of which can better be understood as play for the sake of play. While many anthropologists have interpreted children's games, including the play of Indian children, I propose to focus instead on adult games as instances of sacred play. As Stewart Culin wrote in the introduction to his huge ethnographical compendium, *Games of the North American Indians* (1907), "Children have a variety of . . . amusements, such as top spinning, mimic fights, and similar imitative sports, but the games first described are played only by men and women, or youths and maidens, not by children, and usually at fixed seasons as the accompaniment of certain festivals or religious rites." Such games, "played ceremonially," were part and parcel of fertility ritual, the exorcism of demons, and other aspects of what Culin ethnocentrically thought of as "primitive" religion. Oddly, Culin seemed to forget in his text what he asserted in his introduction. In his 800-page account of these various games he assiduously classified Indian games into "games of chance" and "games of dexterity" (including sports), concluding with the observation that these games "are either instruments of rites or have descended from ceremonial observations of a religious character." Culin seldom discussed the religious elements which he correctly identified as integral parts of Indian sports.[1]

Culin was not the first or the last to describe the spirited sports of the Indian tribes as if they were on the same ontological level as a game of baseball. Robert Gerald Glassford's *Application of a Theory of Games to the Transitional Eskimo Culture* (1976) includes an acknowledgment of the fact that traditional Eskimo games were a part of religious ritual. Glassford's interests, like Culin's, are classificatory. Drawing upon the influential taxonomies of John M. Roberts and Roger Caillois, he has designed a two-by-two matrix of games with specified and unspecified goals and strategies. Glassford has a great deal to say about gender roles and generational differences, but he is not especially interested in the religious significance of traditional games.

Another important anthropologist of play, Alyce Cheska, has also drawn upon the classificatory schemes of Roberts and Caillois. In an article entitled "Native American Games as Strategies of Societal Maintenance," she notes that Indian games sometimes functioned as vehicles for divination, but she—like Glassford—is more concerned with such matters as sex-role differentiation and group identity.[2]

Fortunately for those of us who seek answers to other questions, some anthropologists have been fascinated by the religious element in Indian games. In an essay entitled "Meteorological Play-Forms of the Eastern Woodlands," Michael A. Salter analyzes lacrosse as part of the Iroquois Thunder Ceremony and Arkansas shinny as a ritual contest between the Earth People and the Sky People. In a subsequent essay entitled "Play in Ritual," he concludes that "virtually every social game enjoyed by the eastern natives was, on one occasion or another, employed for ritualistic purposes."[3]

For my present purposes, the most intriguing examples of premodern sports are not the "meteorological play-forms" but the stickball game of the Southeastern tribes and the Jicarilla Apache "relay race." Stickball was the most widely dispersed and popular game of the entire Southeast. The earliest reference to the game by a European was probably that of Pierre François Charlevoix, who observed the Creek version in 1721. Stickball seems to have changed little between that date and the 1830s, when George Catlin, the painter and amateur ethnographer, visited the area and described the game in his *Letters and Notes on the Manners, Customs, and Conditions of the North American Indians* (1844). The Indians' ability to preserve their game through a century of cultural interaction with Europeans suggests that the game was very resistant to change. In all probability, Charlevoix witnessed a ceremony that was already hundreds if not thousands of years old.

Resembling modern lacrosse, stickball was played with a small ball carried in a webbed stick and then thrown at a goal. Villages were matched against each other; there were also intracommunal contests. Although Indian women frequently had their own ball games, ceremonial stickball was played by men only. Each player submitted to strict dietary prohibitions which were, of course, based on religious rather than biomechanical considerations. James Mooney's essay, "The Cherokee Ball Play," which originally appeared in 1890 in *American Anthropologist*, provides the details. Mooney reported that the Cherokee participant "must not eat the flesh of a rabbit . . . because the rabbit is a timid animal, easily alarmed and liable to lose its wits when pursued by the hunter. Hence the player must abstain from it, lest he too should become disconcerted and lose courage in the game. He must also avoid the meat of the frog . . . because the frog's bones are brittle and easily broken. . . ."[4] The taboo usually lasted for twenty-eight days prior to the game because four and seven were sacred numbers. The most important taboo was against sexual intercourse. Thirty days of abstinence preceded the game. Indeed, men whose wives were pregnant were not allowed to take part in the Cherokee version of stickball.

The players spent the night before the game sequestered in a sacred precinct under the supervision of medicine men (now often referred to as shamans) who carefully prepared them for the ritual encounter. Of the Choctaw medicine men, George Catlin wrote that they were "seated at the point where the ball was to be started." While the players danced and "joined in chaunts to the Great Spirit," the medicine men smoked pipes as a form of prayer. Kendall Blanchard, whose *Mississippi Choctaws at Play* (1981) is our best modern source, notes that these "ritual experts . . . administered special medicine to the players, treated equipment, manipulated weather conditions for the day of the planned event, and appealed to the supernatural world for assistance. . . ." The night before the game, the bodies of the players were painted and appropriately adorned for appearance before the Great Spirit. In Catlin's words, "In every ball-play of these people, it is a rule . . . that no man shall wear moccasins on his feet, or any other dress than his breechcloth around his waist, with a beautiful bead belt, and a 'tail' made of white horsehair or quills, and 'mane' on the neck, of horsehair dyed of various colours." Catlin's portrait of Tullock-chish-ko ("He Who Drinks the Juice of the Stone") shows him in this attire. The dance, repeated through the night at half-hour intervals, was "one of the most picturesque scenes imaginable." Appropriately, Catlin drew many pictures.[5]

Mooney's account of the Cherokee ritual dance was even more detailed:

> The dancers are the players of the morrow, with seven women, representing the seven Cherokee clans. The men dance in a circle around the fire, chanting responses to the sound of a rattle carried by another performer, who circles around on the outside, while the women stand in line a few feet away and dance to and fro, now advancing a few steps toward the men, then wheeling and dancing away from them, but all the while keeping time to the sound of the drum and chanting the refrain to the ball songs sung by the drummer, who is seated on the

> ground on the side farthest from the fire. . . . Men and women dance separately throughout, the music, the evolutions, and the songs being entirely distinct, but all combining to produce an harmonious whole. The women are relieved at intervals by others who take their places, but the men dance in the same narrow circle the whole night long. . . .[6]

At intervals, the players left the dance in order to accompany the shaman to the river bank for elaborate ceremonies with sacred red and black beads representing the players and their opponents. Among the other pregame ceremonies described by Mooney was scarification, performed by the shaman with a seven-toothed comb made from the leg bone of a turkey. Twenty-eight scratches (four times seven) were made on each arm above the elbow and then below, on each leg above and below the knee, and on the breast and back. When the shaman was done, the player bled from nearly three hundred gashes. The Great Spirit was not easy to please.

The game was played on a field whose boundaries were not strictly defined. The two goals, which consisted of two posts side by side or lashed together, might be one hundred feet or several miles apart. There were no side lines. Teams varied in size from as few as twenty men to the six or seven hundred whom Catlin observed and painted. The game itself, in the Choctaw version, was accompanied by drums, by frenzied betting, and, often, by female spectators who encouraged their menfolk by lashing their legs with whips. During the game, rival medicine men rushed up and down the field and employed mirrors to cast reflected sunlight (a source of strength) upon their respective teams. The Cherokee and the Choctaw games ended when one team scored a predetermined number of points, usually twelve. Some games lasted a few hours, others went on for several days.

Catlin was struck by the violence of the play (a common characteristic of premodern sports): "In these struggles, every mode is used that can be devised, to oppose the progress of the foremost, who is likely to get the ball; and these obstructions often meet desperate individual resistance, which terminates in a violent scuffle, and sometimes in fisticuffs. . . ." Whiskey, introduced into Indian culture by Europeans, accentuated the violence that was a traditional part of the game. Mooney remarked of the Cherokee melee, "Almost everything short of murder is allowable in the game, and both parties sometimes go into the contest with the deliberate purpose of crippling . . . the best players on the opposing side." Horatio Cushman commented in 1899 on the Choctaws' "scuffling, pulling, pushing, butting—unsurpassed in any game ever engaged in by man." A Creek informant described the game as "younger brother to war." Serious injuries were common.[7]

While the modern observer is struck by a number of premodern elements, such as the ceremonial "mane" which impeded the player's movements, the loosely defined field of play, the lack of standardized equipment, the indeterminate number of players, and the assignment of roles on the basis of ascription, the most obvious difference between "our" sports and "theirs" is the constant presence of medicine men and their performance of elaborate ritual acts which are, from our perspective, extraneous to the game.

Blanchard, who shares Cheska's keen interest in Indian games as vehicles for the maintenance of tribal identity, mentions but does not expand upon the ritual significance of the traditional stickball game. We are left with Culin's generalizations about stickball, which Blanchard quotes from an essay contributed to Frederick W. Hodge's *Handbook of American Indians* (1907): "The ceremonies [associated with the game] appear to have been to cure sickness, to cause fertilization and reproduction of plants and animals, and, in the arid region, to produce rain. . . . The ball was a sacred object not to be touched with the hand, and has been identified as symbolizing the earth, the sun, or the moon." Those of us who are not anthropologists must regret that Blanchard has not analyzed the religious functions of Indian games as carefully as he has interpreted their role as "cultural maintenance devices" and as "a mechanism for the distribution of economic goods and services" (a reference to heavy betting).[8]

Morris Opler's exemplary account of the Jicarilla Apache "relay race" escapes this mild complaint about the relative neglect of religion. Opler shows exactly how the event functioned as a fertility ritual. Apache myth dramatized the delicate balance between the two main sources of food among the Plains Indians of the Southwest. Animal sources were associated with the Sun, vegetable sources with the Moon. As one informant explained to Morris Opler, "The sun is connected with the animal and the moon with the fruit because the sun is a man and the moon is a woman." This traditional dualistic conception of the natural order is one that Claude Lévi-Strauss and many other anthropologists posit as an inevitable facet of "the savage mind." The enactment of the dualistic myth in this instance involved a relay race in which all males participated at least once between puberty and marriage. Boys with sexual experience were excluded from the contest. In conformity with the myths of the tribe, one side, the Ollero or "Sand People," represented animals and the Sun while the other side, the Llanero or "Plains People," represented vegetation and the Moon.[9]

The race was governed by complicated rituals similar to those of the Cherokees and Choctaws. Abstinence from meat and from sexual intercourse was required prior to the race. The track was called the "Milky Way," after the heavenly path over which the Sun and the Moon had originally raced. The "Milky Way" connected two circles around whose circumferences small holes were dug, clockwise, into which the leaders of the two sides, praying all the while, dropped pollen from sunflower, grama grass, limber pine, and wormwood plants. Saplings were then planted in the holes, and leafy branches were woven through the saplings to form an enclosure known as the "kiva." A fire pit was dug in the center of each kiva. Women, especially menstruating women, were warned away from the kivas and from the track that connected them.

Further rituals followed the construction of the kiva. Feasts, songs, and dances were all accompanied by drums representing the Sun and the Moon. The race itself was run on the third day of the festival, at which time a fire was ignited in the center of each circle. The boy runners were painted, dusted with pollen, adorned with feathers, and led to their respective circles by two young girls; each girl carried an ear of corn in one hand and an eagle feather in the other. These emblems symbolized the two sources of food, vegetable and animal, upon which the Plains Indians were dependent. (In pre-Columbian times, in still another association of human fertility with natural abundance, the maidens were married to the winners of the race.) When the teams were in place, four old men inaugurated the track. Then came the race itself.

The leaders of the Ollero and Llanero ran first, followed by the others in no particular order. Some of the boys ran four or five times, but all were supposed to run at least once. Songs, dances, and another feast followed the race—if it was a race. Opler noted that there was "less concern over which side will win the race than . . . that the ceremony take place at frequent intervals."[10]

The sport clearly involved more than a contest to see which group of boys was able to run faster. In fact, we can ask whether the "race" was a sport at all. It was certainly not an autotelic physical contest. It is closer to the mark to say that the ceremony was a religious ritual in which elements of a physical contest were embedded. But it would be a serious error to dichotomize the event into "religious ritual" and "sport," because the race was as religious as the drumming, the singing, and the pollinating.

If one bears in mind the examples of the stickball game and the relay race, one is better prepared than the casual Sunday-supplement reader to assess popular contemporary comments on British soccer or American football as "tribal" or "primitive" games. Desmond Morris, for instance, observed the World Cup of 1978 and concluded that soccer clubs are organized like small tribes, "complete with a tribal territory, tribal elders, witch-doctors, heroes, camp-followers, and other assorted tribesmen." The passions aroused by Manchester United versus Tottenham Hotspurs can be traced to "our primeval past, when our early ancestors lived and died as hunters of wild beasts." Similarly, American scholars such as Geoffrey Winningham have considered American football as a masculinity or initiation rite. Using photographs more effectively than the accompanying text, Winningham contends in *The Rites of Fall* (1979) that Texas high school football "is an obvious rite of passage for the boys who play it." Clearly, there are analogies between the secular rituals associated with modern games and the religious ceremonies observed among the Cherokees, Choctaws, Creeks, and Apaches. The lockerroom prayers of the local priest at a high school football game and the elaborate rites of the shaman on the eve of the stickball game are formally comparable. The cheerleaders who dance at modern football games perform a function recognizably similar to that of the Apache maidens who led the male adolescents of the tribe to the circles of the Sun and Moon.[11]

While it is sometimes entertaining and often sobering to contemplate the "tribal" photographs provided by Morris or by Winningham and to remind ourselves of the similarities between ourselves and our hunter-and-gatherer ancestors, the similarities are too often superficial. The differences are at least as important as the similarities (and less likely to be obvious from photographic evidence). Locker-room priests are expected to ask the Lord's blessings and to remind their psyched-up auditors to leaven the mayhem with a modicum of Christian charity; the shaman, on the other hand, performed a number of symbolic actions associated with human fertility. Without the priest, the football game is unimpaired (some might say enhanced); without the shaman, there *was* no stickball game. The cheerleaders' colorful display of secondary sex characteristics certainly eroticizes the modern game, but their legs and breasts are less essential to the occasion than were the Indian maidens' less revealing evocations of fertility. Important as it is to recognize ourselves in others and thus to promote an awareness of our common membership in the "family of man," it is equally necessary to perceive differences.

A footnote may be appended to this argument for the acknowledgment of otherness. The force of modernization is such that Indian games no longer exemplify otherness as once they did. The Choctaws still play stickball, but the pre-Columbian rituals have vanished, along with the Great Spirit who called them forth. The teams now have uniforms, and there are officials to enforce the rules. There are boundaries, a clock, and a scoreboard. Medicine men linger on with little to do. Sitting on the sidelines, chanting their magic incantations, they dispiritedly seek to influence the outcome of games in which hardly anyone takes much interest. One can lament the disappearance of traditional games and appeal for the revival of ancient rituals, but there is little likelihood of a tribal return to premodern games. Once a central element in the tribal culture of the entire Southeast, stickball has become an ethnographical curiosity.

THREE

Puritans at Play?

Accusations and Replies

"The Puritan," quipped Thomas Babington Macaulay, "hated bear-baiting, not because it gave pain to the bear, but because it gave pleasure to the spectators." Several generations of British historians have shared Macaulay's witticism with their students. For decades American professors asked their classes to read Vernon Louis Parrington's influential study, *Main Currents of American Thought* (1927), which characterized the Puritans as a gloomy lot whose attitude toward play was best represented by kill-joy Cotton Mather on a rampage against the sin of mixed dancing. How can one forget Parrington's chapter on "The Mather Dynasty," which concludes: "The New England of the dreams of Increase and Cotton Mather was sick to death from morbid introspection and ascetic inhibitions; no lancet or purge known to the Puritan pharmacopeia could save it. Though father and son walked the streets of Boston at noonday, they were only twilight figures, communing with ghosts, building with shadows." Parrington's readers have sometimes had the impression that the Puritans came to America mostly to provide the gloom subsequently illuminated by Benjamin Franklin, Thomas Jefferson, and other representatives of the Enlightenment.[1]

Parrington has long since ceased to be viewed as an authority. Perry Miller, Edmund Morgan, and a whole congregation of younger historians have shown that the conventional wisdom about Puritanism was mostly nonsense, but Miller's monumental analysis of the Puritan mind, Morgan's discussion of the Puritan family, and numerous reconstructions of seventeenth-century social structure and religious institutions have done little to dispel the notion that the Puritans were serious to the point of solemnity. That classic story of grim retribution, *The Scarlet Letter*, has also helped to darken the image. Small wonder that the term "puritan" remains a popular synonym for "spoilsport."

Most sports historians have agreed that the English and American Puritans, a dour lot for whom frolic was akin to sacrilege, hindered the development of modern sports. In *Sport and Society: Elizabeth to Anne* (1969), Dennis Brailsford was as direct as, although considerably less witty than, Macaulay: "The Puritans saw their mission to erase all sport and play from men's lives." *A World History of Physical Education* (1971), the widely used text by D. B. Van Dalen and Bruce L. Bennett, summarizes the reasons for the Puritans' opposition to sports. In the first place, the Puritans' religious sanction of labor and their "detestation of idleness" removed play from the sphere of socially approved behavior. "The ideal of serving God through steady application to work came to imply that any innocent amusement was a waste of time and talents." Then there was "the Puritans' desire to eliminate any activity tainted with Catholicism."

Finally, most radically, the "determination to improve morals through spiritual vigilance and external discipline" rigidified into "a fanatic proscription of nearly every natural desire of man." The social historian Foster Rhea Dulles was more moderate, writing in *America Learns to Play* (1940) that the "intolerance of Puritanism was superimposed upon economic necessity to confine life in New England within the narrowest possible grooves. Massachusetts and Connecticut banned dice, cards, quoits, bowls, ninepins, 'or any other unlawful game in house yard, garden or backside,' singling out for special attention 'the Game called Shuffle Board, in howses of Common Interteinment, whereby much precious time is spent unfruitfully.'" Dulles admitted that the builders of Bay Colony and the founders of Connecticut had their playful impulses and that the Puritans "failed to eradicate the early Americans' natural urge for play," but their influence on American culture was ostensibly such that subsequent generations had to *learn* what animals and children know instinctively, i.e., how to play.[2]

Since historians have a penchant for the Hegelian game of assertion and counterassertion, the humanistic indictment of the Puritans as theocratic spoilsports has, inevitably, brought forth a host, or at least a small band, of defenders, most of them Germans. Some scholars brighten the reputation of the Puritan rank and file and tarnish the image of the Puritan leadership. Hans Peter Wagner, for instance, has argued persuasively that "Puritan theology proved ineffective in relation to sport." His evidence, drawn largely from ministerial appeals to the "unregenerate," can, however, be taken as implied support for the case against the clergy, whose "interpretation of recreation found no echo among the body of laymen." While it may have been true that "by the end of the seventeenth century New England had a rich recreational life," Wagner admits that much of this life was a thorn in the eye of the righteous. Christian Graf von Krockow has seized upon Max Weber's interpretation of the Protestant ethic in order to suggest a parallel between the "secular asceticism" (*innerweltliche Askese*) of Puritanism and the self-imposed denials of an athletic regimen. Two other German scholars have sought more directly to refute the accusation that Puritanism retarded the development of modern sports. Gerhard Schneider has written, "In no way have Puritan measures hindered men in the healthy, reasonable physical exercise. . . . The contributions of Puritanism to the shaping of modern physical exercises, including SPORTS, can no longer be overlooked." Erich Geldbach agrees that alleged "opposition between sport and the Puritans does not correspond to the historical facts."[3]

Before joining the Hegelian game and suggesting a resolution to the clash of contradictory opinion, it is imperative to look at the historical record. This is no easy task, partly because the Puritan divines sought to float the arc of their theology on an ocean of words. Since the awesome contrast between goodness and wickedness, leading to salvation and damnation, obsessed the theologians far more than the precise distinction between sports and other forms of recreation (such as dancing, playing cards, or holding hands beneath the orchard boughs), Puritan attitudes are not always clear. In fact, the Puritans seem to have written so little about sports per se that twentieth-century historians usually discuss some larger category like amusements and diversions. But the Puritans did mention sports often enough for the attentive student to determine their views.

Puritan Attitudes and Actions

As early as 1583, Philip Stubbes had thundered against the game of folk-football. In *Anatomy of Abuses* he portrayed it as liable to produce "fighting, brawling, contention, quarrel-picking, murther, homicide, and great effusion of blood." This condemnation tells us little about specifically Puritan attitudes because sixteenth-century folk-football was indeed akin to mayhem; even the exemplary humanist Thomas Elyot denounced the sport as "nothing but beastly fury and extreme violence." A more narrowly Puritan complaint appeared seven years later, in the lament that "Sabbath days and holy days . . . are spent full heathenishly, in taverning, trippling [*sic*], gaming, playing and beholding of bear-baitings and stage-plays." Concerned about the violent passions unleashed among the spectators at animal sports, most Puritans condemned weekday as well as Sunday cockfighting and bearbaiting. Contrary to Macaulay's quip, the Puritans were not indifferent to the pain suffered by the animals. "What christen [*sic*] heart," wrote Philip Stubbes, "can take pleasure to see one poor beast to rent, teare, and kill another, and all for his foolish pleasure?" Such Christian charity did not characterize all Puritan opposition to animal sports. The Reverend Edward Burghall made gleeful journal entries whenever the spectators at such beastly amusements were injured or killed. Such mishaps proved that God will not be mocked.[4]

By 1617, isolated protests against such Sabbath desecrations had become consolidated into a powerful movement effectively restricting them. When James I returned to England that year, after a visit to his native Scotland, he was petitioned by the common people of Lancashire, who complained that Puritan bans had blocked them from their traditional Sunday amusements. The king granted the petitioners temporary relief and, a year later, issued the famous

Declaration of Sports, also known as the *Book of Sports*, in which he took issue generally with those who argued "that no honest mirth or recreation is lawful or tolerable in Our Religion." If the common people of England were not to enjoy their recreation on the one day of the week when they were not hard at work, when were they to relax? James, like rulers before and after him, was also mindful of the necessity for military preparedness. The "common and meaner sort of people" had need of "such exercises as may make their bodies more able for warre, when Wee, or Our Successors, shall have occasion to use them." James ordered, therefore, "That, after the end of Divine Service, Our good people be not disturbed, letted, or discouraged from any lawfull recreation, Such as dancing, either of men or women, Archery for men, leaping, vaulting, or any other such harmlesse Recreation, nor from having of May Games, Whitson Ales, and Morris-dances, and the setting up of Maypoles, and other sports therewith used."[5] Many Puritan clergymen refused to read the *Declaration* from their pulpits. Recalcitrance cost some their positions, but the Puritan resistance was so powerful that James prudently retired from the fray.

When Charles I reissued his father's declaration in 1633, the Puritan response was even more determined. When the balance of power shifted from Cavalier to Roundhead, Parliament damned the *Declaration* and ordered it burned. A year later, in 1644, Parliament ordained "That no person or persons shall hereafter upon the Lords-Day, use, exercise, keep, maintain, or be present at any wrastlings, shooting, Bowling, Ringing of Bells for Pleasure or Pastime, Masque, Wake, otherwise called Feasts, Church-Ale, Dancing, Games, Sport or Pastime whatsoever. . . ."[6] Cavalier-sponsored folk festivals, including Robert Dover's famous Cotswald games (which took place on Thursday and Friday of Easter Week), were banned for the duration of the Commonwealth, only to be revived in 1660, when Charles II gave his *nihil obstat* to "Merrie England."

The Puritans of the New World were at least as strict as those of the Old. The Court of Assistants of Massachusetts Bay reacted with typical severity in 1630, when it ordered that John Baker "be whipped for shooteing att fowle on the Sabbath day." In 1647, the General Court of the colony outlawed shuffleboard; prohibition of bowling followed in 1650. Vermonters who ran, rode, jumped, or danced on Sunday were subject to ten lashes and a forty-shilling fine.[7]

One of the best-known passages in William Bradford's *Of Plimouth Plantation* contains the governor's response to the Christmas revelry of 1621. A number of newcomers to the colony announced that it was against their consciences to work on December 25. Referring to himself in the third person, Bradford commented,

> So the Governor told them that if they made it matter of conscience, he would spare them till they were better informed; so he led away the rest and left them. But when they came home at noon from their work, he found them in the street at play, openly; some pitching the bar, and some at stool-ball and such like sports. So he went to them and took away their implements and told them that was against his conscience, that they should play and others work. If they made the keeping of it a matter of devotion, let them keep their houses; but there should be no gaming or reveling in the streets.[8]

No trace here of the Catholic notion that revelry can be associated with worship, much less of the American Indian sacralization of play.

In another episode, one of the most famous in early American history, Bradford had to deal with the obstreperous Thomas Morton. Morton, who seems to have had some of the same hedonistic impulses as Robert Dover, defied the Puritans and challenged Bradford's control of the colony. Asserting that the Indians were "more full of humanity than the Christians," Morton set up a maypole at "Ma-re Mount" and invited the Indians to join him in a frolic. This was too much for Bradford:

> And Morton became Lord of Misrule, and maintained (as it were) a School of Atheism. . . . They . . . set up a maypole, drinking and dancing about it many days altogether, inviting the Indian women for their consorts, dancing and frisking together like so many fairies, or furies, rather; and worse practices. As if they had anew revived and celebrated the feasts of the Roman goddess Flora, or the beastly practices of the mad

> Bacchanalians. Morton likewise . . . composed sundry rhymes and verses, some tending to lasciviousness, and others to the detraction and scandal of some persons, which he affixed to this idle or idol maypole.

While Bradford's language was a curious mix of outrage and wordplay, his actions were unambiguous. He dispatched Captain Miles Standish, whom Morton irreverently referred to as "Captain Shrimp" (Standish was not a tall man). After a scuffle, the maypole was cut down. Morton endured a brief imprisonment, which did nothing to dampen his love of revelry, and was then sent on his merry way.[9]

Nearly a century later, when Puritan rigor had already been weakened by proponents of a less medieval world view, Judge Samuel Sewall commented in his diary that he had ventured out on a Monday evening to interrupt the unregenerate at play on what is now known as Mount Vernon: "Dissipated the players at Nine-Pins at Mount-Whoredom. . . . Reproved Thomas Messenger for entertaining them."[10]

From these episodes of English and American history one may conclude that the Puritans were indeed hostile to any kind of traditional amusement on the Sabbath and to certain kinds of "heathenish" recreation, such as dancing about the maypole, regardless of the day of the week. How, then, can historians maintain that the Puritans contributed to the rise of modern sports? The argument takes us from the political realm to the theological domain. It is common knowledge that the Puritans of seventeenth-century New England considered themselves Englishmen and Englishwomen guided in their thought and behavior by English scholars. It is at least arguable that the wilderness in which they lived influenced their actions less than did their intellectual tradition of Puritan theology. The English authorities whom they consulted for a godly view of worldly sports agreed that all work and no play made Everyman a poor Christian. In the words of John Downame, who published *A Guide to Godliness* in 1622, shortly before he joined the Puritan exodus to New England, "Let us know, that honest recreation is a thing not onely lawfull, but also profitable and necessary." Downame added that the bow cannot be always spanned, a metaphor that had already occurred to a more influential authority,

William Perkins, who wrote in *The Whole Treatise of the Cases of Conscience* (1614) that "rest from labour with the refreshing of the bodie and mind, is necessary, because man . . . is like a bow, which being always bent and used, is soone broken in pieces." Perkins listed archery, running, wrestling, and fencing among amusements "verie commendable, and not to be disliked." Downame added hunting, hawking, fishing, and fowling. Richard Baxter, who was highly esteemed by the American Puritans, included a section on sports and recreations in his *Christian Directory*. In this influential work Baxter defined lawful recreation as "the use of some Natural thing or Action, not forbidden us, for the exhilerating of the natural Spirits by the Fantasie, and due exercise of the natural parts, thereby to fit the body and mind for ordinary duty to God. It is some delightful exercise."

Edward Elton, interpreting *Gods Holy Mind Touching Matters Morall*, announced confidently in 1625, "There are such movings of the body as bee honest and delightfull exercise of the minde, and serve to the refreshing of the body and minde, as Shooting, Tennis-playing, Stoolball-playing, Wrestling, Running, and such like." Even William Prynne, whose ferocious *Historiomastix* (1633) excoriated playgoers, had some favorable words for more innocent amusements: "Besides, though men are debard from Stage-playes, Dicing, or mixed lascivious Dancing, or any unlawfull sports, they have store of honest . . . recreations still remaining, with which to refresh themselves; as walking, riding, fishing, fowling, hawking, hunting, ringing, leaping, vaulting, wrestling, running, shooting." Apart from the omission of animal sports, the inventory might have been found in the sermons of an Anglican divine.[11]

The American Puritans had somewhat less to say on the relation of play to worship. Increase Mather wrote in 1688, "For a Christian to use Recreation is very lawful, and in some cases a great Duty." His son Cotton admitted, even as he scolded those who "unnecessarily frequent the Tavern," that the Elect required a modicum of innocent recreation: "We would not be misunderstood, as if we meant to insinuate, that a due Pursuit of Religion is inconsistent with all manner of Diversion: No, we suppose there are Diversions undoubtedly innocent, yea profitable and of use, to fit us for Service, by enlivening and fortifying our frail Nature, Invigorating the

Animal Spirits, and brightening the Mind, when tired with a close Application to Business." Cotton Mather's own preference for sedentary diversion was probably intensified when he deviated from his customary regimen and went fishing on Spy Pond. He fell in.[12]

Among the innocent sports, folk-football, which Boston had banned in 1657, was tolerated if the players restrained themselves from breaking one another's bones and were careful not to disturb the peace of more meditative colonists. Shooting matches were looked upon with special favor. The danger of attack by hostile Indians, with or without the Indians' French allies, was present for most of the century. The magistrates and ministers of the colony agreed that a trained militia was essential, and one way to liven up the hours of drill was to institute shooting competitions.

The Puritan affirmation of honest amusements was not, however, unqualified. Indeed, Richard Baxter followed his endorsement of recreation with no less than eighteen restrictions, "the want of any one of them will *make* and *prove* to be *unlawful*." This and every similar list contained the proviso that the Sabbath be devoted to prayer, meditation, and good works rather than to worldly diversions and heedless gambols. When some of the New England "saints" endeavored to justify Sunday sports by reference to Holy Scripture, Cotton Mather was appalled: "Never did anything sound more sorrowfully or more odious since the day the World was first bless'd with such a day." A year later, in 1704, Jeremiah Dummer added his condemnation: it was "strange to see how zealously some Learned men contend for the indulgence of *Sports and Pastimes* on the Lords day in direct contrariety to the Prophet Isaiah." In addition to the adamant defense of the Sabbath, there was always the stipulation that sports and other recreations must be of the right sort. No pastime was to be condoned if it became the occasion for gambling, drunkenness, idleness, cupidity, cruelty, wastefulness, extravagance, or lascivious behavior. The divines were also careful to warn, in Perkins's words, that recreation "must be moderate and sparing." Most insistently, the saints reminded each other that they were placed upon this earth in order to serve and glorify God. In Baxter's view of lawful sport or recreation, "The *end* which you really intend in using it, must be to fit you for your *service to God*; that is, either for your Callings, or for his *worship*, or for some work of obedience in which you may *please* and *Glorify* him." Thomas Gouge, author of *The Young Man's Guide Through the Wilderness of This World to the Heavenly Canaan* (1672), used more colloquial language to express this same sense of the purpose of sports and recreation. They "should be as Sauces to your Meat, to sharpen your appetite unto the duties of your Calling and not to glut yourselves with them, so as to make your selves the more unfit, both for the duties of your callings, and of Gods service." We can be sure that clerical New England nodded its approval of such sentiments.[13]

Can these authentically Puritan opinions be construed as an affirmation of sports? Wagner is surely correct in asserting that there was always a discrepancy between what the clergy dictated and what the farmers, bakers, smiths, and wheelwrights of New England did. It is difficult to believe that ordinary New Englanders always heeded ministerial admonitions, sought invariably to "performe service unto God" in their sports, and never lost themselves in the excitement of the contest. It is improbable that the majority of Puritans, English or American, gave much thought to Election, or even to Innate Depravity, as they ran, jumped, wrestled, shot, and whacked away at the stoolball. But that is not really the issue. Did the Puritan elite encourage the development of modern sports, as Schneider and Geldbach maintain? Or did they not? The debate is over their attitudes and intentions, not over the putative behavior of their indentured servants.

There is no reason to accept the popular notion that Puritan ministers were sullenly opposed to any kind of play. The Puritans were not "puritanical" in the twentieth-century Menckenesque sense of the word, and Brailsford certainly did them an injustice when he wrote that they saw it as "their mission to erase all sport and play from men's lives." Their asceticism has been exaggerated. They were certainly stern and capable of self-denial, but they allowed for "reasonable and lawful" pleasures and were disinclined to inflict upon themselves the mortifications of Saint Anthony in the desert or Saint Simeon upon his pillar. The divines were in agreement on the lawfulness, necessity, and propriety of a wide range of physical diversions. To acknowledge this, however, is not to agree that the Puritans contributed to the rise of modern sports. In the first place, most allowable recreations were not sports at all but versions of what was, in the nineteenth century, called "calisthenics." Other acceptable pastimes (running, wrestling, and ball games) were indeed sports under almost any definition, but the Puritan affirmation of such activities lacked the enthusiasm of a Robert Dover (not to speak of the reckless abandon of a Thomas Morton). The acceptance of sports was *sotto voce* in comparison to the thundered denunciations of sinners in the hands of an angry God. When the clergy did list sports among the other "lawful recreations," their justification was traditionally Christian. Within the Puritans' hierarchical worldview, sports were instrumental—means to an end (rest, recreation, diversion, defense), rather than ends in themselves. The theological justification for rest, recreation, and diversion was that *mens sancta* required *corpus sanum*. That sports might also be done for the intrinsic pleasure of a "peak experience" or the quest for "excellence of the body" was a thought too hedonistic to be contemplated by the Puritan mind. Downame was typical when he demanded that his fellow men "performe service unto God" in their "lawful sports and recreations" as well as in their vocations. We can be sure he contemplated nothing remotely like the modern feast-of-fools theology that predicates God as the spirit of play.[14]

There is, therefore, good reason to reject Schneider's and Geldbach's unconventional argument that Puritanism actually *furthered* the development of sports. While negative universals are always susceptible to disproof by further research, I am not aware of a single document in which a Puritan minister or magistrate demonstrates any enthusiasm for sports per se. Puritan attitudes towards sports were—not surprisingly—premodern. It may have been that their root-and-branch hostility to traditional pastimes, like maypoles and Morris dances, inadvertently cleared the way for the growth of modern forms of recreation just as their "Protestant ethic" of hard work and sober thrift contributed—in Max Weber's analysis—to the eventual emergence of modern capitalism, which was certainly one of the last things the Puritans consciously intended. Whether modern capitalism might have developed more quickly *without* the Puritan efforts to establish a Bible-based commonwealth is for others to debate. That the English and American Puritans retarded the emergence of modern sports, which "took off" only when Puritan magistrates were replaced by more worldly rulers, seems undeniable. To argue the contrary, as the revisionists have done, is a distortion of the historical facts.

FOUR

The Southerner as Sportsman

Cavalier versus Yankee

The aristocratic Englishmen who fought for Charles I were often neighbors of the Puritans who followed Oliver Cromwell into battle. Cavaliers and Roundheads had their areas of greater and lesser concentration, but the civil war that replaced the monarchy with the Commonwealth was not a case of regional strife. In the New World, geography interacted with religion to produce regional differences that have fascinated several generations of American historians. One can make too much of the contrast between Massachusetts and Virginia; the culture they shared was doubtless as important as their more superficial differences. Nonetheless, Henry Adams in his autobiography remembered a childhood visit to Virginia as the exploration of a strangely unfamiliar world, and Basil Ransom, Henry James's scarcely less fictional southern hero, hardly knew what to make of the Bostonians.

Social historians interested in leisure and recreation have utilized the symbolic opposition between New England and the South. In its most exaggerated form, the contrast degenerates into a parody that sets Puritans too busy at their prayers to play a harmless game of stoolball against Tidewater aristocrats too engrossed in horse races and cockfights to agonize over the state of their souls. Like other contrasts that enliven and distort historiography, this one has its germ of truth. As we have seen, ordinary New Englanders may have lost themselves in play, but their Puritan leaders, secular as well as clerical, really did harbor deep suspicions about sports as autotelic activity. And southern culture really did include the affirmation of hardy outdoor sports.

There was ample justification for Jane Carson to publish a book entitled *Colonial Virginians at Play* (1965). In addition to checkers, backgammon, dominoes, dice, and an array of card games that included piquet, basset, ombre, commerce, loo, ace of hearts, faro, and slam, colonial aristocrats enjoyed contests such as quoits and bowls, which required a modicum of physical skill. William Byrd of Westover, whose *Secret Diary* has been a boon to all historians of early Virginia, recorded cricket matches in 1709 and 1710, the first American references to the game, but cricket never became popular in the South (as it did, for a time, in the North). As Nancy L. Struna indicates in a study of the Chesapeake gentry, an obsession with physical prowess hindered the development of " 'artificial contests' such as ball games."[1]

The demonstration of physical prowess, closely related to conceptions of personal honor, took various forms. Although aristocrats such as William Byrd occasionally fenced, they were seldom enthusiastic about the sport. Injured honor demanded the redress of a duel, but gentlemen preferred to settle their quarrels, which occurred with distressing frequency, with pistols. Backcountry southerners were less punctilious; they competed in feats of strength, like lifting and throwing, and they wrestled for the animal pleasure involved. When they were angry, they often crossed the imaginary line between a friendly tussle and a feral stomp-and-gouge match in which they tore at each others' testicles and sought, with sharpened fingernails, to rip out each others' eyes. Such combats were, as Elliott J. Gorn observes, "focal events in the culture of lower-class males." As such they were a significant part of social history. Northerners who witnessed and wrote about such combats put as much rhetorical distance as possible between themselves and the combatants. Visiting Hanover Court House on election day, 1778, Elkanah Watson was

> attacked by a wild Irishman, who insisted on my "swapping horses" with him. . . . Treating his importunity with little respect, I was near being involved in a boxing-match, the Irish-

> man swearing that I did not "trate him like a jintleman." I had hardly escaped this dilemma, when my attention was attracted to a fight between two very unwieldly, fat men, foaming and puffing like two furies, until one succeeded in twisting his forefinger in a side-lock of the other's hair, and was in the act of thrusting . . . his thumb into his adversary's eyes, when he bawled out, "King's cruse," equivalent, in technical language, to "enough."

Philip Vickers Fithian, a Princeton-educated Presbyterian, was horrified by the southerners' sudden shifts from rough play to deadly encounter and shocked by the sight of gleeful spectators gathered to enjoy these "odious and filthy amusements." It must be acknowledged that southern aristocrats were almost as appalled as Fithian and Watson. Their attitude toward the stomp-and-gouge fight was best dramatized in Augustus Baldwin Longstreet's satirical *Georgia Scenes* (1835), where the educated narrator amply indicates his disdain for the barbaric lower-class combat.[2]

The hard-to-trace imaginary line that separated the sports of boxing and wrestling from the animal behavior of a stomp-and-gouge fight also separated hunting as a sport from hunting as a source of food. (The very ambiguity of the act was the salvation of New Englanders, who justified their pleasure by the food it provided for the godly.) Hunters rich and poor have roamed through southern history and literature from Robert Beverley's *History and Present State of Virginia* (1705) to William Elliott's *Carolina Sports* (1859) to William Faulkner's novels and stories of Yoknapatawpha County. Isaac McCaslin, the hero of "The Bear," is one of the most vividly memorable creations in American literature. There is plenty of evidence that real southerners were as keen on hunting as fictional southerners have been. If the excitement of the chase ended with a supply of bear meat or venison or with a bag of ducks, all the more reason to rejoice. Hunters have never worried much about paradigmatic definitions of work and play.

There is, in short, good reason to accept the conventional wisdom that outdoor sports were more various, more popular, and more socially acceptable in the South than in the North. The southerner rode and hunted and was proud of his personal vigor, which he frequently contrasted to the pallid ill health of the average New Englander (who was, indeed, if Oliver Wendell Holmes, Sr., was to be believed, a sickly sort). But does this enthusiasm for outdoor sports mean that the southerners' attitudes were more modern than those of the Puritans, who sought to instrumentalize sports into what we now recognize to have been physical education and hygiene? The best way to respond is to look more closely at two of the region's most popular pastimes: cockfighting and horseracing.

Cockfights

"The common planters," wrote Hugh Jones in *The Present State of Virginia* (1724), "leading easy lives, don't much admire labor or any manly exercise except horse-racing, nor diversion except cock-fighting."[3] Cockfights are certainly not true sports, because the birds, not their handlers, are the active participants. But horse races are, because the physical skills of the jockeys are an important part of the contest. What is at stake for the moment is not the categorization of the activity but the attitudes of the southerners involved in it.

Cockfights are common to many cultures past and present. They were popular in Greek and Roman antiquity and they were, until recently, an important part of traditional Balinese village life. Cockfights enjoyed royal favor in sixteenth-century England. Henry VIII was an enthusiast, and Elizabeth and James I shared his taste. Needless to say, the Puritans disapproved of cockfights and banned them. The Restoration restored them (or made it possible to enjoy them openly), but middle-class opinion waged a relentless campaign against every variety of animal sports. By the end of the eighteenth century, sentimental poets, rationalist philosophers, and Methodist ministers had more or less won the war for public opinion. Early in the nineteenth century, blood sports that pitted animals against each other were outlawed by Parliament (but hunters still had the legal right to bring down deer and to set their dogs after foxes).

Cultures that place heavy emphasis on demonstrations of physical prowess rejoice in opportunities for vicarious as well as direct assertions of manhood. The psychological processes at work during a cockfight have been described by the anthropologist Clifford Geertz: "the deep psychological identification of Balinese men with their cocks is unmistakable. The double entendre here is deliberate. It works in exactly the same way in Balinese as it does in English, even to producing the same tired jokes, strained puns, and uninventive obscenities."[4] The historical record of the antebellum South has not preserved whatever jokes, puns, and obscenities appeared in the cockpit conversation of Tidewater planters and backcountry woodsmen, but there is ample evidence of a widespread passion for cockfights.

Rhys Isaac notes of eighteenth-century Virginia, "The excitement engendered by the mortal combat between the birds extended to all ranks of society." John Brickell's *Natural History of North Carolina* (1737) noted, "Cock-fighting the North Carolinians greatly admire, which Birds they endeavor to procure from England and Ireland, and to that intent, implore Masters of Ships, and other Trading Persons to supply them." Political and economic independence from the mother country interrupted the supply of birds but did not diminish the passion for cockfights. The *North Carolina Journal* for July 28, 1806, announced that "a number of gentlemen of two of the lower counties of North Carolina, and of two southern counties of Virginia, offer to meet the gentlemen of Maryland at Norfolk, any time between the 20th of March and 18th of July, 1807, to show fifty cocks, and match not less than twenty-one in the main. The main is to be from one to ten thousand dollars." A generation later, a Mecklenburg County resident called cockfights "one of the fashionable amusements of the day."[5]

The first known cockfight in Virginia was advertised in the *Virginia Gazette* for February 19, 1751. In May 1768, Robert W. Carter traveled all the way from Northern Neck to Chesterfield County in order to witness and bet on a main of sixty cocks owned by Colonel Edward Carter and Colonel Anthony Thornton. The fact that betting on the ferocious birds had been illegal in Virginia since 1740 deterred no one, and young Carter lost over £21. A few years later, at the plantation of Robert Carter III, Fithian observed the passion for cockfights at both ends of the social spectrum. On Easter Monday, 1774, the slaves "are all disbanded till Wednesday morning and are at Cock Fights through the County." Six days later, on April 10, Fithian noted that "a Ring of Negroes" had gathered before breakfast in order to fight cocks at the stable. Their masters shared the servile enthusiasm. Eight years later, almost to the day, the French traveler François Jean de Beauvoir, Marquis de Chastellux, came upon a cockfight at Willis's Ordinary in Louisa County. He noted that, "when the principal promoters of this diversion propose to match their champions, they take care to announce it to the public, and although there are neither posts nor regular conveyances, this important news spreads with such facility that planters come from thirty or forty miles around, some with cocks, but all with money for betting, which is sometimes very considerable." The marquis was most struck by the participation of "a child of fifteen, who was near me." The child "leaped for joy and cried, 'Oh, it is a charming diversion!'" Chastellux disagreed. He was astonished by "the insipidity of such diversion" and by "the stupid interest with which it animates the parties."[6]

Such aristocratic disdain was followed by middle-class disapproval when, five years later, Elkanah Watson journeyed from New England to the South. Watson's detailed account can be taken as emblematic of the cultural divergence in attitudes between Yankees and Cavaliers:

> The roads, as we approached the scene, were alive with carriages, horses, and pedestrians, black and white, hastening to the point of attraction. Several houses formed a spacious square, in the centre of which was arranged a large cock-pit; surrounded by many genteel people, promiscuously mingled with the vulgar and debased. Exceedingly beautiful cocks were produced, armed with long, sharp, steel-pointed gaffles, which were firmly attached to their natural spurs. The moment the birds were dropped, bets ran high. The little heroes appeared trained to the business, and not the least disconcerted by the crowd or shouting. They stepped about with great apparent pride and dignity; advancing nearer and nearer, they flew upon each other . . . the cruel and fatal gaffles being driven into their bodies, and, at times, directly through their heads. Frequently one, or both, would be struck dead at the first blow; but they

> often fought after being repeatedly pierced, as long as they were able to crawl, and in the agonies of death would often make abortive efforts to raise their heads and strike their antagonists.

Watson was shocked to see "men of character and intelligence giving their countenance to an amusement so frivolous and scandalous, so abhorrent to every feeling of humanity, and so injurious in its moral influence." Watson expressed his distaste for the scene in metaphors that might have occurred to Puritan writers like Jonathan Edwards or Edward Taylor. "I soon sickened at this barbarous sport, and retired under the shade of a wide-spread willow, where I was much better entertained, in witnessing a voluntary fight between a wasp and a spider." It is curious that Watson's disapproval of the Virginians' addiction to the sport mingles with his obvious admiration for "the little heroes" who fought on despite their mortal wounds. Did he, too, despite his Puritan heritage, feel his manhood enhanced by the prowess of the cocks?[7]

As sectional tensions increased, cockfights were increasingly denigrated by northerners who agreed with Watson that the cockpit was a barbaric anachronism appropriate to a region that still insisted upon the "peculiar institution" of slavery. In northern eyes, cockfights were too depraved for civilized tastes. The May 1857 issue of *Harper's New Monthly*, for instance, included a vividly drawn cockfight scene. The two brutishly depicted handlers, presumably the owners of the cocks, have quarreled and are about to grapple with each other. The spectators, black and white, appear thrilled at the prospect of a stomp-and-gouge fight.

Horse Races

Scornful criticisms from north of the Mason-Dixon Line may have been effective. Some antebellum southerners with visions of themselves as aristocratic descendants of the Cavaliers became uneasy about cockfights. For them the horse and not the gamecock. A few southerners allowed themselves to become intoxicated by the myth of chivalry and attempted, in consequence, to revive the institution most closely associated with that myth: the medieval tournament. (In this, as in countless other ways, Southern aristocrats imitated their English cousins, who staged the century's most famous tournament at Eglinton in 1839.) Although tournaments never rivaled horse races or cockfights as popular Southern amusements, they sprang up in Virginia, South Carolina, and Louisiana. Mounted on thoroughbreds, dressed in makeshift armor, bedecked with the colors of their ladies, armed with lances, "their shields emblazoned with heraldic devices," and announced by trumpeters, "knights" with sobriquets such as Brian de Bois-Guilbert and Wilfred of Ivanhoe jousted against each other or competed to see who was best at managing a galloping mount while spearing a dangling ring. Were the men and women who staged these elaborate reconstructions addled by too many volumes of Sir Walter Scott—as Mark Twain opined in *Life on the Mississippi?* It is difficult to avoid that conclusion when one reads of a tournament held at Thomas Jefferson's Monticello. This particular enactment of the fantasy of knighthood occurred in the fall of 1863—a few weeks after the battle of Gettysburg.[8]

While a handful of dreamers revived the medieval tournament as their defiant response to the specter of industrial capitalism, most southerners preferred horse races. Here was an aristocratic pastime that had, like cockfighting, enjoyed royal favor; horseracing had an additional advantage in it might be defended instrumentally as a means to "improve the stock." In an age when all but the most impoverished owned horses or at least knew how to ride, horse races seemed to epitomize the South. Andrew Jackson, who relinquished his youthful passion for cockfights in order to advance his political prospects outside the South, continued to pride himself on his knowledge of horses. "I do not know much," he boasted, " but I do know men and horses." He was certainly not the first or the last southerner to make the smug assertion. As cockfights declined in popularity, the southerner continued to think of his horse as an instrument of his prowess and as an extension of the self. Thoroughbred horses were, in the words of a modern historian, "surrogates for their master as they exhibited their strength and courage on the track." This interpretation is certainly not willfully imposed by psychoanalytically oriented historians. John B. Irving, a member of the Carolina Jockey Club, wrote in 1857 that the horses were "the impersonation of Carolina chivalry—the *embodied spirit* of Carolina blood and Carolina honor."[9]

Charles II and his entourage frequented the races at Newmarket, which became the model for Williamsburg. The British actor John Bernard, who toured the United States between 1797 and 1811, thought the Virginians had succeeded in copying the original. Of the races at Williamsburg he wrote, "better order and arrangement I had never seen at Newmarket." Thomas Anburey, who had campaigned with Burgoyne during the Revolution, was also impressed by the Williamsburg races, then organized into a series of three four-mile heats, rather than the single quarter-mile races common in the seventeenth century. Anburey thought the track "a very beautiful course" and opined grandly that the horses "would make no contemptible figure at Newmarket." A generation earlier, the hard-to-please Philip Vickers Fithian had to admit that the crowd assembled for a race at Richmond Court House was "exceeding polite in general." In the 1830s, the Carolina Jockey Club and the Augusta (Georgia) Jockey Club, of which the aristocratic James Henry Hammond was a member, also aspired to the politeness and decorum of Newmarket.[10]

Visitors to the interior of the South, however, had few occasions to compliment the crowd on its civilized behavior. Horse races in the hinterlands were often scenes of rowdy disorder. Rough and ready quarter-mile races between two riders mounted on their own horses were still common long after Tidewater contests had become well organized three-heat events. Anburey noted that these races were "much laughed at and ridiculed by the people in the lower parts." He was also surprised by the lack of specialization in the backcountry, where horse races were often accompanied by "those horrid boxing-matches." Bernard the actor reported the same medley of sports and called the scene "one of the most animated and primitive I had the fortune to stumble upon." He described the crowd as "a motley multitude of negroes, Dutchmen, Yankee peddlers, and backwoodsmen, among whom, with long whips in their hands to clear the ground, moved the proprietors and betters, riding or leading their horses." Victory was "always proclaimed by a tornado of applause from the winner's party, the niggers in particular hallooing, jumping, and clapping their hands in a frenzy of delight, more especially if the horses had happened to jostle and one of the riders been thrown off with a broken leg."[11]

In 1806, another English traveler, Thomas Ashe, looked on in horror when a backwoods race at Wheeling spawned a rough-and-tumble fight. The delighted spectators took bets on the outcome and "shouted with joy" when one of the combatants gouged out the other's eyes. After this satisfying conclusion of the quarrel, the townspeople, "refreshed with whiskey and biscuit," went back to betting on the nags.[12]

Adherence to a code of honor, which Bertram Wyatt-Brown considers the key to southern history, did not mean that all backwoods gamblers were completely trustworthy. On one of his famous journeys through the Cotton Kingdom, Frederick Law Olmsted shuddered at a story of callous deception. How, Olmsted asked, could a young man possibly run up debts of $16,000 in a single year? "Well," replied his informant, "he gambled some, and run horses. He don't know anything about a horse, and, of course, he thinks he knows everything. Those fellows up at Natchez would sell him any kind of a tacky for four or five hundred dollars, and then after he'd had him a month, they ride out another and make a bet of five or six hundred dollars they'd beat him. Then he'd run with 'em, and of course he'd lose it."[13] Olmsted's disapproval of such shenanigans was almost as intense as his condemnation of slavery. His sober inability to respond to clever rogues, like Elkanah Watson's failure to see any purpose to a cockfight, vividly illustrates the cultural opposition between North and South, an opposition in which slavery played the most important but by no means the only part.

Given the ubiquitous passion for horseracing and the force of regionalism in nineteenth-century America, one can imagine the tension and excitement when the first great intersectional race took place on May 27, 1823. Colonel William R. Johnson of Warren County, North Carolina, known to his contemporaries as "the Napoleon of the turf," challenged Northern owners to race against his Sir Henry for a stake of $20,000. John Cox Steven accepted the challenge and backed Cornelius W. Van Ranst's Eclipse. Newspapers reported that 60,000 spectators crowded the Union Course on Long

Island for the three-heat race. The estimate is surely exaggerated, but the throng of spectators was undoubtedly immense. Sir Henry won the first heat by a length, but Eclipse had been ridden by William Crafts, a substitute for the horse's regular jockey, Sam Purdy, who had quarreled with Van Ranst. The quarrel was patched up, and Eclipse ran the second heat with Purdy in the saddle. Eclipse won by a length. For the final heat, Sir Henry's backers decided that their horse needed a new jockey, too, and entrusted the South's hopes to Arthur Taylor. Eclipse won by two lengths. Southern sportsmen reacted with disbelief, as if their honor had been impugned, as if their sense of self had been wounded, which it had been. John Randolph of Roanoke had sought during the race to slow Sir Henry by shouting, "You can't do it, Mr. Purdy! You can't do it, Mr. Purdy!" Afterward, Randolph explained, "It was not Eclipse but the lobster that beat Henry," an arcane reference to a wine-and-lobster-induced illness that kept Colonel Johnson from the track and thus handicapped his favorite horse. Few northerners accepted Randolph's limp excuse.[14]

The South's Contribution to Modern Sports

If the southerners' behavior at cockfights and horse races can be taken as evidence, then it is clear that they were sportsmen in an older sense of the term, i.e., they sought diversion and amusement. Some of the formal-structural characteristics of modern sports can be detected in their horse races, which were certainly secular events distressing to the sensibilities of Baptist preachers (but not to those of more worldly Anglican divines). The concept of the handicap testifies to an incipient realization that equality within the rules of the game makes for a better contest. There was even some degree of specialization, rationalization, and quantification. Horses were bred for speed, and amateur jockeys were recruited from among the best riders. Horses were exercised, if not trained, and some thought was given to how best to feed them. As early as the middle of the eighteenth century, stopwatches were available to quantify the results of the races. Jockey clubs were founded (for the owners, of course; not for the jockeys, many of whom were slaves), but there was certainly no effort at bureaucratic organization and apparently little enthusiasm for setting records.

There were limits to the modernization of southern sports. The mania for equestrian events did not extend to harness racing, which Melvin L. Adelman refers to as "the first modern sport." Harness racing, "which emerged as a popular American pastime after the Revolution," encountered "strong opposition in the rural South because southern turfmen generally regarded the gaited racer as inferior to the thoroughbred." The sport was definitely "an urban product. Trotting first emerged on urban roads and developed its most salient modern characteristics in the city, with New York playing a more critical role than any other urban area." In New York and other northern centers, the sport was rationalized and exploited commercially. "In common with other forms of popular entertainment the emergence of trotting as a spectator sport was the result of two dynamic forces, urbanization and economic expansion, which was transforming and modernizing American life."[15] Material factors, however, are only part of the explanation for the North's advances, even in an area traditionally dominated by the South. After all, the antebellum South had its flush times, too, as northern and European textile mills developed an apparently insatiable demand for cotton. By most objective measures (other than their use of slave rather than free labor), antebellum planters were part of an international capitalist economy, but they consciously cultivated what Eugene Genovese refers to as a "precapitalist" mentality. In their play, if not in their work, they continued to think of the Cotton Kingdom as an aristocratic alternative to Yankeedom.

And it certainly mattered what they thought. Just as the study of clerical motivations demonstrates the difference between the Puritan acceptance of physical recreations and the modern affirmation of sports as autotelic activity, an examination of motives clarifies the subtle differences between southern pastimes and modern sports. The southerner approached horse races as he approached cockfights: as a gambler. I make the distinction between the gambler and the participant not as a moralist, but simply as an analyst. James Michener has recently asserted that gamblers are sportsmen, and indeed they are, in an older usage of the term. But there is a fundamental distinction between the person who participates actively in a sport and the person who watches, whether or not the watcher is also a bettor.

Admittedly, some northerners risked their money on horses as well as in the Lowell mills and the China trade, but southern gamblers were a breed apart. They often seem to have taken leave of their senses. As T. H. Breen remarks in an important essay on "Horses and Gentlemen," gambling was "a distinguishing characteristic of gentry culture," " a ritual activity." At a time when the average grower harvested some 1,500 pounds of tobacco a year, bets of as much as 4,000 pounds were recorded. To risk one's entire fortune on a horse, a cock, or a hand of cards is obviously irrational. In his analysis Breen follows Clifford Geertz, whose famous essay on the Balinese cockfight drew upon Jeremy Bentham's concept of "deep play," i.e., gambling that defies rational behavior. The southerners' need to uphold their honor made the acceptance of seemingly irrational risk a necessity. The degree to which southerners' behavior can be interpreted as an attempt to reassure themselves about their masculinity is impossible to say, but Geertz (and Breen) have made a persuasive case for the interplay of virility, prowess, and risk.[16]

That the colonial and antebellum South contributed little to the rise of modern sports can be seen from another perspective. Where exactly in these United States *did* modern sports first appear? In New England and New York. As everyone knows, the Puritan mind evolved into the Yankee mentality and Dutch burghers became New York businessmen. Water-driven mills dotted landscapes where church spires had been the most remarkable architecture. Vermont-born William T. Porter launched the first American sports weekly, *The Spirit of the Times* (1831), in New York because "sports" meant horse races and New York "offered the biggest purses, the largest crowds, and the most important races." Anglophile students at Harvard and Yale began, in the 1840s, to row against each other. At the same time, John Cox Steven of Hoboken, New Jersey, a steamboat and railroad entrepreneur, gave the land on which the first baseball game was played. In 1851 Steven commissioned George Steers to build the yacht that won the America's Cup and inaugurated the most famous boat race of modern times. In 1859, little more than ten years after the invention of baseball by a New York bank clerk, two New England colleges, Amherst and Williams, made the game into an intercollegiate sport. After the Civil War, institutions such as the New York Athletic Club (1868) sprang up, flourished, and banded together in the urban centers of the North to form the Amateur Athletic Union (1890). In the 1870s, northern students organized regattas and track-and-field contests. They domesticated rugby football and turned the English game into an American one. In the 1890s basketball and volleyball were invented, the former in Springfield, Massachusetts, the latter in nearby Holyoke. By the early twentieth century, the National League and the American League had established professional baseball throughout the Northeast; only two southern cities had major-league baseball teams—if Washington and St. Louis can be considered southern cities.[17]

The one southern city that *did* participate fully in the rise of modern sports was New Orleans, but the Crescent City was an exception, a milieu culturally as well as geographically distant from Tidewater plantation life. In some ways, of course, New Orleans was typically southern. Horse races were the city's most popular sport; cockfights were also common. The first track was built in 1814 or 1815 on Wade Hampton's plantation, and the Metairie Course was built in 1837. In other ways, however, the city's sports were exceptional. By the late 1850s New Orleans had oarsmen, boxers, male and female "pedestrians" (who ran foot races), and clubs for gymnastics, cricket, and baseball, but the vitality of the city's sports owed a great deal to impulses not typically southern. In *The Rise of Sports in New Orleans, 1850-1900* (1972), Dale A. Somers notes that citizens of French or Spanish descent "seldom shared the Anglo-American's love of sports." On the basis of his own carefully gathered evidence, Somers might have added that the rise of sports was powerfully abetted by the influx of immigrants from the North or from Europe. The most influential horse race promoter of antebellum New Orleans was Richard Ten Broeck from Albany. (Ten Broeck, a modernizer, rebuilt the stands at the Metairie Track, installed special parlors for the ladies, and demanded that the jockeys wear the owners' colors.) James O. Nixon, a newspaperman from Philadelphia, purchased the *New Orleans Crescent* and used the paper to advocate and publicize modern sports. Along with John Egerton, a New York banker, Nixon helped to found the Southern Yacht Club in 1849. Most of the boxers who fought in the Crescent City were Englishmen, such as James "Deaf" Burke, or Irishmen, such as Samuel O'Rourke. The gymnastics club was, not unexpectedly, a *Turnverein* organized by German immigrants. In a word, New Orleans is an ambiguous example of "southern" sports.[18]

If we discount the exceptional case of New Orleans, we can ask, What exactly did the plantation South contribute to the transformation of American sports from premodern to modern forms? Very little. The Cavalier neither ran nor rowed. The thought of his playing baseball is almost as absurd as Mark Twain's hilarious account of the game in *A Connecticut Yankee in King Arthur's Court*, where Hank Morgan has only limited success fielding two teams of armored knights. Of course, a few southerners always stood ready to approach sports in a new manner, but they did surprisingly little to develop the formal-structural characteristics of modern sports or to join the Yankees in the further diffusion of such sports.

An insightful 1773 comment by Josiah Quincy reveals with startling clarity the dichotomy between Massachusetts and Virginia and suggests some of the deeper causes of the South's relative "backwardness." In the South, "he who won the last match, the last main, or the last horse-race assumed the airs of a hero or a German potentate. The ingenuity of a Locke or the discoveries of a Newton were considered as infinitely inferior to the accomplishments of him who knew when to shoulder a blind cock or start a fleet horse." In short, modernization was, in the judgment of Richard D. Brown, "substantially arrested in the South." Brown makes no effort to analyze antebellum sports, but it should not surprise anyone that men for whom urban-industrial society was anathema were understandably reluctant to restructure their sports in accordance with the dictates of modernity. Not until the twentieth century—not until reformers had fought to create a New South, not until southern society had begun to lose its distinctive characteristics and, more and more, to resemble northern society—did modern sports become a central element of southern culture. The colonial Virginian was passionately involved in his cocks and horses and more tolerant in general of life's diversions than was his Massachusetts cousin, but the descendants of the Puritans were far more likely than the offspring of the Cavaliers to spread the gospel of modern sports. Whether one applauds or laments the South's "backwardness" in this matter depends on one's evaluation of the world whose coming the South resisted.[19]

FIVE

The National Game

A Park Full of Numbers

For approximately a century, from the 1850s to the 1950s, baseball was considered our national pastime. Commentators as different as Mark Twain, Morris Raphael Cohen, and Jacques Barzun agreed with the fans in the bleachers that baseball was an expression of a distinctively American culture. The alleged correspondence of national game to national character stimulated an intellectual metagame the point of which was to explain exactly what the correspondence meant. No one has played this metagame more enthusiastically than Albert G. Spalding, a former baseball player who became a prosperous sporting goods manufacturer. Writing in 1911, he proclaimed magisterially that it was absurd to doubt baseball's appropriateness as the national game: "To enter upon a deliberate argument to prove that Base Ball is our National Game; that it has all the attributes of American origin, American character and unbounded public favor in America, seems a work of supererogation. It is to undertake the elucidation of a patent fact; the sober demonstration of an axiom; it is like a solemn declaration that two plus two equal four."[1] Although no one wants to labor at works of supererogation, something more in the way of deliberate argument is called for.

Until its transformation in the 1960s and 1970s, baseball was an odd combination of premodern and modern elements. On the one hand, baseball was associated with what Irwin Shaw referred to lyrically as "the American sounds of summer, the tap of bat against ball, the cries of the infielders, the wooden plump of the ball into catchers' mitts." Thomas Wolfe may have said it even better: "Is there anything that can evoke spring—the first fine days of April—better than the sound of the ball smacking into the pocket of the big mitt, the sound of the bat as it hits the horse hide: for me, at any rate, and I am being literal and not rhetorical—almost everything I know about spring is in it—the first leaf, the jonquil, the maple tree, the smell of grass upon your hands and knees, the coming into flower of April."[2] A host of American novelists and poets followed Wolfe and Shaw into the green pastures of baseball fiction.

The pastoral associations were so powerful that the myth of Abner Doubleday and his Cooperstown cow-pasture was invented in order to wipe away the memory of the game's actual invention, in its modern form, by a New York bank clerk named Alexander Cartwright. The myth of Abner Doubleday was cut from whole cloth in 1907, when Spalding appointed a commission, chaired by his friend Abraham Mills, to investigate the origins of baseball. The rigged nationalistic commission which put the undeserving Doubleday in the ludic pantheon was determined to disprove the (correct) theory that baseball was derived from the British children's game of rounders. On the basis of a letter from an octagenarian named Abner Graves, Mills obligingly informed the delighted Spalding that the game was an American invention. Patriotism did not require that Cooperstown be named as its birthplace, but the pastoral impulse entered the equation, too. Apparently it went against the grain for a midwesterner like Spalding to associate the national game with the sidewalks of New York.

However deserved the irony that historians have heaped upon the heads of Mills, Spalding, and generations of gullible Cooperstown pilgrims, one must grant the game its pastoral elements. Baseball was indeed "the summer game," played on grassy fields during sunny afternoons, the perfect ludic embodiment of what the literary historian Leo Marx refers to, in *The Machine in the Garden* (1964), as "the middle landscape." Although most modern ballgames are played in some rectangular space of standardized dimensions, baseball fields are bounded on two sides by lines that extend, in our minds, to infinity. The stands into which the home-run ball is swatted are there for commercial and not for intrinsically ludic reasons. Moreover, although most modern ballgames are characterized by a back-and-forth oscillatory motion, the baseball player takes off on a circular course that ends where it started. In other, more anthropological, words, the movement is circular, as in the eternal return of myth, rather than linear, as in history's one thing after another.

Urban imagery *did* become an important part of the folklore of baseball (one need think only of the Brooklyn "Trolley Dodgers" and the "Gas-House Gang"), but pastoral associations lingered on —until recently. The partial transformation of the game in the last quarter-century has greatly reduced the pastoral dimension. Where are the "sounds of summer" when baseball is played in October? Night games on artificial turf in a domed and weatherless stadium equipped with cocktail lounges and a razzle-dazzle electronic scoreboard are not exactly what Abner Doubleday would have had in mind if Abner Doubleday had actually invented baseball. The game experienced on television—fragmented by advertisements for automobiles and computers, interrupted by telephone calls and children who need to be put to bed, distorted by the inescapably narrow focus of the camera's eye, now on the pitcher, now on the batter or fielder or runner—is something other than pastoral.

But the game has *always* been something other than simply pastoral. The modern elements have always existed simultaneously, paradoxically, side by side with the premodern pastoral dimension. They were there even on that June day in 1846, when Cartwright led his fellow New Yorkers to Hoboken to play the first game of baseball on land donated by the ubiquitous John Cox Steven (whom we have already met as an entrepreneur and sports promoter). For Mark Twain, an enthusiastic fan, baseball was a symbol of modernity, which is why he used it to such comic effect in *A Connecticut Yankee in King Arthur's Court*. The game was "the very symbol, the outward and visible expression of the drive and push and rush and struggle of the raging, tearing, booming nineteenth century!"[3]

Quite apart from the secularism and equality that baseball shares with all modern sports, the game was, even in the nineteenth century, characterized by a high degree of specialization, e.g., the division of the defensive side into nine separate playing positions. Rationalization dictated a constant revision of the rules. (Between 1876 and 1889, for instance, the base-on-balls rule was altered seven times.) In comparison, the closely related game of cricket resisted change once its rules were codified in the late eighteenth century. Furthermore, as Keith Sandiford has shown, the implements of cricket have changed scarcely at all.[4] The "static technology" of the game was in marked contrast to baseball's constant experimentation with balls (lively and "dead"), bats (wooden and metal), and gloves (bigger and bigger). The beginnings of bureaucratic organization can be dated from the founding of the National League in 1876. Most importantly, baseball was from the start marked by quantification and by the proliferation of records that quantification alone makes possible. Baseball requires not *literacy*, which might have limited its appeal; rather, it demands what Patricia Cline Cohen and other historians of science refer to as *numeracy*, i.e., the ability to work with numbers. Half the drama of the game (the invisible half, which European spectators cannot perceive) lies in the calculations of the fan who understands the significance of a 3-2 count and *knows* that a player batting .347 can bring in the tying run from second base. What other game, with the possible exception of cricket, has complexities of quantification as abstruse and arcane as the rules governing the foul ball (which counts as a strike for the first two strikes but not for the third)? In comparison, the level of quantification represented by the Byzantine charioteer's counting his wins or the medieval herald's jotting down the number of splintered spears seems primitive.

The quantified action, which includes four balls, three strikes, three outs, and nine innings, leads to an abstract world of batting averages, fielding averages, earned run averages, and all the other spectral numbers that haunt the ballpark, flicker at the side of the televised images, fill the columns of *The Sporting News*, and come to rest, finally, in the hallowed pages of *The Baseball Encyclopedia*. While records, in the sense of an unsurpassed quantified achievement, characterize every modern sport, baseball seems to have a greater variety of them. The times and distances of track and field are certainly important, and crowds can go wild when a runner sprints to what looks like a new record in the 1500 meters, but baseball has a special kind of quantified frenzy that, for instance, accompanied Hank Aaron's 715th home run and Pete Rose's 4,192nd hit.

In short, the formal-structural characteristics of baseball in its heyday, from 1850 to 1950, were an odd, perhaps even a unique, combination of pastoral and modern elements. In the late twentieth century we have seen the diminution of the premodern and the accentuation of the modern elements. Traditionalists bemoan the changes in the game, but baseball no longer needs to function as it did when it was the national pastime. Alexander Cartwright's inspired invention eased the difficult transition from an agrarian to an urban-industrial society. Playing and watching the game allowed nineteenth-century Americans to experience the comfortably familiar and the thrillingly novel, the bucolic sounds of summer and "the drive and push and rush and struggle of the raging, tearing, booming nineteenth century!"

Baseball, Social Class, and Fair Play

Let us consider two statements: "That's not cricket," and "Nice guys finish last." The first statement refers disapprovingly to behavior that violates the rules of the game. It implies recognition of the fact that agreement on the rules is what makes a sport possible. It evokes the spirit as well as the letter of the law. The second statement, an epigram by the immortal Leo Durocher, strongly suggests that excessive attention to the rules makes one a patsy, a wimp, a fall guy, a loser. While the epigram does not specifically endorse cheating, the folklore of baseball honors the successful trickster. As the dusk gathers, the last batter hits the ball squarely and the center fielder races backward, leaps into the air, shouts gleefully, and runs to the dugout. The ball continues on its unseen way into the deepening shadows, but cleverness has won the game. A stickler for the rules might be tempted to say, "That's not baseball," but the fans know better. All's fair in love and baseball. Nice guys finish last.

C. L. R. James, a Trinidadian cricketplayer and a Marxist scholar, testified that cricket had taught him fair play: "I never cheated, I never appealed for a decision unless I thought the batsman was out, I never argued with the umpire, I never jeered at a defeated opponent." When James visited the United States, he attended a baseball game and was appalled by "the howls of anger and rage and denunciation . . . hurled at the players as a matter of course."[5]

Is the difference implied by the two statements a matter of national character? British commentators have asserted this at various times, e.g., when American officials complained at the 1908 Olympics that British officials had dragged an exhausted Italian marathoner across the finish line in order to deprive plucky Johnny Hayes (U.S.A.) of victory. German scholars like Rudolf Kircher and Hans Indorf have written admiringly of fair play as an expression of English character (or, as they prefer to put it, *Geist*). National character may well be a factor in the way the British and the Americans respond to the demands of fair play, but there is reason to be skeptical. When Kircher became too lyrical on fair play as an English trait, he was confronted with evidence that factory workers and miners at a soccer match did not always behave as if they were at Lord's, the legendary venue of the Marylebone Cricket Club. He responded simply that such spectators were "un-English," but he might more logically have considered the difference in social class between soccer fans and cricket enthusiasts.[6]

Cricket is the game of England's elite. It is associated with Tom Brown's school days, with country squires, with colonial administrators manfully shouldering "the white man's burden," with spotless flannels and impeccable manners and time out for afternoon tea. Its greatest player, W. G. Grace, was the son of a prosperous Gloucestershire medical man. Baseball is associated with the lower classes. Its legendary hero, Babe Ruth, came from the slums of Baltimore and learned to play the game at St. Mary's Industrial School, an institution that one of Ruth's biographers referred to as "a medium-security prison for children."[7]

The folklore of baseball is complex and contradictory, but it certainly includes Ty Cobb sharpening his spikes and countless tobacco-chewing pitchers cleverly rubbing the ball with a little forbidden juice to give it that extra unpredictable illegal drop. Quite by accident, George Hildebrand of the Eastern League discovered in 1908 that an unevenly dampened ball flew in an unpredictable trajectory. The spitball was born, followed in time by the mudball, the shampoo ball, and a long list of others. Dave Duncan, a coach for the Cleveland Indians, estimates that nearly half of today's pitchers avail themselves of the illegal trick. Batters have a few tricks of their own, which Graig Nettles of the Yankees openly defends: "I don't begrudge the pitchers. . . . But until the umpires have the guts to stop them from marking the ball, I see nothing wrong with using a corked bat." For a *Sports Illustrated* article cataloging the many ways to cheat, former Detroit Tiger Norm Cash demonstrated in eight photographs "how he doctored his bats when he won the American League batting title in 1961." The article names dozens of past and present players who have been suspected of illegally meddling with ball, bat, base, and glove. Many players are candid about the ethics of the game: "When asked last season what percentage of the time he cheats on the DP [double play], Phillie Infielder Ramon Aviles said, 'All the time. Last Sunday I participated in four double plays. I cheated on three of them.'" The article concludes that cheaters are more sophisticated than in Ty Cobb's day, but "the rule of thumb still is: if you can get away with it, do it."[8]

None of this chicanery should surprise the historian who understands the social origins of the game. The folklore of the disadvantaged has always included the trickster and the clever rogue who gets around the rules. The ideal of fair play, in its Victorian and Edwardian heyday, was a *class* ideal. It was, to use Marxist terminology, an element of bourgeois liberalism, which has always emphasized legal and juridical guarantees (the rules of the game) rather than substantive and structural changes (a new game entirely). In the realm of sports, as in other realms, the ruling class makes up the rules.

Needless to say, the class relationships can change. Baseball, like soccer, began as the invention of the middle class and was taken over by society's less privileged members. And there are always exceptions—bankers' sons who throw spitballs and truck-drivers' sons who admit to the umpire that they really were tagged out. But the argument about class, sport, and fair play holds up as well as most sociological generalizations. This argument brings forth vigorous protests from American scholars who are pained to think that chicanery is a permanent part of their favorite sport; however, their pain at the thought that baseball is not always associated with fair play should be pleasure at the realization that here, at last, is a sport for underdogs. Baseball may not be an occasion for the wretched of the earth to revolt against their oppressors, but it is at least an opportunity for the downtrodden and frustrated American to admire the successful trickster or, at the very least, to stand up and scream, "Kill the umpire!" You can't do that at Lord's.

The Game, the Ghetto, and the Boss

In the first pages of Abraham Cahan's novel *Yekl* (1896) baseball functions as a symbol of Americanization. The novel opens in a sweatshop where Yekl, who now calls himself Jake, attempts to gain prestige in the eyes of his fellow immigrants because he understands the mysteries of sports. He tells the other Jews all about John L. Sullivan. Indicating that Yekl still communicates mainly in Yiddish, Cahan used italics for interspersed English words, many of which are sporting terms: "Jimmie Corbett *leaked* him, and Jimmie *leaked* Cholly Meetchel, too. *You can betch you' bootsh!*" When Yekl's fellow workers, simultaneously impressed and appalled, point out that boxing is a brutal activity unsuited for an educated and civilized person, Yekl has an answer that silences them. "*Alla right*, let it be as you say; the *fighters* are not *ejucate*. No, not a bit! . . . But what will you say to *baseball*? All *college boys* and *tony peoplesh* play it." The others are abashed by the force of these assertions. That "college boys" were actually more likely to play football than baseball is irrelevant. Baseball was the national game. To know baseball was to be a real American.[9]

The sportswriter Hugh Fullerton exaggerated his point and probably confused causes and effects, but there was a germ of truth in his claim, published in the *Atlanta Constitution* in 1919, that baseball "is the greatest single force working for Americanization. No other game appeals so much to the foreign-born youngsters and nothing, not even the schools, teaches the American spirit so quickly, or inculcates the idea of sportsmanship or fair play as thoroughly." Doubts are in order about the inculcation of fair play, but baseball was unquestionably a vehicle for Americanization. Because it was perceived as the archetypically American game, baseball won the allegiance of immigrants who wished to cast their lot with their new homeland. Indeed, the children of the immigrants, at home in America and eager to demonstrate their loyalty, became the most enthusiastic fans of all.[10]

Middle-class Americans of British descent invented and first played the game, but they were not to be its mainstay. One reason for the decline of their enthusiasm for baseball was that they had so many other sports to choose from. In addition to cricket, which many British-Americans continued to prefer over baseball, there were track-and-field events (often referred to as "athleticism"), rowing, golf, tennis, and yachting. Indeed, the distinctly upper-class *Book of Sport* that appeared in 1901 had no reference at all to the "national game." Just as the English upper middle class, having invented the modern game of soccer, then lost its popular invention to the lower classes, the American middle class was forced to give up its monopoly on baseball.

By the end of the nineteenth century the Irish-Americans and the German-Americans had all but taken over. Baseball had become popular with the poor whites (and blacks) of the South, and British-American players such as Adrian C. "Cap" Anson had their followers; but it was Michael "King" Kelly who packed the National League's stands and inspired the song, "Slide, Kelly, Slide!" Kelly was "a free spender, a fancy dresser, and an avid pursuer of night life." He was also a resourceful cheater. Nonetheless, when Arthur Soden of the Boston Braves paid an unprecedented $10,000 to bring Kelly to Beantown, he invested wisely in the economics of ethnicity. When Ernest L. Thayer wrote the most famous of all American poems about the national game, he entitled it "Casey at the Bat" and thus acknowledged the representative role of Irish players.[11]

Irish immigration to America was followed, a few years later, by a new wave of German *Auswanderer*. The German immigrants founded gymnastics clubs and organized these *Turnvereine* into the Nordamerikanischer Turnerbund. The Turnerbund had a powerful influence on physical education in American schools, but the children and grandchildren of the immigrants were less committed to the preservation of German culture. They deserted the well-drilled gymnastics ranks and learned the excitement of sandlot baseball. In time, Herman "Germany" Schaefer and John Peter "Honus" Wagner were heroes even to the *bei-unsers* (who insisted annoyingly that almost everything had been better "*bei uns* back in Germany"). A generation later, George Herman Ruth and Lou Gehrig were authentic American heroes whose ethnic origins disappeared in the Olympian mists of Yankee Stadium, where even a German-American could be nicknamed "Bambino."

Italian-Americans came later and had to wait longer for places on the team. The immigrant generation remained loyal to *bocce*, but two Italian-Americans signed major-league contracts in 1920, and Tony Lazzeri eventually joined Ruth and Gehrig in the Yankee lineup. By 1941, 8 percent of the players were Italian-Americans, with Joe DiMaggio about to become the most famous player of the era. DiMaggio's exploits at bat, and those of hundreds of other Italian-Americans, helped the *paisano* survive the hard knocks of discrimination.

After the Italians came the Jews, but Cahan's novel overstates the suddenness of the Jewish love affair with baseball. Orthodox Judaism was centered on Talmudic law, and the culture of Eastern Europe's ghettos and *shtetls* was hostile to sports. The children of the Talmudic scholars, however, turned away from the past in order to worship the modern equivalent of the golden calf. When the local team had no Jewish baseball players to idolize, the kids—like the protagonists of recent novels by Eric Rolfe Greenberg and Robert Mayer—dreamed of Christy Mathewson or Pee Wee Reese and waited impatiently for the day when the first Jewish star would arrive to inaugurate the ludic millennium.[12]

And then came the Afro-Americans. In fact, they had played in the major leagues in the 1880s, until the tide of segregation swept them out of the game, and they continued to play in their own leagues. While white Americans thrilled to the antics and exploits of Babe Ruth, black Americans were often ambivalent. They, too, admired the white stars, but they had a wholly justified sense of injustice when they alone applauded Judy Johnson, Cool Papa Bell, and Satchel Paige. Although a place in history may seem poor recompense for the exclusion suffered in one's lifetime, historians have written extensively on the Negro leagues and on the struggle to integrate the majors (about which more later). It was, of course, not until 1947 that Branch Rickey determined to break the color barrier and sent Jackie Robinson to bat for the Brooklyn Dodgers.

The performance of black players since those days has earned them a place in baseball disproportionate to what one might expect from their share of the population. Stars like Reggie Jackson now enjoy the adulation (and the income) denied an earlier generation. Baseball continues to Americanize.

The enthusiasm of the "ethnics" for baseball did not escape the attention of urban political leaders. Politicians rushed to identify themselves with the local team, a task undoubtedly made easier by the fact that most of the politicians were probably sincere in their enthusiasm. In no city was the political leadership more demonstrative in its affection than in Boston. In 1914 the Braves climbed from last place in July to first place in October, unexpectedly winning sixty of their last seventy-six games on their way to the National League pennant. "For this season, at least," writes Stephen Hardy, "they were Boston's darlings." In the World Series the Braves faced Connie Mack's powerful Philadelphia Athletics, a team that had won three of the previous four World Series. After Boston trounced Philadelphia in the first two games, the entire political establishment showed up at the ballpark to cheer the Braves on to a third victory. John "Honey Fitz" Fitzgerald and his great rival, the incumbent mayor James Michael Curley, were both on hand along with Governor David Walsh, Lieutenant Governor Edward Barry, Assistant Attorney General Thomas Riley, and a host of other hopefuls eager to demonstrate their loyalty to the team. It was a great day for the Irish.[13]

Happy as they were to harvest votes, urban political leaders were also well aware of the fact that baseball was a profitable business. Franchises made money. They offered employment to groundskeepers, ticket-sellers, and refreshment vendors, and there was no reason why these jobs should not have gone to loyal voters. Since economically viable franchises required land for a ballpark and some means of mass transit to bring the fans to the game, there were bids to be accepted, deals to be cut, and opportunities for "honest graft." Like other popular sports, baseball attracted gamblers, and gamblers frequently needed some sort of protection from the police. Good relations with the "machine" were an inestimable advantage.

In *Touching Base: Professional Baseball and American Culture in the Progressive Era* (1980), Steven A. Riess has published the results of his detailed investigation of the sports-politics-crime nexus. Paradoxically, although Americans of the Progressive Era regarded baseball as the epitome of "the finest American beliefs, traditions, and values," the men who controlled the major leagues were often machine politicians "who symbolized all that progressives and small-town Americans believed was wrong with American society." In the Progressive Era, "professional baseball was a nexus between politics and organized crime." In New York, for instance, William M. Tweed, the notorious boss of the Tammany Hall machine, controlled a supposedly amateur baseball team known as the Mutuals. "The players were ostensibly city employees in the coroner's office or the sanitation department, but they were actually . . . subsidized to play baseball." The team played in the nation's first professional league, the National Association of Professional Base Ball Players, and was a charter member of the National League. The Mutuals were eventually replaced by the New York Giants, owned by Andrew Freedman, a member of the machine's Finance Committee and a crony of Richard Croker, who became Tammany's boss in 1886.[14]

When Byron Bancroft Johnson founded the American League in 1900, he and his fellow owners sought to place a franchise in New York. There were profits to be earned, but there was also a political price to pay. "New York politicos were adamant in their demands for stock in any new club before they would permit an interloper into the city, and they had the power to back up their threats." Johnson acquiesced. The syndicate that received the franchise, which eventually became the New York Yankees, was supposedly headed by Joseph Gordon, a minor political appointee, but was actually controlled by Frank Farrell, a powerful gambler, and William Devery, a former police chief and close friend of Richard Croker. "During his flamboyant and crooked tenure, Devery usually could be found each evening meeting with bail bondsmen, dive owners, and pool room operators in the heart of the Tenderloin. His regime was so blatantly corrupt that in 1901 the state legislature decided to abolish his position and replace it with a commission system." When Farrell and Devery decided to sell their franchise in 1914, another Tammany insider, the brewery owner Jacob Ruppert, Jr., took over. In Chicago and other cities, the interaction of baseball magnates, political machines, and gamblers was similar to what occurred in New York.[15]

If Americans averted their gaze from the profit margins, personal lives, and political connections of the franchise owners, it was because they preferred, then as now, to follow the action on the field. When the gamblers got to the players, as they did to the Chicago White Sox before the 1919 World Series against Cincinnati, the public responded with a sense of outraged innocence. Although never convicted in the courts, the "Black Sox" players were purged by the new commissioner of baseball, Kenesaw Mountain Landis. Meanwhile, avowals of integrity were made by White Sox owner Charles Comiskey, who had almost certainly been involved in a coverup. The reassured public trooped back to the ballpark for blissful enjoyment of "the national game."

Flood v. Kuhn versus Common Sense

Until very recently, when hundreds of millions of dollars flowed from network television into the coffers of the National and American Leagues, baseball was small business. The Carnegies and Rockefellers of the Gilded Age looked with condescension if not with contempt on baseball entrepreneurs like Andrew Freedman and Charles Comiskey. Nonetheless, there was money to be made in baseball, and the owners, with rare exceptions such as Tom Yawkey of the Boston Red Sox, have always been more interested in maximizing profit than in providing wholesome entertainment for their beloved fellow citizens. In case of any doubt about their priorities, the existence of "gypsy" franchises, moved by their owners from city to city, should remind us of the actual state of affairs.

In the very first years of organized baseball, it was clear to the owners that paying high salaries to the players was not the way to maximize profits. Since competing for players had the not unexpected effect of driving up salaries, economic logic called for monopsony, i.e., control of the labor market. In 1879, three years after launching the National League, the owners agreed that each team should henceforth have the right to "reserve" certain players. In order to make absolutely sure that everyone respected the "hands off" agreement, the players were asked to sign contracts that "reserved" their future services to their present employers.

The reserve clause condemned each player to bargain with a single owner. If the player refused to sign a new contract at the termination of the old one, he was nonetheless committed to play on—at 80 percent of his previous salary. If, on the other hand, the owner decided to dispense with the player's services, he was free to sell or trade the hapless recalcitrant to another owner. "The major impact of the reservation system was to cause an extreme imbalance in bargaining power between owners and players." From the owners' point of view, the market operated nicely.[16]

The players responded to their plight by forming the National Brotherhood of Professional Ball Players (1885). In 1890 they attempted to break away from the system by creating the Players' League, which, for two short years, offered real competition for ballplayers and sent salaries soaring. In 1889, before the organization of the Players' League, four typical Philadelphia players earned an average salary of $2,025. While the rival organization was active, their contracts brought them $2,900 each, an increase of nearly 45 percent. Once the Brotherhood abandoned the unequal struggle, the Philadelphia players' average salary dropped to $1,800.

It was not the players who mounted the next really serious challenge to the system. Instead, rival entrepreneurs destabilized the baseball business. In 1914 and 1915 the Federal League competed with the two older circuits. Predictably, salaries in the National and American Leagues rose dramatically. For Ty Cobb and Walter Johnson, the benefits of competition were obvious. During the brief life of the Federal League, Cobb went from $12,000 to $20,000 a year and the miserably underpaid Johnson from $7,000 to $20,000. After a fierce struggle for the mind, hearts, and dollars of the fans, the upstart league collapsed. Defeated at the turnstiles, the Federal League owners resorted to the courts and sued the National and American Leagues. They accused their successful rivals of unlawful and monopolistic restraint of trade in violation of the Sherman Act and other antitrust legislation.

In 1922 Oliver Wendell Holmes, speaking for the majority, delivered the Supreme Court's opinion adjudicating the claims of the defunct Federal Baseball League. The court considered the facts (i.e., that the National and American Leagues had sought to monopolize the major league baseball business) and then ignored them. Baseball, concluded the learned jurists, was not an instance of interstate commerce. Although the teams traveled thousands of miles each year between cities as far apart as Boston and St. Louis, each of the thousands of games was played within the boundaries of a single state. "The business is giving exhibitions of baseball, which are purely state affairs." Therefore the Sherman Act, which had been used to send labor leaders off to the penitentiary, did not apply to baseball. Two decades later, in *U.S.* v. *Crescent City Amusement Company* (1944), the Supreme Court held that film distributors *were* acting in restraint of trade. Motion pictures were shown in theaters that never straddled state lines, but the films themselves went from California to the other forty-seven states. The industry, therefore, was engaged in "a regular exchange of films in interstate commerce," and that fact was "adequate to bring the exhibitors within the reach of the Sherman Act."

Lawyers interested in baseball noticed that the court seemed to have rejected the line of argument taken by Holmes in the Federal League case. Indeed, the decision used the word "exhibitors," which echoed the very language of the Federal League case. Their legal suspicions seemed confirmed in 1949 by the decision in *Gardella* v. *Chandler*. Danny Gardella of the New York Giants, along with seventeen other players, had been lured by Jorge and Bernardo Pasquel to "jump" to the Mexican League. When Gardella thought twice about his move, he found that he had been banned from north-of-the-border baseball by Commissioner Albert "Happy" Chandler. Gardella sued. Judge Jerome Frank, writing for the Federal Court of Appeals for New York, ruled in Gardella's favor and opined that the reserve clause held the players "in something resembling peonage." Judge Learned Hand agreed. Rather than appeal to the Supreme Court, Chandler dropped his blacklist. George Earl Toolson, who had a grievance against the New York Yankees, took heart and went to court. Some legal experts expected a new era, but they were wrong. In *Toolson* v. *New York Yankees* (1953) the Supreme Court reaffirmed the 1922 decision in the Federal League case.

In the years that followed *Toolson*, however, owners of baseball franchises watched their peers in other sports lose case after case. When the Supreme Court ruled in 1955 that a New York firm had violated the Sherman Act by conspiring to monopolize boxing, Justice Felix Frankfurter commented that it "would baffle the subtlest ingenuity to find a single differentiating factor between other sporting exhibitions . . . and baseball." His bafflement was intensified two years later when William Radovich took the NFL to court. In *Radovich* v. *National Football League* (1957), the justices ruled that the blacklisting violated federal antitrust legislation. The confusion was confounded in 1966. As if to make a point of judicial irrationality, the Wisconsin Supreme Court decided, in *Wisconsin* v. *Milwaukee Braves*, that the *states* had no legal grounds to regulate organized baseball because baseball is, after all, interstate commerce. Since the state court was obviously not empowered to reverse the Supreme Court's decisions in the *Federal League* and *Toolson* cases, the Wisconsin judges appealed to Congress to act, but Congress opted for continued inaction.

Legalities were not the owners' only argument in defense of the reserve clause and the "free agent" draft. (The latter institution granted individual teams exclusive rights to bargain with unsigned prospective players. The players then had two options: to play for the teams that picked them, or to hope for a career in Canadian or Latin American baseball.) The owners' principal defense of the reserve clause and the free agent draft depended on the peculiar logic of sports competition. General Motors could flourish without competition from Chrysler and Ford (much less from Volkswagen and Toyota), but competition is a sine qua non of sports. Although the Boston Red Sox and the New York Yankees are longtime rivals, it is in the interest of neither to drive the other out of business. It is, moreover, in the interest of *all* the teams that none of them dominates the league to the point where the fans become bored by all-too-predictable outcomes. Armed with this logic, the owners have argued that the reserve clause and the free agent draft are simply instruments to maintain a requisite degree of equality among the teams. That such instruments also act to deprive players of the right to bargain among prospective employers is simply a side effect.

The argument has some plausibility, but economists have challenged it. Thomas N. Daymont, for instance, has compared data from years when various sports leagues did or did not have the reserve clause, the free agent draft, and/or competition from rival leagues. Using the simplest of statistical devices, the standard deviation (which measures the distance of the data from their mean), Daymont claims that restrictive devices do not really preserve equality among the teams. In short, Daymont and other economists who have adopted similar strategies have sought to disarm the owners of their principal weapon.[17]

The debate over the reserve clause reached its climax in the 1970s. Since the decision handed down in *Wisconsin* v. *Milwaukee Braves* asserted that baseball really was a form of interstate commerce, Curt Flood of the St. Louis Cardinals might justifiably have anticipated a favorable decision in his case against Commissioner Bowie Kuhn. The opinion in *Flood* v. *Kuhn* (1972), written by Justice Blackmun, is one of the most curious in the history of the Supreme Court. Blackmun's decision begins conventionally enough: "For the third time in fifty years the Court is asked specifically to rule that professional baseball's reserve system is within the reach of the federal antitrust laws. Collateral issues of state law and of federal labor policy are also advanced." Immediately after this sober start, Blackmun bursts into lyric historicism: "It is a century and a quarter since the New York Nine defeated the Knickerbockers 23 to 1 on Hoboken's Elysian Fields June 19, 1846, with Alexander Jay Cartwright as the instigator and the umpire." After a brief history of the game, Blackmun comes to "the many names, celebrated for one reason or another, that have sparked the diamond and its environs and that have provided tinder for recaptured thrills, for reminiscence and comparisons, and for conversation and anticipation in-season and off-season." This rush of metaphor is followed by a list of eighty-eight names, beginning with Ty Cobb, Babe Ruth, and Tris Speaker, and ending with Rabbit Maranville, Jimmie Foxx, and Lefty Grove. As the baseball-inspired jurist truthfully remarks, "The list seems endless." A moment later, Blackmun cites the fiction of Ring Lardner and quotes from Ernest L. Thayer's "Casey at the Bat." By the time Blackmun began to deal with the legal issues involved, the plaintiff must have wondered whether he had appealed to the Supreme Court or to the Hot Stove League. Blackmun concluded that baseball's exemption from antitrust legislation had been a mistake, but he was content to accept the status quo as an "established aberration." The court repeated the suggestion made six years earlier in *Wisconsin* v. *Milwaukee Braves*: If the Congress wanted to correct the aberration, it was up to Congress to take remedial action. What is most extraordinary about *Flood* v. *Kuhn* is not the court's unusual restraint, but its remarkable candor. In all innocence, Blackmun and the three justices who agreed with him in the 4–4 decision not only revealed but seemed actually to glory in their prejudices. As one legal expert remarked, "It is an uphill fight to apply . . . the antitrust laws to the mythological kingdom of professional sports." Confronted with an economic injustice and a legal absurdity, the justices wallowed in nostalgia. Lovers of the "national game," they basked in their roles as the fans on the bench.[18]

Although Congress seemed happy with the judicial doctrine of "established aberration," lower-court judges have repeatedly ruled in favor of aggrieved players and have whittled away at baseball's exempt status. Unionization has probably done even more than legal action to better the players' economic lot. The Major League Ball Players Association was organized in 1954 and stirred from its doldrums in 1966, when Marvin Miller became its full-time executive director. The players began to bargain collectively and, in 1972, went out on a thirteen-day strike. A system of arbitration, established in 1968, was revised in 1974. In 1975, when Andy Messersmith of the Dodgers and Dave McNally of the Expos turned to arbitration in order to escape the bonds of the reserve clause, the arbiter upheld them and ruled that the clause was invalid. The owners promptly sued and were rebuffed at the district-court level. At this point the owners realized that their luck was not likely to last forever. They decided to compromise: they agreed to allow players with six years in the major leagues to declare themselves free agents. There were restrictions on the number of teams that could bid for any given player, and players who did move were bound to stay five years with their new clubs, but the compromise, subsequently modified, effectively curtailed the reserve system and did what the players had hoped for and the owners had feared. Salaries rocketed beyond the million-dollar mark.

Throughout these labor-management conflicts, typical in most ways of economic controversies in other modern industries, the fans have shown a notable lack of sympathy for the players. Dedicated members of the United Auto Workers seem to agree with the physicians of the American Medical Association that it is wrong, perhaps even un-American, for professional athletes to bargain collectively and sell their skills to the highest bidder. Whenever *Sports Illustrated* reports on the economic aspects of baseball, which it does surprisingly often, peevish letters berate the players for their greed and the journalists for their neglect of sports—as if economics were not a part of modern sports. Fans today are probably more sophisticated about the business of baseball than they were when Holmes wrote the decision in the Federal League case, but many Americans desire nothing better than to dream on of a pastoral world where the grass is green, the sun is bright, and the crisp spring air carries the delightful sound of bats and balls, where the ever-resourceful Kelly, skipping second base (who's looking?), slides safely into third.

SIX

Muscular Christianity and the Point Spread

Christian Science Invents a Game

Not even Aristotle knew when the Olympic Games were first celebrated or who began them. The legendary version most widely accepted by the ancients and commemorated by a falsified inscription on a discus was that the rulers of Elis, Pisa, and Sparta inaugurated the games in 776 B.C., but other versions had their supporters too. The consensus of twentieth-century scholars is that we are unlikely ever to unearth the data needed to settle the two-thousand-year-old controversy over origins.

About basketball, the prototypical modern sport, we have better information. The game was invented in 1891 in Springfield, Massachusetts, at the School for Christian Workers, later renamed the International Young Men's Christian Association Training School. Basketball's inventor was a thirty-year-old Canadian immigrant named James Naismith. The game was, in Naismith's words, "a synthetic product of the office. The conditions were met, and the rules formulated . . . before any attempt was made to test its value." Naismith had been given the task of inventing the game by the twenty-five-year-old superintendent of the school, Luther M. Gulick, who encouraged Naismith's ingenuity by arguing, with illustrations drawn from the chemistry of synthetic drugs and dyes, that novelty is merely the result of new combinations of known elements. Specifically, Gulick challenged Naismith to devise a game complicated enough to maintain the involvement of adults and spatially confined enough to be played indoors when New England winters daunted faint-hearted Christians. Naismith tried prisoner's base, sailors' tag, rounders, town ball, battle ball, and leapfrog, but all failed the first criterion: adults lost interest. He tried indoor baseball, football, soccer, and lacrosse, but all failed the second criterion: they caused too many injuries when played in the gymnasium. Whereupon the resourceful Canadian invented basketball. It was, in his own words, "a deliberate attempt to supply for the winter season a game that would have the same interest for the young man that football has in the fall and baseball in the spring."[1]

The attempt succeeded beyond Naismith's expectations. The first game was played in the school's gymnasium on December 21, 1891. The YMCA's *Triangle* published Naismith's rules on January 15, 1892, the *New York Times* described the game on April 26, and Amos Alonzo Stagg, better known for a long career in football, introduced the game at the University of Chicago in 1893. Intercollegiate basketball began on February 9, 1895, when Hamline lost to the Minnesota State School of Agriculture. A year later the YMCA organized national championships. By the end of basketball's first decade, Columbia, Cornell, Harvard, Princeton, and Yale had organized the Intercollegiate League. Amherst, Dartmouth, Holy Cross, Trinity, and Williams had joined in the New England League. Basketball reached Asia before it arrived in Europe because Naismith's first team included future missionaries to China, India, and Japan.

The athletic festivals of antiquity and the modern game of basketball were both responses to a cultural need. The ancient Olympic Games were a religious ritual as well as an athletic encounter; basketball was meant to serve as an instrument to bring young men to Christ. The Olympic Games evolved slowly, over centuries, under the direction of the priestly *hellanodikoi*; in contrast, basketball's development, controlled at first by the YMCA and then by the Amateur Athletic Union and the National Collegiate Athletic Association, was swift. Moreoever, basketball's development has been *rational* in Max Weber's sense of the term, i.e., there has been an instrumental means-ends relationship. In a 1914 article published in the *American Physical Education Review* and in a short book entitled *Basketball*, which he published in 1941 to celebrate the fiftieth anniversary of the game's invention, Naismith reconstructed the sequence of logical steps he took as he reasoned his way to the solution of his problem. Perhaps the best indication of his instrumental approach was the placement of the basket (which was, in 1891, quite literally a peach basket). Fearful of potential injury from balls hurled forcefully at a ground-level vertical goal (like soccer's), Naismith elevated the goal above the players' heads and designed it so that its aperture was horizontal and narrow. The ball *had* to be thrown softly if its arc was to pass through the center of the basket. Constructed rule by rule, basketball represented a rational design.

Once it had sprung full-blown from the high-minded Mr. Naismith's brow, basketball was continuously reshaped by the YMCA, the AAU, the NCAA, and various other national and international bureaucratic organizations anxious to perfect the game. One result of this eminently scientific approach to play has been that the historian can chronicle the development of the rules in the minutest detail. The pivot was allowed in 1893, the dribble in 1896. Fouls were penalized by points at first, but the free throw was introduced in 1894. Naismith began with nine players (because his class consisted of eighteen), but the AAU reduced teams to five in 1897. The peach-basket goals of the first game made retrieval of the ball something of an inconvenience, so the problem-solvers knocked out the basket's bottom. The modern net, "basket" in name only, was introduced in 1906. The out-of-bounds rule was imposed in 1913 to end mad scrambles for the ball. There is no need to trace the steps from Naismith's clever placement of the basket to the twenty-four-second and the three-point rules. Everyone realizes that basketball, like the internal combustion engine and the computer, is an invention that has been and will be modified.

The instrumental means-ends approach to basketball provides good answers to technical questions: What rules will minimize the probability of injury? How can the game be modified to maximize the excitement of players and spectators? But those were not the only questions asked by Gulick and Naismith in 1891. Gulick's challenge to invent an indoor game for adults was related to the moral purpose of the YMCA. In their approach to sports, Gulick and Naismith were similar to such Puritan theologians as Richard Baxter and William Prynne. They were, in fact, directly influenced by

Charles Kingsley, the nineteenth century's great preacher (in novels as in sermons) of the gospel of "muscular Christianity." The immediate purpose of basketball was to provide exercise and amusement for eighteen young men who were bored by calisthenics and too rambunctious for indoor football. Ultimately, however, basketball was meant as an instrument to bring these young men to Christ.

Behind the inventive deliberations of the YMCA workers lay the doctrine of "muscular Christianity," behind which loomed the imposingly moral and interestingly misunderstood figure of Thomas Arnold, headmaster of Rugby School from 1828 to 1842. Since Arnold encouraged his students to play team games like cricket and football (Rugby version) rather than to waste their time and jeopardize their souls in ale-houses and brothels, he has often been described as a believer in sports as an instrument of moral reform, but Arnold cared little for sports and had no faith in them as ethical inculcators. For moral reform he relied on sermons replete with Christian doctrine. It was Arnold's admiring student, Thomas Hughes, who misconstrued his preceptor's message and dramatized it in one of the nineteenth century's classic boys' books, *Tom Brown's School Days* (1856). It was Hughes, rather than Arnold, who imagined that piety and manhood were learned on the cricket field and the soccer pitch. The strength of character that could be taught by sports was a good deal more important than calculus and Greek, which were drummed into boys by a set of sickly pedants. Charles Kingsley agreed: "Games conduce not merely to physical, but to moral health; in the playing-field boys acquire virtues which no books can give them; not merely daring and endurance, but, better still, temper, self-restraint, fairness, honour, unenvious approbation of another's success." The phrase "muscular Christianity" was coined by T. C. Sander in a *Saturday Review* notice of Kingsley's novel *Two Years Ago* (1857). Kingsley was initially stung by the phrase, but in 1863 he wrote to his Christian-socialist friend F. D. Maurice that he was "content to be called a Muscular Christian, or any other impertinent name, by men who little dream of the weakness of character, sickness of body, and misery of mind, by which I have bought what little I know of the human heart." With or without the tag, the doctrine of "muscular Christianity" caught on. As A. N.

Mangan has shown in *Athleticism in the Victorian and Edwardian Public School* (1981), by the 1890s there was hardly an English school where the "games ethic" did not reign supreme.[2]

The faith that moved Hughes and Kingsley inspired Gulick and Naismith as well. Generations of American physical educators, those employed by schools and colleges as well as those committed to the YMCA, have preached the sermon of "muscular Christianity" and have insisted dogmatically that sports teach young men (and even young women) to be reverent, adventuresome, courageous, cooperative, loyal, etc., etc. Perhaps they do, but the personality tests devised to measure the psychological differences between athletes and nonathletes have produced such contradictory results that most psychologists have abandoned this approach. If psychologists had studied the history of basketball, skepticism about the efficacy of the game as a teacher of ethics might have arisen sooner.

The Permanent Crisis

Quite apart from the officially sanctioned modifications of basketball as the game is described in the basketball rulebooks, there has been a continuous transformation of the unwritten rules that actually govern what happens on the boards. Rulebooks, after all, seldom adequately reflect the norms that regulate play. Although Naismith played and loved football, his notion of basketball excluded body contact between players. Coaches, players, and officials have long since determined otherwise. Naismith, dismayed by the transformation of the game, wrote plaintively, "How anyone can make a rough game of it and follow the rules is hard to understand."[3] It *is* hard to understand—but it is easy to see that not everyone follows the rules. The norms are established by the players and by the coaches and officials who do or do not enforce the written rules. They have collectively determined that the intercollegiate game should be a rough-and-tumble affair and that the National Basketball Association should feature a "physical" approach in which shoving, elbowing, holding, and clawing are legitimate.

Deviant officials who decided to enforce Naismith's rules would bring the contemporary game to a standstill.

The reasons for such a radical departure from Naismith's original norms are certainly complex, but demographic changes in American society are one important factor. In the 1890s the game had the aura of muscular Christianty and the social gospel. It was part of a missionary impulse, an instrument in the hands of earnest, young, mostly middle-class, mostly British-American men (and, somewhat later, women). The game was taught to the children of the immigrants in order to imbue them with the competitive-cooperative spirit of strenuous fair play. Settlement House and YMCA worked hand in hand to Christianize the social order.

Times changed. In the 1920s and 1930s, basketball established itself as one of the nation's most popular sports. It was played with enthusiasm in the Midwest and in the South, but the associations and folkways of the game (as opposed to its written rules) remained urban. Basketball became the archetypal "city game," played by teams representing the Young Men's Hebrew Association and the Newman Club as well as by stalwarts from the YMCA. Naismith's invention became the favorite sport of metropolitan high schools and colleges. Boys whose fathers had been Talmudic scholars in Polish ghettos dribbled and shot against teams from parochial high schools or Catholic colleges. In the 1930s an astute sportswriter, Paul Gallico, asserted that the game "above all others seems to appeal to the temperament of Jews, and for the past few years Jewish players on the college teams around New York have had the game all to themselves."[4] Eventually, at the intercollegiate as well as the openly professional level, the game came to be dominated by urban blacks. Decade by decade, basketball became a faster and rougher game, hardly a "non-contact sport." National invitational tournaments are not reminiscent of the YMCA physical-education classes of nearly a century ago. The unwritten rules now allow for rougher play—and for fixed games.

That some players cheated and that some games were fixed "was no secret to anybody on the collegiate athletic scene" in the 1920s, 1930s, and 1940s, but the real blockbuster exploded in 1951. On January 14 Junius Kellogg, a black student who had been recruited from Virginia to play for Manhattan College, met Henry Poppe, the previous season's star. Kellogg agreed to keep the point spread below ten points. Manhattan College beat DePaul 62–59, but Poppe failed to show up with the money. Kellogg had already spoken with coach Kenneth Norton, President Bonaventure Thomas, and the police. Poppe was arrested and confessed that he and John Byrnes had received thousands of dollars from Cornelius Kelleher in return for fixing games during the 1949–50 season. Kelleher was arrested, along with Benjamin and Irving Schwartzberg, brothers who were "bookmakers, felons, and ex-cons." The investigation that followed revealed that a whole network of fixers, like Eli Klukofsy and Salvatore Sollazzo, had reached dozens of players at CCNY, Long Island University, Manhattan College, New York University, Bradley, Toledo, and the University of Kentucky.[5]

Most of the players confessed, which sent several of the gamblers to prison and cast suspicion on a number of coaches. Kentucky's famed Adolph Rupp assured the world that *his* players were immune to the kind of sickness which had overcome the New Yorkers. There was no corruption in the bluegrass country; gamblers "couldn't touch our boys with a ten-foot pole." Although this assertion of innocence was widely believed, Alex Groza and a number of his University of Kentucky teammates had "apparently . . . set up shop as soon as they returned from the [1948] Olympics, and their splendid 1949 season is all the more amazing when it is remembered that they won thirty-two of thirty-four games while controlling their point spreads." Coach Nat Holman of CCNY was probably honest in his recruitment of players, "but with the deliberate involvement of an assistant to whom he delegated authority, some of his players had been illegally recruited, their transcripts and records falsified." Did the gamblers sense that dishonestly recruited players were fair game?[6]

In 1961 another series of scandals occurred, with fifty players from twenty-seven schools implicated for fixing forty-four games played from 1956 to 1961. A grand jury returned true bills against four North Carolina State basketball players. Among them was Don Gallagher, who had won the 1960 alumni trophy as outstanding senior athlete. Since the gamblers involved were mostly New Yorkers who had contacted the southern players during the summer season in the Catskills, many North Carolinians felt as University of

Kentucky stalwarts had felt a decade earlier; evil lurked in New York City and its environs, and the best way to prevent its spread was, in the words of Everett Case, "to play our basketball with North Carolina boys." This conception of the geography of sin may explain why the bribed North Carolina players escaped prosecution. None was indicted, but Jack Molinas, who had acted as a middleman for the gambler Aaron Wagman, was less fortunate. He had earlier been suspended from the National Basketball League for betting on games in which he had played. Found guilty now of gambling, conspiracy, and perjury, Molinas was sentenced to thirty-six years in prison, served a fraction of that time, was released on probation, and was subsequently murdered by an unidentified gunman. Wagman admitted years later that he "had fixed more than one hundred college basketball games in his heyday."[7]

While there is no need to reconstruct the complete history of the basketball fixes, a difficult and unpleasant task, it must be said that intercollegiate basketball continues to be marred by an apparently interminable sequence of scandals, which has come to include accusations of rape and drug trafficking as well as fixed games. A final example should suffice. At Tulane University, John "Hot Rod" Williams and two other players were arrested in the spring of 1985 for allegedly manipulating the point spread in games against Southern Mississippi and Memphis State. Two other players were indicated but granted immunity from prosecution in return for their testimony. Three non-athletes, Gary B. Kranz, Mark Olensky, and David Rothenberg, were also arrested. Williams, a marginal student whose combined SAT scores were below 500 and who had failed psychology three times, admitted to having been paid $10,000 for matriculating at Tulane. He did not seem fully to comprehend the controversy which raged around him. He was later released on a defense motion for a mistrial, retried, and acquitted, whereupon he signed a $675,000 contract with the Cleveland Cavaliers. Tulane's athletic director, head basketball coach, and two assistant coaches all resigned, and Tulane's president, Eamon Kelly, did what Father John LoSchiavo of San Francsico University had felt compelled to do in a similar situation: he eliminated the entire basketball program. Only the most sport-crazed fan can maintain that these recurrent scandals are isolated incidents.[8]

Marvels of the Point Spread

The mysterious motivations impelling men and women to gamble need not long concern us. The French anthropologist Roger Caillois lists *alea* (i.e., chance) as one of four universal categories of play, but Caillois is no more successful than others in his attempt to indicate *why* some of us seek out opportunities to wager and others do not. John M. Findlay's *People of Chance* (1986), which draws upon the work of Caillois, demonstrates clearly enough that Americans of all places and periods have gambled, from John Smith's Jamestown to Benjamin ("Bugsy") Siegel's Las Vegas, but Findlay seems as baffled as Caillois by their motivations. Why do some risk life and limb in a sport like football while others are impelled to pecuniary risk? Presumably there are not only personality differences between athletic risk-takers and gamblers but also between different types of gamblers. There are, for instance, contestant gamblers, who match their wits against each other in games like poker or in bets at the horse track, and fatalistic gamblers, who submit entirely to chance in lotteries and in games like roulette. If we can assume that people who place bets on sporting events have some insight into the probable outcome (UCLA will probably vanquish Amherst College), then we can conclude that such bettors are contestant rather than fatalistic gamblers. But this does not take us very far. It may also be that most of the money wagered on sporting events is put down by fans who want simply to demonstrate their commitment to their favorite team, to have a stake on as well as in the game, and thus to identify themselves more intensely with their sports representatives. If this is the case, then the money bet on sporting events is very unlike that bet in the hope of sudden unearned munificence.

That millions of Americans *do* gamble on sports is beyond question. In 1974, the Michigan Survey Research Center reported that 61 percent of American adults gamble and that sporting events are their favorite occasions for indulging. A 1983 Gallup poll found that 23 percent of the nation's men (eighteen and over) and 12 percent of the women bet on sports. In 1985 nearly twice that number, 41 percent of the population, told the pollsters that they favored legalization of betting on baseball, basketball, and football. Although, as I have indicated, there must be some kind of personality difference to account for the fact that 61 percent of the American people gamble while 39 percent do not, a recent study conducted by a trio of anthropologists concludes that there is scarcely any difference in the demographic profiles of gamblers and nongamblers. Indeed, contrary to the conventional wisdom, the gamblers in their sample were more likely to be employed and married than the nongamblers.[9]

Public responses to gambling, like public responses to prostitution, seem to be ambivalent if not confused. Although in most states it is illegal to wager on NCAA games, no laws prevent the media's dissemination of information on the odds. Coaches have asked the media not to publicize the point spreads, but journalists have defended their role with the usual appeals to "the public's right to know." Estimates of the amount of betting on intercollegiate athletics are notoriously unreliable, but it is certainly in the billions if not the tens of billions of dollars. Such sums have an appeal to organized crime.

As for the motivation of the fixer: he is no ordinary gambler. He has no desire to match wits with the experts or to fling himself blindly into the arms of Lady Luck. He is no risk-seeker. On the contrary, he seeks to obviate expertise, to eliminate chance, to avoid risk, and to cash in on a "sure thing." The fixer's only real gamble is that he can escape detection by the authorities.

Why has Naismith's well-meant invention attracted more than its fair share of fixers? There are several factors at work. Basketball's popularity is obviously important. Large numbers of people *care* who wins. The size of the team is also important; it is easier to bribe one or two basketball players than to go after half a dozen "Black Sox." The high scores and the quick turnovers are also factors. When a good player can shoot at least fifty times per game, it is difficult to prove—or even to notice—that he purposely missed five of his shots. Charles K. McNeil's invention of the point spread matters, too, in ways that may not be obvious at first glance. Honest bookmakers seek a contest in which each team is backed by exactly the same amount of money. When this occurs, the bookmaker is automatically insured against a loss; his percentage cut (the vigorish) is assured no matter which team wins. The invention of the point spread made it much easier for honest bookmakers to quote odds that encourage bettors to wager exactly as much on one side as on the other. Unfortunately, the optimal situation for the bookmaker also makes it possible for the dishonest gambler to say to a player, "You don't have to throw the game. You don't have to look bad. You don't have to be *disloyal* to the coach, the team, and the school. All you have to do is win by five points instead of ten." In the eyes of the fixer, boxing has many of the advantages of basketball; indeed, one need bribe only one man to control the outcome. But the boxer who takes a dive suffers defeat, humiliation, an impaired sense of masculinity, the loss of the purse, and the risk of serious physical injury. The basketball player who keeps down the point spread can still think of himself as a winner.

Other factors predispose basketball players to accept bribes, quite aside from the rather obvious fact that they too are attracted by large sums of money earned by no extra effort. Today, as in the 1950s, a disproportionately large number of first-rate players come from economically and socially disadvantaged homes. If they reach the National Basketball Association, their astronomical incomes immunize them from gamblers' offers of a few thousand dollars. The problem, accordingly, is most severe at the college level. Many NCAA stars are economically deprived urban black youths who lack the academic preparation necessary for college work. Many are apparently recruited in violation of NCAA rules, offered cash for their valuable services, sent to take special "Mickey Mouse" courses, and encouraged by their coaches to get away with rule infractions. If the situation of the college basketball star is indeed as it has been described, it is difficult to imagine why he should shun the fixer. Money delivered in a shoebox as a reward for choosing a university does not look appreciably different from money delivered in a shoebox as a reward for shaving points. The problem is *not* simply that the bribe-taker has not internalized YMCA values. The point-shaver is enmeshed in a system which makes corruption all but inevitable.

Reforms have been urged in response to the problem of fixed games, and to myriad related problems in intercollegiate basketball. Insist that all players can read and write before they are admitted to a university. Inform them of James Naismith's original high-minded Christian intentions. Give academic tenure to coaches and take the pressure off them so that they will not feel driven to violate the rules. Do not allow boosters to give players automobiles or pecuniary tokens of esteem. These suggestions are doubtless well meant, but the problems associated with intercollegiate basketball are the problems of intercollegiate athletics writ large, as Chapter 7 will indicate. Before looking at the anomaly of intercollegiate athletics, we do well to examine children's sports, where the future collegians are nurtured and socialized into the win-at-all-costs world of modern big-time team sports.

SEVEN

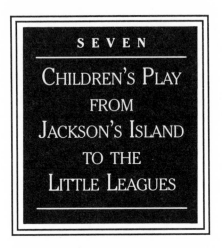

Children's Play from Jackson's Island to the Little Leagues

Playgrounds as Social Control?

When there were no fences for Tom Sawyer to paint, he was able to join Huckleberry Finn and head for Jackson's Island. Once safely on the island and out of Aunt Polly's and Pap Finn's reach, the boys were free to amuse themselves, to imagine themselves pirates or Indians, to enact whatever fantasies came to mind. The sidewalks of New York were distant—socially as well as geographically—from Jackson's Island, but Tom Sawyer's urban contemporaries played hide-and-seek, Red Rover, marbles, crack-the-whip, capture-the-flag, sandlot baseball, and hundreds of other children's games. (An 1896 survey of Worcester, Massachusetts, listed over four hundred such games.) As Mark Twain's readers knew and as twentieth-century folklorists have shown, nineteenth-century children were often supervised when at work but seldom when at play.[1]

Although boys enjoyed a greater number of traditional games than girls did, and were less likely to suffer from parental interference, children of both sexes were simply left alone to a degree unknown in today's middle-class family. We, however, have grown accustomed to the concept of adult-sponsored child's play. Long before they reach their teens, the juvenile descendants of Tom Sawyer and Becky Thatcher are driven by harassed members of parental carpools to their gymnastics classes and Little League games.

They are watched, supervised, coached, instructed, and judged by adults.

This transformation of children's play did not occur overnight. Historically, "regulated and administered sport programs by interested individuals and organizations solely for the use of small boys did not begin until after 1900."[2] The change was gradual, incremental, sometimes intentional, sometimes accidental. It is convenient to divide the evolution of adult-organized children's sports into two phases: the playground movement of the Progressive Era, and the mid-twentieth-century invention of sports leagues for children. The first stage was intentional and ideological; the second was not—at least not with the programmatic tenor of the nineteenth-century reformers.

The playground movement, which can be defined broadly enough to include such closely related institutions as the Public Schools Athletic League, was not the only Progressive Era effort to bring children's play under the control of reform-minded adults. In 1902 Ernest Thompson Seton organized the Woodcraft Indians, which encouraged boys to develop the skills needed for wilderness survival and to strive for the harmony with nature that Seton saw in the Indians' way of life. Sports, however, were not a significant part of Seton's program; nor were they originally of much importance in the Boy Scouts of America, founded in 1910 by the YMCA worker E. M. Robinson in imitation of Robert S. S. Baden-Powell's organization for British boys. For their efforts to show to the scoutmaster that they were trustworthy, loyal, helpful, friendly, courteous, kind, obedient, cheerful, thrifty, brave, clean, and reverent, Scouts earned merit badges testifying to their mastery of individual skills. At Scout camps, sports were tolerated rather than encouraged.

As David I. Macleod has clearly demonstrated in *Building Character in the American Boy* (1983), the boys who joined the Woodcraft Indians and the Boy Scouts of America were recruited almost exclusively from the middle classes. This was definitely *not* the case for the boys and girls whose moral improvement through sports was a central purpose of the playground movement. That movement has recently been characterized as an effort by middle-class and upper-class reformers to control the behavior of lower-class immigrant children. As a first step in assessing the validity of this characterization, it is important to recognize that the initiative for reform often came from the people most intimately involved with urban problems. Stephen Hardy makes this point well: "The major initiative for [Boston's] public playgrounds came from neighborhood lobbies who were sold on the simple proposition that outdoor exercise was wholesome, a deterrent to crime and disease. . . . Only when the drive for playgrounds was well under way did genteel reformers exalt the movement with sophisticated theories about play, child development, and social behavior."[3] In *Eight Hours for What We Will* (1985), a study of patterns of leisure in Worcester, Massachusetts, Roy Rosenzweig comes to a similar conclusion.

Although the "neighborhood lobbies" and the "genteel reformers" needed each other, the historical debate has focused on the latter. There is no doubt about who they were. Many of their names are familiar to every historian: Jane Addams, Felix Adler, Luther Gulick, G. Stanley Hall, Joseph Lee, Jacob Riis, Lillian Wald. There is disagreement over the nature and value of their achievement. Dominick Cavallo's *Muscles and Morals: Organized Playgrounds and Urban Reform, 1880–1920* (1981), is relatively mild in its judgments: "The reformers viewed organized play as a vital medium for shaping the moral and cognitive development of young people. Equally important, organized play, particularly team sports for adolescents, was seen by reformers as an ideal means of integrating the young into the work rhythms and social demands of a dynamic and complex urban-industrial civilization."[4] Cary Goodman's *Choosing Sides: Playground and Street Life on the Lower East Side* (1979) is much more critical. Its thesis is accurately summarized in the foreword by Stanley Aronowitz: "The transition from autonomous play to organized play and sports is the switch from the notion of abandon, where body and mind range freely in time/space, to the rigorously enforced game rules that control body and mind, regimenting them to the iron cage of military and industrial disciplines."[5] Before deciding to praise the reformers for their idealism or to condemn them for their desire to regiment the young, one should examine the evidence. By the end of the nineteenth century, the unplanned urban development that still occurs throughout the United States was already felt as a severe social problem. Hysterical books like

Josiah Strong's *Our Country* (1886) warned against the bars and brothels of the slums, where ignorant immigrants caroused by night, from whence they emerged, bleary eyed, to make their way to the polls, where good government perished in an avalanche of corruption. The settlement house, with which the names of Jane Addams and Lillian Wald will forever be associated, was a more positive response to the problems of the slums. In the minds of many Progressives, playgrounds and parks were as necessary as settlement houses.

In 1887 Charles Stover persuaded the city of New York to authorize the establishment of small parks and playgrounds, but the city failed to provide the funds necessary to clear the ground and build the facilities. A model playground was opened in 1891 with private funds, but public money was not forthcoming. In 1898, with the help of Felix Adler, Jacob Schiff, Richard Watson Gilder, J. G. Phelps Stokes, Jacob Riis, and Lillian Wald, Stover founded the Outdoor Recreation League, which was able to open Seward Park in 1899 and Hamilton Fish Park in 1900. (Both were reopened as playgrounds in 1903.) There were running tracks, lockers, public baths, and—at Fish Park—tennis courts.

In 1903 Luther Gulick, who had left the Springfield YMCA to become director of physical education for New York City's schools, widened the reach of his program by founding the Public Schools Athletic League, which featured sports festivals, contests, badges, buttons, and secular sermons on good sportsmanship and fair play. Three years later Gulick became the first president of the Playground Association of America. (He also became a director of the Boy Scouts of America. Progressive Era reform was characterized by the same kind of "interlocking directorate" that economic historians have found typical for the modern corporation.)

The PAA was a typically Progressive institution. Its founder, Henry Curtis, garnered financial aid from the Russell Sage Foundation. Curtis had been a student of G. Stanley Hall, the influential psychologist of childhood and adolescence whose ideas formed the intellectual framework of the playground movement. Curtis was strongly supported by Jane Addams, already nationally famous for her nearly twenty years at Hull House, and by Joseph Lee, the founder of the Massachusetts Civic League. Clark Hetherington of the University of

Wisconsin was the PAA's consultant and the designer of its training program for playground instructors.

The movement flourished. In 1905, twenty-four cities operated a mere eighty-seven playgrounds. In 1917, 481 cities operated 3,940 playgrounds with 8,748 directors. Although the movement was in decline by 1920, it had achieved its purpose in that urban school boards had generally acknowledged their responsibility for providing school-year recreational opportunities.

The background of the playground movement was strongly Darwinian. Addams, Curtis, and most of the other playground reformers accepted Hall's notion of the child as a primitive. Recapitulation theory held that the wild behavior of the adolescent was not an aberration but a developmental—one might almost say evolutionary—stage. Lee's *Play in Education* (1915) expanded on some of Hall's ideas. As children move from infancy to adulthood, they pass through what Lee referred to as the "Big Injun" or self-assertive stage, which he thought occurred in six-to-eleven-year-olds. The trick was not to stifle the exuberance of this phase, which was a necessary part of the child's development, but to supervise and control it. The necessity for supervision seemed obvious. When playgrounds were not supervised, they were vandalized and ruled by bullies. Lee asked a Boston boy why he avoided the North End playground and was told, "Oh, dere's a tough crowd down dere who would knock the stuffin out of yer."[6]

All the playground reformers agreed that some kind of civilized physical activity was essential. Modern life was too sedentary, too intellectualized. G. Stanley Hall warned against "intelligence . . . separated from action" and thus rendered "mystic, abstract, and dessicated." Vigorous outdoor play was his answer to the debility created by modern life. Play was a rehearsal of racial history, a means to preserve past motor habits in a milieu that discouraged physical activity. The lack of physical activity was associated, in Hall's mind, with ethical laxness. In Cavallo's epigramatic synopsis of Hall's attitude, "flabby muscles inevitably fostered flabby morals."[7]

Hall was less dedicated than he might have been to firming up the flabby muscles of American girls. Writing in *Youth* (1906), he opined that women rejoiced in placidity while "a real man rejoices in noble strife." Of girls Hall wrote, "It is hard for them to bear defeat in games with the same dignity and unruffled temper as boys."[8] He was not the only Progressive to accept conventional stereotypes about masculinity and femininity. Influenced by popular Darwinism, such reformers assumed that men and women were physiologically destined to play complementary social roles; accordingly, boys and girls had differing recreational needs. They agreed with Catharine Beecher and numerous nineteenth-century physicians that American women, especially middle-class women, were in wretched health and in urgent need of moderate exercise, but their approach to children's play was based on the assumption that the boys, rather than the girls, had to be guided through the "Big Injun" and adolescent stages. Nonetheless, Jane Addams and most other reformers thought team sports appropriate for girls as well as boys—provided, of course, that the girls were decently clothed and avoided overexertion. The PAA provided facilities for girls' softball and basketball.

No one was more committed than Gulick to socialization through team games. (It was he, after all, who challenged James Naismith to invent the game of basketball.) His primary efforts were aimed at the Americanization of immigrant children. Interpreting the psychological needs that led to the organization of youth gangs, he wrote that the gang "is a masculine unit. It is the modern counterpart of the tribe. It is the germ out of which the club, the society, the corporation—every effective organization—develops."[9] Organized team games were Gulick's answer to the random destructive behavior of the street gang. Swept up in his enthusiasm for baseball, basketball, and football, the savage adolescent learns the complementary virtues of individualism and cooperation. Obedience to the rules of the game becomes the self-discipline prized by middle-class reformers.

Curtis, too, was a believer in socialization through team games. In *Education through Play* (1915) he argued, "The playground is far more democratic than the school." In Cavallo's words, "Because the team experience forged social unity out of individuals from diverse ethnic, class, and religious backgrounds, play organizers viewed it as an antidote to the alienation, violence, and loneliness seemingly inherent in urban society."[10] While Cavallo refuses to take the reformers at their word, he has some sympathy for their program of Americanization.

Cary Goodman, in contrast, has no such sympathy. Cavallo's criticisms pale when compared with those found in *Choosing Sides*, Goodman's Marxist study of New York's Lower East Side. In Goodman's view, the supervised playground appears as a form of social control imposed on "street life . . . vibrant and alive with children and adults, images and fantasies." The upper-class reformers felt "threatened by the radical nature of street life in the Jewish quarter." In response, they imposed their "hegemonic" control over the world of play, just as upper-class industrial entrepreneurs had imposed their will in the world of work. Luther Gulick was to the captive children of the playground what Andrew Carnegie was to the exploited laborers of the steel mills. "Children from Scranton, Pennsylvania, to Detroit, Michigan, were plotted, packaged, and had their spontaneity purloined under the guise of giving them what they asked for." Although the unwary reader might expect a radical analysis of play to be critical of the sabbatarian restrictions that lingered in some areas until the 1930s, Goodman interprets the campaign for Sunday play as desecration of the Sabbath. When the Playground Association and the settlement houses instituted programs celebrating Christmas, St. Valentine's Day, and Washington's and Lincoln's birthdays, the hidden motive was to distract the lower classes "from an identification with class-based holidays like May Day which had helped to sustain a culture of struggle within the working class." The team games sponsored by the reformers were engines of repression and domination. Spontaneous play was replaced by a rationalized system that prepared children for the disciplines of modern factory labor: "How many tens of thousands of children were readied for the robotized Taylorized factory system as a result of accommodating their time sense to time schedules, play directors, and a stopwatch?"[11]

While Cavallo acknowledges the reformers' inclusion of girls within their programs, Goodman stresses the playground directors' lack of enthusiasm for girls' participation in serious competition. He suggests that the reformers were not at all progressive in their attitudes towards adolescent sexuality: "Every play leader . . . believed in eliminating coed play with the onset of puberty." The reformers' discrimination against the girls did not, however, give an advantage to the boys. Deprived of playful interaction with the opposite sex, boys were "desensitized psychologically." During World War I, when the PAA cooperated with the War Camp Community Service, the results of such deprivation were apparently pathological. The men whom the armed forces inducted for military service were "psychologically crippled, handicapped in their ability to reach out to women and one another with affect and in a spirit of equality."[12]

Since Cavallo and Goodman more or less agree on names and dates and deeds, we must understand their disagreements as differences in interpretation. Neither is content to accept the notion that the reformers were simply men and women of good will who responded to the cry of the cities and forthwith constructed parks and playgrounds to brighten the lives of deprived children, but Goodman seems to view the Playground Association as little more than a capitalist plot aimed at enslaving proletarians before they are old enough to work. He often writes as if a citation from Marx or Engels sufficed to unmask the disguised exploitive motives of the upper-class reformers.

The reformers were unquestionably anxious to change the unruly ways of New York's Lower East Side and Boston's North End. Their conception of disciplined play was indeed meant to socialize boys and girls into the more or less rationalized modern world. They did not, however, intend team games to eradicate individual initiative, nor did they imagine that organized play was the basis for industrial exploitation. If their conception of modernity was flawed by their traditional view of gender roles, they were nonetheless more modern in their attitudes towards girls' physical activity than were the Polish or Sicilian parents who were horrified at the very thought of their daughters playing basketball. The Playground Committee of the Massachusetts Civic League reported in 1901 that its "hockey and football teams ignored, to a great extent, the race lines between Irish, Jews, and Italians, which are so marked in the North End." The desire to minimize ethnic differences, universalistic in Talcott Parsons' terminology, should not be dismissed with dark remarks about "social control."[13]

Behind Goodman's dark accusations there seems to lurk a romanticized notion about what unsupervised children's games are like. One example from Brooklyn in the 1880s offers a helpful reminder. The game described by Stewart Culin is "hide the straw": "Bounds are agreed upon, and the new boy is made 'it.' All close their eyes while he hides the straw, and afterwards they search for it, apparently with much diligence. At last they go to the boy and say: 'I believe you have concealed it about you. Let us search him.' Then they ask him to open his mouth, and when he complies they stuff coal and dirt and other objects in it."[14] Such pranks seem good natured when compared to a switch blade assault, but it is important not to become too misty eyed about nineteenth-century play. Goodman is not only forgetful of what children's play was like; he is also confused about the very nature of socialization. Since culture can be defined as a symbolic world that each generation inherits, modifies, and seeks to pass on to the next, it is naive to complain that the reformers sought to impose their values upon the children of the immigrants. Of course they did—in what utopia do educators delight in pupils whose values diametrically oppose their own? The real question is not whether children were encouraged to adopt the reformers' liberal-democratic values, but whether the process of socialization left them more free or less free than they might otherwise have been.

Research into turn-of-the-century children's play has barely emerged from the taxonomic stage. Apart from grand European works such as Philippe Ariès's *Centuries of Childhood* and *Renaissance Games*, historians have done relatively little with children's play. Most of the research has been done by sociologists and psychologists who have limited themselves, understandably enough, to studying today's children. Historians need to know more about what actually went on when children played. Psychologists need to discover more about the kinds of personality traits encouraged by different modes of play. Tom Sawyer and his urban counterparts may indeed have been better off without the intervention of the play professionals, but it is foolish simply to assert that a romp in the woods or stickball in the street was socially superior to playground basketball or fifteen minutes on the teeter-totter.

One cannot generalize from the experiences of a single person, but, having survived childhood in the streets of Chicago's South

Side, I look back with gratitude on the do-gooders who offered me the sanctuary of Woodhull Playground Park.

The Six-Year-Old Champions

The Playground Association of America was consciously intended as a reformist organization. The same cannot be said of Little League Baseball and its equivalents in a dozen other sports. Little League was created not by educators, social workers, and philanthropists but by an ordinary citizen, Carl Stotz of Williamsport, Pennsylvania. Stotz conceived of Little League in 1938 and inaugurated play in 1939. In 1947 he organized a tournament for boys from Pennsylvania, New York, and New Jersey. By 1974, over 2,000,000 boys and girls played in a network of 8,500 leagues that covered the entire United States and a number of foreign countries. (World championships were established—and became a source of tension between the United States and Taiwan when the Chinese boys won four years in a row. After their 12–1 victory in the final game of 1974, they were temporarily banned from further competition.)

Pop Warner Football actually preceded Little League Baseball. In 1929 Joseph Tomlin, a Philadelphia stockbroker, formed a league named for Glenn Scobie "Pop" Warner, the famed coach at the Carlisle Indian School, for whom Tomlin also named his son. By 1975 some 175,000 boys aged seven to fifteen were enrolled in 5,700 Pop Warner teams in thirty-nine states and Mexico.

There are now children's leagues and national championships in almost every sport. The tendency, moreover, has been to organize children's sports for younger and younger age groups. The "Pee Wee" category for motorcyclists consists of children from two and a half to six years old.

The relentless modernization of children's sports has meant not only bureaucratic organization on a national basis but also specialization (in the form of ten-year-olds who are settled in at second base or as goalie), rationalization (in the form of regular practice and workout schedules), quantified performance, and, of course, an obsession with records. Among *Sports Illustrated*'s "Faces in the

Crowd" (July 28, 1986) was six-year-old Stephen Cassaday of the Gloucester Track Club; Cassaday set a national record of 19 seconds for the hundred-meter dash. Modern children choose professional athletes as their models, which is certainly not new; but children now wear uniforms, inspire enthusiasm in prepubescent cheerleaders (also uniformed), worry about local television coverage, and dream of possible appearances in the "Mighty Mite Bowl" or one of its many equivalents.

Little League Baseball and other children's programs have been controversial. As Jack Berryman observes, "From the 1930's on, physical educators and professional recreation leaders denounced the overt emphasis placed on winning, the physical and emotional strain, and the attempt to organize competition into leagues for championship play." In an article provocatively entitled "Backyard versus Little League Baseball: The Impoverishment of Children's Games," Edward C. Devereux drew upon the psychological theories of Jean Piaget and argued that "informal peer group experiences and their accompanying dissonance contribute to the development of moral autonomy in children" while "authoritarian control by adults has precisely the opposite effect." Unfortunately, Devereux does not indicate if *democratic* guidance by adults might have more benign results than authoritarian control. Perhaps Devereux believes that it is simply impossible for adults to organize children's sports in a nonauthoritarian way.[15]

The bill of indictment against adult-organized children's sports is lengthy. Empirical studies have shown conclusively that children enter Little League with a preference for the pleasures of participation—or, in their words, for having fun, rather than for winning. The psychologist Terry Orlick investigated a thousand children involved in children's leagues and found that 95 percent gave "fun" as their motive; 90 percent preferred playing and losing to sitting on the bench and watching their teammates win. Critics of children's leagues have blamed parents for their refusal to accept the children's priorities. The trouble is that fathers and mothers are vicariously involved in their sons' and daughters' performances. Through the psychological mechanisms of identification and projection, middle-aged men and women relive their own childhood triumphs and expunge the memory of their own athletic failures.

This view of the psychic dynamics of parental involvement seems especially plausible in light of data gathered by Geoffrey Watson, who reported that fathers who were themselves athletically active are more likely than other fathers to encourage their sons to participate in Little League Baseball.[16]

Many parents demand a return on their psychological (and material) investment. When driven children fail to act out parental fantasies, frustrated fathers and mothers can bully, humiliate, and physically punish their offspring. "After one [motorcycle] race, a father who thought his son had lost through a stupid mistake . . . was seen to vent his frustration by hitting the boy with a wrench."[17] Spare the rod and spoil the super-star.

Since children cannot perform well if they are deprived of the opportunity to play, parents frequently pressure the coaches to send their children into the game. Fathers have been known to lug cases of cold beer to the ballpark in order to win the favor of thirsty coaches. One disillusioned father complained to *Sports Illustrated* writer John Underwood about the unfair tactics of attractive young mothers: "Mama comes around in a tight pair of pants and a halter and wants to engage [the coach] in a philosophical discussion about football. At her place."[18]

Disappointed parents of defeated players have also been known to turn to violence. In Kissimmee, Florida, "a mob of adults attacked four coaches of a winning team of twelve-year-olds with clubs and pipes, sending one coach to the hospital. A cry from the crowd, 'He's dead!' apparently satisfied the mob and it withdrew just before the police arrived. The coach was not dead, only unconscious for four hours." Watson, who probably studied Little League Baseball more extensively than any other sociologist, saw social class as a factor in parental behavior at the games. If his results from an investigation of thirty-six middle-class and sixty-five working-class families can offer a basis for generalization, it is the blue-collar rather than the white-collar parents who interfere with the game by jeers, applause, and "coaching" from the sidelines.[19]

Coaches, most of whom are also fathers of Little League players, are involved in the same psychological processes as the parents. Jonathan J. Brower concluded, after a ten-month study of motivational research into Little League Baseball, that "the thirst for victory and its accompanying competitiveness was far stronger among managers and coaches than players." The coaches' ego identities merge with those of their players to the point where they lose their perspective and become obsessed with their won-lost ratio or the pursuit of a championship. In such a state they have been known to berate, intimidate, and even assault the children who failed to perform well. One parent who can claim to be an authority on football, the former Miami Dolphin star Larry Csonka, refuses to entrust his two sons to the care of such coaches: "Csonka went out to watch a boys' team practice one afternoon in Fort Lauderdale and was appalled. Csonka is not a man who recoils from spilled blood, his or anybody else's, but he was horrified by little league football. 'The coaches didn't know much about what they were doing,' he said. 'They just yelled a lot. They acted like they imagined [Vince] Lombardi or [Don] Shula would act.' "[20] The Fort Lauderdale coaches demanded that the eight-year-olds run postpractice windsprints. Since windsprints are not the average eight-year-old's idea of fun, many children begin to hate football before they are old enough to play the game properly. "The burned-out football player is not unusual," writes Underwood, and some boys decide early on that they are fed up with the world according to Vince Lombardi. "The coach," complained one disillusioned thirteen-year-old, "thinks football is the only thing in the world." That boy retired from the game.[21]

Some of the best data on children's leagues come from British Canada, but the consensus among sociologists and social psychologists is that the data are valid for the United States as well. Children's hockey in North America is usually organized under the sponsorship of the National Hockey League. The children are divided into Tykes (seven to nine years old), Novices (nine to eleven), Peewees (eleven to thirteen), Bantams (thirteen or fourteen), Midgets (fifteen or sixteen), and Juveniles (seventeen or eighteen). Each group is further divided into teams constituted on the basis of ability. Edmund Vaz, who suggestively entitled his book *The Professionalization of Young Hockey Players* (1979), deplores the fact that the children "are given no formal instruction in obeying rules. They do receive informal instruction in violating rules and in the use of illegitimate tactics, and they are taught conditions under which these acts are expected." The coaches do not encourage the children to inflict permanent injury, but their bag of dirty tricks is full of other ways to cheat. Among the tactics taught by the coaches are knocking the skates out from under an opponent, hanging onto his pants, holding his stick, and slamming him up against the boards. "Players who want to excel at the game are obliged to violate rules and to engage in certain forms of violence. Failure to do so seriously jeopardizes their chances of success." One of the coaches instructed the children, "If you can't skate with them, then the only way is to knock them down." Another coach told his charges to "go out and take your man out, and show him you're there." The young players soon learn the message. Vaz found that the coaches who emphasize roughness and aggressiveness are much more likely than other coaches to have players who attempt to "take out" opposing players by resorting to "instrumental" fouls. Hypocrisy seems not to be a problem. The children are aware of what is expected of them. As one hardened ten-year-old remarked, "If you hit some people once in a while then they'll be afraid of you." Asked what to do in the corners, another child answered, "First man is supposed to take the man out, the second guy's supposed to get the puck."[22]

The National Hockey League is the model to be imitated. "This means fearless, aggressive, physically intimidating hockey, including disciplined use of the body as well as the ability to play in spite of pain." In a similar study of 751 minor league players aged twelve to twenty-one, Michael D. Smith also found evidence of modeling. Smith asked the children if they had learned to hit illegally by watching the professional game; 56.9 percent said that they had. The same effect can be seen in children's football. Consider one child's letter to Jack Lambert of the Pittsburgh Steelers: "I hit some kid the other day and broke his arm, and when I did I thought of you."[23]

The longer a child plays in organized sports, the more likely he or she is to approve of instrumental violence. In Smith's study, the children were asked to comment on the statement, "One professional player has said, 'I get paid to beat up the other guys.' In your opinion, does he deserve or not deserve the high salary he gets for this?" Only 10.1 percent of the twelve-and-thirteen-year-olds, as compared with 23.7 percent of the eighteen-to-twenty-one category, thought the player deserved his salary.[24]

Despite a century of optimistic rhetoric about sports and character, there is a clear correlation between years of Little League play and a predisposition to cheat. The sociologist Harry Webb devised a pencil-and-paper attitudinal test that purports to measure professionalization. Children are said to be "professionalized" when they rank winning and improving their playing skills above playing fairly. Webb and others who employed his test found that the commitment to fair play declined with increased exposure to Little League and comparable sports. When Vaz rated young hockey players by their commitment to good sportsmanship, 21 percent of the Tykes and 76 percent of the Juniors were classified as "low." The most skillful players were also the most cynical about fair play.[25]

One of the most notorious instances of kids who cheat (with the connivance of their elders) occurred during the Soap Box Derby of 1973, when fourteen-year-old James Gronon conspired with his uncle, Robert B. Lange, to build a better "soap box." Although the rules stipulated that the vehicles be built by the children and at a cost of no more than $75, Lange employed the engineers and the equipment of his ski factory to build his nephew a fiberglass marvel (which he then tested in the factory's wind-tunnel). Not satisfied with this advantage, he installed a hidden electromagnet for a bit of additional acceleration. Jimmy Gronon won what the *Ladies' Home Journal* called "Watergate on Wheels," but his fate was analogous to Richard Nixon's: he was disqualified. Neither he nor his uncle, whose son had won the previous year's Derby, seemed to feel any moral qualms. They described themselves as the victims of jealousy. They seem not to have commented on the irony of a race for computer-designed cars that still bears a name reminiscent of nineteenth-century children's play.[26]

The misdeeds of Little League coaches include the administration of drugs. Robert Cupp, a golf-course designer, former professional golfer, and former scholarship baseball player at the University of Miami, told *Sports Illustrated*'s John Underwood that he knew of a coach who "decided to give his team a little boost by injecting a stimulant—Benzedrine, Dexedrine, something—into the oranges he always fed them before a game. He used a hypodermic and kept upping the dosage. After the third or fourth game the players started complaining of headaches and throwing up. The coach later admitted to me what he'd done." *Sport*, another mainstream magazine, reported in 1976 that fourteen-year-old Craig Blum was given pills by coach Jim Guandolo and Athletic Director Gene Bovello of the Bethesda (Maryland) Boys Club. The purpose of the pills was to allow Blum to gain enough weight to play Intermediate Division football. When exposed, Bovello responded with the conventional justification: "Let's face it, it's a competitive world, and football prepares kids for life." Despite this appeal to common sense, Bovello was expelled from the club. In reprisal, the Blum family was victimized by obscene telephone calls from angry parents who presumably endorsed the use of drugs if drugs promise to enhance their children's athletic performance. While Blum was given pills to help him gain weight, other children have taken drugs in order to stay in lightweight competition. Underwood quotes an unidentified Florida coach who has seen children "flying around so high on diet pills they can barely tell you their names."[27]

German psychologists who have studied children's sports have found statistical evidence to support the claim of American observers that intense competition leads to emotional "burn out." Swimmers and gymnasts often "retire" at fifteen or sixteen. The forced achievements of teenage (or younger) athletes seem also to reduce long-range athletic potential. For instance, swimmers who train intensely when very young not only peak sooner but also attain levels of performance lower than swimmers who are developed more slowly.[28]

More obvious to all observers is the fact that intense competition can be physically destructive. Childrens' softer bones and weaker ligaments and tendons make it likely that Little League pitchers will suffer from arm injuries. Pop Warner football players emulating their heroes in the NFL have attempted to "spear" their opponents with their helmets. But NFL linesmen have necks strengthened by years of exercise; children don't. The result is that an unknown number of children have broken their necks and become paraplegics or quadraplegics.

All of these disadvantages must be weighed against the fact that countless children have enjoyed adult-sponsored sports and have escaped serious physical injury. When Vaz asked the nearly 2,000 hockey players in his sample what they liked *least* about the game, 45.6 percent responded that there was nothing to dislike. If John Underwood's informants can be trusted, there was only "one broken bone in 17 years of play in Pop Warner ball in Boston." While some children have become quadraplegics because of injuries, millions of others have suffered no damage more serious than bruises and blisters.[29]

Damage to the psyche is even harder to evaluate. It may damage a fourteen-year-old girl to appear on the cover of *Sports Illustrated* and to be touted nationally as "the next Mary Lou Retton," but it is important to bear in mind that actors and violinists have also had instant fame visited upon them and that few social critics have protested. Robert C. Townsend's autobiographical essay, "The Competitive Male as a Loser," is a vivid account of the trauma visited upon a "macho" young man by his mother, but most psychologists seem ready to agree that sports participation is likely to increase, rather than decrease, a child's self-confidence. On the assumption that self-confidence is healthy (even if machismo is not), one should give credit where credit is due. Psychological tests usually indicate that children involved in organized sports are more extroverted and better integrated into their peer groups than are children who do not participate. Whether one groans or cheers at this news depends, of course, on one's values. It must also be stated that other studies have found no personality differences at all between the athletically involved and uninvolved.[30]

While it is probably wise not to place great faith in personality tests, which have produced some dishearteningly contradictory results when administered to athletes and non-athletes, attitudinal surveys are somewhat more reliable. They do not indicate that Little League participation results in total depravity. One study found that boys and girls playing in an organized community-wide league thought that playing fairly was *more* important than improving one's skills, while children in an elementary-school-sponsored !eague thought the opposite. Another study reassures us that not all children involved in Canadian hockey are enchanted by the prospect of blood on the ice; 61 percent of the players wanted to experience fewer fights.[31]

Nor do all the parents in the stands commit atrocities. A count of "adult observer verbalizations" at Little League Baseball games played by five-to-eight-year-old boys and girls logged positive, neutral, and negative remarks made by the spectators; only 0.42 percent were negative. Nor are all coaches the ogres that they sometimes seem to be. Research into the behavior of fifty-one Little League Baseball coaches in the Seattle area led a team of three scholars to conclude that the coaches instructed and encouraged the children far more often than they scolded them. Of 57,213 "behaviors," only 2.8 percent were categorized as punitive.[32]

It is unlikely that anyone can make a conclusive case that modern adult-organized children's sports are unambiguously good or bad. The most insightful exploration of the problem may be Martin Ralbovsky's oral history of "destiny's darlings," which is what sportscaster Mel Allen called the 1954 Little League Baseball world champions from Schenectady, New York. Twenty years after the tournament, Ralbovsky asked the former players what it had meant to them to have won the title and how they felt now about Michael Maietta, who had coached them to their victory. For some, like Joseph Loudis, the only Jew on the team, "Winning that world championship in 1954 was the greatest thing that's ever happened to me." As a high school basketball coach still committed to the importance of winning, Loudis reads none of "those radical books that say sports are bad." He cannot object to Maietta's authoritarian coaching because his own approach to sports is similar: "I'm the boss; they do it my way, or they don't do it at all." William Masucci, who described himself as a sadist who loves a good fight, also had positive memories. Of Maietta and another coach he remarked, "They taught me how to win, not only in baseball, but in life." Warren Jerome Fennicks remembered that the white boys on the team treated him as an equal; there was "no racial stuff at all." When opponents from the South screamed, "Nigger, nigger, nigger, we're gonna kill you," Maietta put his arm around him and told Fennicks's outraged teammates to express their resentment by defeating the taunters—which they did, by a score of 17–0. Little League Baseball gave Fennicks the happiest moments of his life.[33]

But not all the memories were positive. James Barbieri remembered that "we were the meanest bunch of kids in the tournament."

Maietta encouraged a killer instinct and advised the boys to intimidate their opponents by first sliding into and then pretending to comfort the other team's catcher. Ernest Lotano also recalled Maietta's influence: "We were like twelve-year-old pros when we won that title, that's what he did to us." "We were pawns on the chessboard," said Barbieri, "and he made all the moves." Perhaps the most revealing remark came from Maietta: "I had to make the kids hate me. . . . I knew that if they hated me and got mad at me, they would go out there and take it out on the other team."[34]

Whether one affirms or castigates adult-organized children's sports, one should acknowledge the fact that most children seem to prefer Little League to the sandlot baseball games of the past. Those who participate in adult-sponsored children's sports are statistically more likely than others to participate actively in sports when they reach adulthood, and they are more likely to coach the next generation of Little Leaguers. In the last analysis, the intense competition and the intermittent violence which characterize children's sports must be seen as part of the larger configurations of American society. Nor should one allow himself to forget that the unsupervised play has its problems, too. How many children have been left out of pickup games? How many children have been bullied by older children? Beaten? Terrified? How many children have fallen from how many trees? How many have been killed by automobiles as they rushed to retrieve a ball? In our assessments of children's play, we would do well to remember the general historical admonition against the romanticization of the past.

EIGHT

THE ANOMALY OF INTERCOLLEGIATE ATHLETICS

CREATION

From 1935 to 1942, Louisiana State University sponsored an internationally admired literary magazine, *The Southern Review*, with which were associated such famed figures as Cleanth Brooks, Allen Tate, and Robert Penn Warren. In the dark days of World War II, the financially pressed university had to choose between *The Southern Review* and an adequate supply of fresh meat for the tiger that the school kept as the football team's mascot. No contest. The tiger won. It was an easy victory, one that American professors are likely to find quite predictable; but it is difficult to imagine a similar choice at Oxford, the Sorbonne, or Tübingen. British, French, and German centers of higher learning are seldom renowned for the excellence of their rugby players, cyclists, or soccer team. Only in America can colleges and universities become famous for their basketball and football triumphs.

There are, of course, arguments in favor of the American system of intercollegiate athletics. The inner logic of sports competition seems to demand them. If one grants that sports offer an opportunity for men and women to test their physical skills against one another, then it follows that students searching for the most challenging opponents will want to search as widely as possible, i.e., beyond the campus.

Intercollegiate contests, however, have more than individual significance. They help to demarcate social boundaries between groups and thus to reinforce collective identity. If athletes rather than scholars are seen as representatives of educational institutions, the probable reason is that sports are a lowest common denominator, a signifier whose significance anyone can understand. Unlike the genetic code, Roman law, and Japanese grammar, the rules of the game—any game, even cricket—can be learned in a day. Finally, as John J. MacAloon has noted, modern sports festivals can provide the secular rituals which Emile Durkheim thought essential to modern social solidarity or, in the lingo of the educationists, "school spirit." MacAloon's focus is on the Olympic Games, but intercollegiate athletics are equally amenable to his analysis. Although the rituals associated with intercollegiate athletics are as much the consequence as the cause of Durkheimian collective representations, they tend to take on a life of their own. Around them rise associated rituals: the rallies, parades, dinners, and formal dances on the eve of the game; the drunken brawls afterward. The result is the Big Game that Edwin H. Cady calls at once a popular art form and "the most vitally folkloristic event in our culture." For students, faculty, alumni, and administration, the football weekend is the closest American equivalent to a Roman holiday. The motto on our currency should also be printed on the tickets to the Big Game: *E pluribus unum*.[1]

The most remarkable aspect of this situation is that American academics, apart from a bemused or embittered minority, accept this curious state of affairs as if it were part of the unalterable order of nature. Suggestions that academic life might not only survive but actually be improved by the abolition of intercollegiate athletics are received not with hostility but with astonishment. Yet this hallowed tradition, with an emphasis on football and basketball, is little more than a century old.

Intercollegiate athletics began at the initiative of students who sought to test their physical skills against those of rival colleges, despite faculty preference for rivalries of a more intellectual sort. English students began the tradition in the early nineteenth century, when Oxford met Cambridge in rowing (1829) and then in track and field (1864). Varsity sports in England remained more or less in the hands of the students. In contrast, intercollegiate athletics in

America grew rather quickly into an institution governed not by undergraduates but by faculties, administrations, and, in many cases, alumni. Guy Lewis, Ronald Smith, and other sports historians have made familiar the story of institutional growth. The first intercollegiate sport, in America as in England, was rowing. Yale had a boat club in 1843, Harvard in 1844. The first intercollegiate contest occurred at Lake Winnipesaukee in 1852. Six years later Brown, Harvard, Trinity, and Yale organized the College Rowing Association. Princeton students formed a baseball society in 1859, but, before they found suitable rivals with whom to begin a tradition, Amherst and Williams played the first intercollegiate game (1859). Harvard and Yale took up baseball in 1864. Track and field meets were inaugurated after the Civil War. Eventually the associations formed to promote baseball, football, crew, and track and field laid the foundation for a national administrative organization for intercollegiate athletics.

The first impulse of most mid-nineteenth-century faculties and administrations was to forbid intercollegiate sports, which were left by default in the hands of students and alumni. By the beginning of the twentieth century, however, prohibition and benign neglect had been replaced by that same desire for supervision and control that characterized the playground movement. Since undergraduates were young adults, they were usually included on the athletic committee along with faculty, administration, and, sometimes, alumni. Departments of physical education and athletics were established. It was agreed that intercollegiate sports were a proper extension of physical education and that physical education was an important adjunct to moral education. Those whose knowledge of Latin had dwindled away to the *amo-amas-amat* level were nonetheless able to rise to their feet and quote Juvenal: *mens sana in corpore sano*.

Corruption

The National Collegiate Athletic Association (originally called the Intercollegiate Athletic Association of the United States) was born amid controversy in 1905–6. But the controversy was engendered not by the debate over sports' legitimacy but by the secondary question of their excesses; not whether to allow intercollegiate contests, but how to prevent the bloodshed and mayhem that had become associated with the Big Game. While American educators were generally sanguine about football's contribution to manly character, they were upset when the young men who actually played the game began to cripple and even kill each other on the field. After the particularly brutal Harvard-Yale game of 1904, Harvard discontinued the sport. At this point, Theodore Roosevelt invited the presidents of Harvard, Yale, and Princeton to the White House for a discussion of football violence.

Roosevelt demanded reforms in order to preserve the game (which he much admired) from its critics, among whom President Charles William Eliot of Harvard was especially outspoken. As John Higham and other historians have often remarked, Roosevelt was a self-advertised exemplar of the strenuous life and a tireless censor of what he considered to be a decadent elite urgently in need of physical and moral revitalization. In an essay on "The American Boy" (1900), Roosevelt echoed sentiments expressed earlier by such muscular Unitarians as Oliver Wendell Holmes and Thomas Wentworth Higginson:

> Forty or fifty years ago the writer on American morals was sure to deplore the effeminacy and luxury of young Americans who were born of rich parents. The boy who was well off then . . . lived too luxuriously, took to billiards as his chief innocent recreation, and felt small shame in his inability to take part in rough pastimes and field-sports. Nowadays, whatever other faults the son of rich parents may tend to develop, he is at least forced . . . to bear himself well in manly exercises and to develop his body—and therefore, to a certain extent, his character—in the rough sports which call for pluck, endurance, and physical address.

Roosevelt certainly practiced what he preached. "Although Roosevelt's strenuous life invited voguish press coverage and faddish imitation," comments Donald J. Mrozek, "it also stood as a model of sport's efficacy in molding a man for an active and creative life in the business of the nation." It was largely because of the president's energetic appeals that football escaped abolition.[2]

It was a close call. At a famous meeting held at New York's Murray Hill Hotel on December 8, 1905, representatives from Columbia, NYU, Stevens Institute, Union College, and the University of Rochester were in favor of a resolution calling for the abolition of football, but the majority—from Fordham, Haverford, Lafayette, Rutgers, Syracuse, Swarthmore, Wesleyan, and West Point—were for reform. Together with NYU's Chancellor Henry McCracken and West Point's Palmer Pierce, Columbia trustee Francis S. Bangs then drew up a list of reforms. Offered to the larger group at a second Murray Hill meeting on December 28 the reforms were accepted. From the travail of 1905–6 the NCAA was born.

Rules were rewritten; problems remained. Surveying "The Evolution of Athletic Evil" in 1909, Wilbur P. Bowen lamented that what had begun as recreation for the students had degenerated into amusement for the multitude. "As long as the purpose of athletics is commercial, the spirit will not rise above the spirit of the stock exchange, no matter what rules the faculty committee try to enforce." By 1929 the Carnegie Commission had ample evidence to prove that the quest for athletic glory was attended by distortions and dishonesties that mocked the ideals of higher education. The authors of the 1929 report noted mildly that a "system of recruiting and subsidizing has grown up, under which boys are offered pecuniary and other inducements to enter a particular college." Although recruiting was "the most disgraceful phase" of the problem, the report commented bleakly on the commercialization of college sports and on the special treatment accorded to strapping young men of negligible intellectual ability. The preface to the report expressed the authors' conclusions:

> In the United States the composite institution called a university is doubtless still an intellectual agency. But it is also a social, a commercial, and an athletic agency, and these activities have in recent years appreciably overshadowed the intellectual life for which the university is assumed to exist. . . . The question is not so much whether athletics in their present form should be fostered by the university, but how fully can a univer-

sity that fosters professional athletics discharge its primary function.

(The reference to "professional" athletics was presumably justified in part by the sums of money given to student-athletes and in part by the more important fact that the young men in question were specialists who devoted most of their time to sports.) The response to the widely publicized report was a call for reform—a call that was already forlorn and that has since become ridiculous.[3]

Despite periodic efforts to institutionalize some kind of restraint upon intercollegiate athletics, the evils lamented in 1929 have grown worse. In 1938 President Robert M. Hutchins, of the University of Chicago declared that "a college which is interested in producing professional athletes is not an educational institution." The following year, to the dismay of many alumni, Hutchins withdrew Chicago from intercollegiate football, an action taken by dozens of presidents since. In 1956 football coach Herman Hickman wrote of the crisis in his sport and quoted Michigan's Fritz Crisler, chairman of the NCAA Rules Committee: "We have discarded the principles on which college football was established. . . . We are nourishing a monster which can destroy us if we admit we are powerless to direct, resist or control it." In 1974 Indiana's Bobby Knight remarked, "When they get to the bottom of Watergate, they'll find a football coach." Summarizing the situation in 1980, John Underwood concluded, "From the moment the student-athlete sets foot on campus, the name of the game is 'majoring in eligibility,' and it is a vulgar, callous, shameful, cynical—and perfectly legal—exploitation of the system by and for the American college athlete."[4]

Once the tradition was established that athletes—football, basketball, and baseball players; swimmers, runners, and wrestlers—*represent* the university and provide models for students and alumni to admire and emulate, the juggernaut of intercollegiate athletics was set in motion. The psychological mechanisms of identification were (and are) such that victory or defeat of a football team was (and is) felt as a *personal* triumph or humiliation by thousands and tens of thousands of students. To obtain psychic satisfaction and avoid vicarious humiliation, administrations are ready to pay coaches salaries that are far beyond the limited imaginations of mere professors. Texas A&M, for instance, offered football coach Jackie Sherrill $267,000 a year, plus perquisites. When interrogated about educational priorities, the chairman of the Board of Trustees was candid: "Higher education is a business, and I think Sherrill's contract is part of that process." Bear Bryant of Alabama earned an estimated $450,000 a year.[5]

Where does the money come from? For the "minor sports," such as baseball and tennis, most of it comes from the university's budget, but the "revenue-producing sports" can generate income from ticket sales. Except for universities in the NCAA's Division I, the revenue is almost never enough to offset the expenses. The "football powers" of Division I do show a profit; furthermore, these schools can count on large sums from the sale of television rights. Under a four-year contract with the NCAA, two networks (ABC and CBS) agreed to pay $280,000,000 for such rights. A 1985 regular-season TV appearance earned a university $650,000. If the university rescheduled a game for the convenience of the networks, the compliant institution received another $250,000. In 1983 their Rose Bowl appearance brought $2,900,000 (each) to UCLA and the University of Michigan. Universities who sent teams to play in the Sugar Bowl and the Cotton Bowl had to be content with less than $2,000,000 each.

Although many smaller schools have ended their football programs because of financial losses, the football powers have done well. It seems, however, that the large schools have not done well enough. The University of Georgia and the University of Oklahoma successfully sued the NCAA and won their cases before the Supreme Court. In *Board of Regents of University of Oklahoma* v. *NCAA* (1984), the NCAA's regulations were found to be "paradigmatic examples of restraints of trade that the Sherman Act was intended to prohibit." Universities were freed from the fetters imposed upon them by the organization that universities had created to save them from themselves. Informed observers can only wonder at the court's claim to be furthering the cause of amateur sports by encouraging schools like Georgia and Oklahoma to wrest even larger payments for even more frequent television appearances.[6]

For the coach, the rewards of success (i.e., a winning season) are psychological as well as economic. A Bear Bryant of Alabama or a

Woody Hayes of Ohio State can enjoy national fame and take modestly concealed satisfaction in the fact that he is far better known than the governor of the state—not to mention the president of the university. The results of failure (i.e., a losing season) are punitive: coaches whose teams have done badly can expect to be pilloried in print, burned in effigy, and separated from the university. John Robinson, a football coach at Southern California, complained to *Sports Illustrated* writer John Underwood about the psychological burden of the incessant death threats that are an occupational hazard of college coaching. Although some institutions grant coaches tenure as members of the faculty, most do not. The casualty rate among coaches is high. Of 130 head football coaches in the NCAA's "University Division" in 1970, 50 had been fired or forced to resign before the beginning of the 1974 season. Only 37 were at the same school in the same position. The turnover in other sports is comparable.[7]

Since intercollegiate football and basketball attract large crowds of spectators, money from the "revenue-producing" sports has become a regular item in the budgets of departments of athletics and physical education. Often much less revenue is produced than is claimed. By such elementary accounting devices as excluding from the balance sheet the costs of salaries and stadium construction, universities can often claim huge profits from big-time sports when they are actually losing money. Still, when income from the TV networks is added to income from ticket sales, some of the more successful institutions (say, UCLA or Penn State) really do earn significant profits. In the process, they can also become dependent upon a source of income that is, of course, signficantly influenced by athletic victory or defeat. An invitation to the Rose Bowl or an appearance on TV can make the difference between a budget deficit and a "healthy" surplus. Moreover, the conventional wisdom is that alumni and state legislators are more generous to their alma mater or state university when the football or basketball team has done well. In fact, a careful study based on data gathered by the Council for Financial Aid to Education found no statistical relationship between success or failure in football and basketball and increases or decreases in alumni support. A recent study of Washington State University alumni revealed that most ranked sports far below "traditional academic programs" in their list of priorities. There are, however, exceptional situations. When Ohio State's football record dropped from 7–2 one year to 4–5 the next, the alumni fund dropped by almost $500,000; Missouri's improvement from 6–5 to 10–1 was accompanied by a 95 percent increase in gifts. That state legislatures are interested in intercollegiate athletics, or at least in football games, can also be inferred from a 1951 incident. When the NCAA limited its members to two television appearances yearly, the Oklahoma legislature threatened to pass a law ordering the university to defy the NCAA. When the university finally, in 1984, won its Thirty Years War against the NCAA, the legislature must have felt itself vindicated.[8]

Confronted, as most coaches are, by the stark contrast between success and failure, between being lionized and tossed to the lions, many are tempted to do whatever is necessary in order to win. They justify infractions of the rules with the ancient rhetorical argument *tu quoque*; in modern form, "Everybody does it." Since professors once were students, they know fairly well what it is that everybody does.

Bear Bryant of Alabama commanded a small fleet of private airplanes to ameliorate the recruiters' hardships. The appeals of football fame at Alabama and the promise of a crack at the National Football League were supplemented by the tangible evidence of Paul W. Bryant Hall, where scores of football players and a scatter of other athletes resided in fully air-conditioned comfort. The dormitory has a marble-columned entry and prints of Roman ruins—inappropriate symbolic suggestions of gladiatorial glory crumbled into dust? At Oral Roberts University, basketball rather than football was perceived as the royal road to academic glory. Talented athletes were recruited, and the hypocrisy of their "student" status was refreshingly admitted by an assistant coach who was asked how many players in the program actually graduated: "Do you know what my job is at that school? It's to teach those kids how to use a bar of Dial soap and a tube of Ipana toothpaste. I'm the guy who has to get them to turn down their goddamn stereos at three A.M. so my family can get some sleep." Although Moses Malone had a C average in high school, he received scholarship offers from over 300 colleges and universities. None of the schools could match the $3,000,000 contract offered by the Utah Stars; Malone went directly to the American Basketball Association. After Chris Washburn failed to answer a single question correctly on his verbal SAT, he was recruited by 150 universities. (He chose to attend North Carolina State, but his career was compromised in 1985, when he pled guilty to the theft of an $800 stereo set.) When Marcus Dupree approached the age of college matriculation, men and women throughout Mississippi waited breathlessly to see whether that awesome athletic ability was headed for Ole Miss or for some alien center of scholarship. More than a hundred universities sent their recruiters to Philadelphia, Mississippi, to court the football phenomenon of the year. Dupree eventually chose the University of Oklahoma, which had sent a private jet to fly him to Norman for a campus visit. A white oil executive and a black millionaire flew with Dupree and extolled the wonders of an Oklahoma education. At the end of Dupree's freshman year, the university showed its appreciation by honoring him with an award intended for students who combine "excellence in scholarship and athletics." At the time Dupree had a C− average.[9]

The inducements to matriculation are not always limited to the package of benefits authorized by the NCAA. Billy Harris, who went to Northern Illinois to play basketball, explained: "I had guys come to my mother's house and put five, six, seven thousand dollars on the table and say, 'Here, all you gotta do is sign this piece of paper.'" Alumni who are not always concerned for excellence in the classics or physics departments have been known to give generously to purchase athletic greatness. Morris "Snake" Bailey, a Texas Christian University booster, told the *Chronicle of Higher Education* that head football coach F. A. Dry approached him in 1980 and asked for a monthly slush-fund contribution of $7,500. Kenneth Davis, one of seven football players suspended when the TCU scandal finally broke, claimed to have been approached by a university trustee who offered him the equivalent of $38,000; the promises included an initial cash payment of $3,700. At nearby Southern Methodist University, a booster admitted to having donated $200,000 to the football program over a three-year period. While SMU was in the second year of a three-year NCAA-imposed probation, "former linebacker David Stanley told Dallas television station

WFAA that school officials had paid him $25,000 to come to SMU in 1983 and gave him and his mother $750 per month thereafter." At this point, some two hundred SMU faculty members lost patience with the football program and signed a Garrisonian petition calling for the "immediate, unconditional and permanent abolition of quasi-professional" sports. The president of the university opted for early retirement. It was revealed in March 1987 that Bill Clements, the newly elected governor of Texas, had been involved in the scandal while head of the SMU Board of Governors. The NCAA's chief enforcement official, David Berst, remarked, "If he's typical of people who are in charge at the highest level, then there really isn't much hope for integrity in collegiate athletics." The NCAA ordered the cancellation of SMU's 1987 football season.[10]

Dishonest recruitment has its comic side as well. Some kind of ultimate may have been achieved when Thomas Affinito, an imaginative journalism student, invented a high school basketball star whom he named after himself, Tom Fini. After sending out a number of faked newspaper clippings and a letter of application, "Tom Fini" was inundated by telephone calls, telegrams, letters, and offers of full scholarships.[11]

Recruitment of the academically unqualified has gone beyond the discovery and matriculation of Americans with no marked interest in higher education. It has become common to recruit abroad, especially for track and field events. The University of Texas at El Paso, for instance, boasted a cross-country team made up entirely of Africans. Track coach Ted Banks arrived on campus in January 1973 and, by 1980, had won five indoor and three outdoor championships. It is, of course, possible that these athletes were recruited by idealistic coaches eager to spread the benefits of American higher education to Kenya and Tanzania; however, there is no sign of missionary zeal on behalf of African boys distinguished in more sedentary endeavors. While informed observers assume that the abuses of recruitment occur mainly at the big-time universities and least often at the elite schools that refuse to offer "athletic" scholarships, there is reason to suspect that even the Ivies will open their doors more quickly for a football player with a C average than for an academically superior student whose talents are exclusively bookish.

Once the athlete has been recruited, in accordance with or in violation of NCAA rules, there is a tendency for him or her to concentrate on athletics rather than on less spectacular academic activities. As every professor knows, in order to remain eligible the student must comply with certain rules, e.g., maintain an acceptable GPA. This is not always easy to arrange. By 1902, corruption was so rife at Columbia University that the dean of the law school, who chaired the university's athletic committee, reported to President Nicholas Murray Butler that the illness of the football program was incurable. Among the problems was a secret fund to reimburse players for their college expenses and an attempt "to subvert a Faculty Committee's disqualification of Columbia's outstanding football player." The situation has not improved. When confronted by the press with the fact that twenty-seven football and nine basketball players were listed as eligible although they were on academic probation, Dan Winters, an athletic academic advisor at Arizona, admitted, "We recognize the farce of putting some of our kids into regular classes with regular students." Reports of "Mickey Mouse" courses have been common for decades, but coaches have recently developed deceptive skills undreamed of by the Carnegie Commission in its 1929 report. One strategy is to provide junior-college transfer credit for courses the athlete may or may not have taken. During the 1979 season assistant basketball coach Manny Goldstein of the University of New Mexico was accused of bribing Oxnard Junior College's dean of admissions, John Woolley, to falsify a student's transcript by adding credits for courses supposedly taken at Mercer Junior College. Goldstein's defense was, "I didn't do anything illegal until I had to." Two years after New Mexico dismissed coach Norm Ellenberger for complicity in this scandal, he was convicted of twenty-one counts of fraud. He had, for instance, billed the university for $6,000 worth of illegal travel. Judge Phillip D. Baiamonte sentenced Ellenberger to one year of unsupervised probation and justified lenience as follows: "How fair is it to incarcerate a coach who is basically doing what almost everybody in this community wanted him to do? Namely, win basketball games at any cost and by whatever means necessary to do that." Meanwhile, the University of Southern California discovered that twenty-eight of its athletes enrolled in Speech Communication 380 were neither attending class regularly nor doing very well. The campus newspaper printed part of an essay done by an anonymous athlete who had been asked to evaluate a debate: "I when went John because He had a point on girl that I couldn't not again, so that made me think girl don't have body for lady unless they wont that why I went with John." After four years of playing basketball for Creighton University, Kevin Ross courageously decided to return to elementary school in order to learn to read at better than a fourth-grade level.[12]

At the University of Georgia's School of Developmental Studies, students with academic deficiencies are offered noncredit remedial courses that they must pass in order to transfer to a regular program of studies. When Jan Kemp, an English instructor, protested the transfer of eight football players who had failed to pass the remedial course, she was dismissed from her position. When she sued her superiors, spokesmen for the university defended recruitment of the functionally illiterate. As the defendants' lawyer explained, "We may not make a university student out of him [the academically unqualified athlete], but if we can teach him to read and write, maybe he can work at the post office rather than as a garbage man when he gets through with his athletic career." (The use of the word "career" is revealing.) Fred Davison, president of the university, admitted that football and basketball players were theoretically eligible for scholarships even if they failed to answer a single question correctly on the verbal and mathematical Scholastic Aptitude Tests; other athletes had to score at least 650 points. When asked if the discrepancy might be explained by the fact that football and basketball earned money for the school, Davision answered, "If you want to ask me if they have utilitarian effect to the university, certainly they do." When pressed for a justification of academic skullduggery, Davison was mysterious: "We have to compete on a level playing field." The court awarded Jan Kemp $2,579,681.95 and the American Association of University Professors honored her for her "unwavering commitment to academic integrity."[13]

And what do faculty members think of campus-based professional sports? Since most professors at American schools are

Americans born and bred, it is probable that most of them support the status quo. They, too, go to the Big Game and talk it over at the Faculty Commons. The more thoughtful among them see sports as secular rituals in the service of school spirit. When confronted with evidence of gross dishonesty and comic-opera travesty, the average professor is likely to develop a bad conscience. When asked to award academic credit to a semiliterate who has neither attended class nor turned in the assigned papers nor taken the final examination, the professor is likely to feel that his code of ethics has been threatened. The customary response in such instances is to call indignantly for reform.

Reform

Suggestions for reform are many and have come from those who know the system best. Feeling that they are trapped in the academic equivalent of the international arms race, some ethically responsible coaches and athletic directors have called for stricter NCAA rules and for more sustained enforcement efforts. If every coach knew that no coach offered sub-rosa cash payments to prospective stars, then all coaches would suffer less anxiety. But self-regulation invariably raises the question best formulated by Juvenal, who knew a thing or two about the Colosseum and the Circus Maximus: *Quis custodiet ipsos custodes?*. One answer (offered by Edwin Cady, a scholar with considerable NCAA experience) is that the faculty should become more active in the governance of intercollegiate athletics. Since faculties proved unable to control sports when sports were in their infancy, comparatively speaking, one wonders how the overworked professoriat, torn between teaching, writing, and doing time on college committees, can assert any kind of authority over the athletic leviathan. When Ohio State's faculty council bravely voted 28–25 to decline the Rose Bowl bid for 1962, three nights of rioting followed. "With characteristic objectivity and good taste, the Columbus *Dispatch* published on its front page the names, addresses, rank and salaries of faculty members who supposedly had voted against the Rose Bowl." Those on the paper's inaccurate list received obscene mail and telephone calls. Their colleagues on the faculty examined their values and elected more malleable representatives.[14]

Hopeful signs do exist. When twenty-two college presidents demanded reform of the system, the NCAA voted in January 1983 to require new eligibility standards for freshmen: beginning in January 1986, students must have C averages in a set of given high school subjects and have scored at least 700 points on the combined SAT (or the equivalent on other standard tests). In 1983 the Ivy League and the "Little Three" (Amherst, Wesleyan, Williams), which do not award athletic scholarships, were joined by a newly formed Colonial League made up of Bucknell, Colgate, Davidson, Holy Cross, Lafayette, and Lehigh. The University Athletic Association followed in 1986. Johns Hopkins, Carnegie-Mellon, Emory, Case Western, Washington (St. Louis), NYU, Rochester, and Chicago all agreed to end athletic scholarships and to treat athletes like other students. The ideal of the UAA is to organize regular contests in baseball, basketball, football, and soccer, as well as yearly tournaments in eight men's and eight women's sports. What the geographical dispersion of the UAA members will mean for the students involved in regular contests remains to be seen. It is certainly too soon to celebrate the end of university-sponsored professional sports.

Knowing that reform of the present system is improbable, some critics have attempted to cut the Gordian knot. They have boldly suggested that colleges and universities remove the hyphen from "student-athlete" and separate the academic from the athletic. Let the academy sponsor openly professional football, basketball, track and field, etc. James F. Rooney, who has written about recruitment patterns in two important books, calls for "an honest business operation designed to entertain the university community, alumni, and other interested parties." Using his knowledge of the geography of American sports, Rooney has sketched out his plan in considerable detail.[15]

The proposal is an attractive one. With one stroke, hypocrisy is ended. There is, however, at least one fundamental question raised by this call for radical reform through overt professionalism: Should institutions of higher learning be involved in the entertainment business? James Michener, himself a successful entertainer, feels that major universities like Notre Dame "are obligated to provide nationwide entertainment and they would be delinquent if they sought to avoid the responsibility."[16] On the other hand, John C. Weistart of Duke University School of Law is appalled by the fact that athletic departments frequently operate "as the entertainment division of the university."[17] Most of academe seems to disagree with Weistart and to share Michener's peculiarly American conception of the aims of education. As the processes of modernization transformed traditional institutions, Americans entrusted more and more of the socialization function to governmental agencies. Foremost among those agencies, at least until recently, was the educational system, in which Americans seem to have had unbounded faith. If it seems appropriate to Americans that universities provide rural housewives with advice on home economics, contract to do research for the Department of Defense, and offer courses in the use of contraceptive techniques, why should it appear strange that universities also produce Broadway musicals and stage spectacular sporting events? Michener's typically American acceptance of the university as an entertainment provider displays an ethnocentric inability to imagine alternatives to the American system of intercollegiate athletics.

There *are* alternative possibilities. The most attractive one has long been institutionalized in Europe, especially in the Federal Republic of Germany. In the German system, universities devote themselves to education (including physical education and the scientific study of sports) while private clubs provide for both participant and spectator sports. The corruption of the university is avoided by the elimination of temptation. Semiliterate coalminers are not lured to play soccer for Heidelberg because Heidelberg has no varsity soccer team. The omission does not signify a lack of interest in sports on the part of either the students or the professors. It means only that the intense interest has been institutionalized in the private club, rather than in the public university.

The club system has another advantage over the American model of university-based sports. One of the continual complaints against

American physical education is that it concentrates on team sports that adults seldom have a chance to play. Americans are familiar with the stereotype of the forty-year-old alum, physically unfit, positively unhealthy, still fixed on that inevitably receding moment of glory when he or she shot the winning basket for State. The options for the graduate include fitness-center aerobics, country-club golf and tennis, swimming in one's own pool, and jogging. This may seem like a rich assortment, but it is impoverished compared to the dozens of organized activities available to Germans of all ages.

German clubs are open to everyone. They presently include more than 19 million people, 30 percent of the entire population. They enroll children of elementary-school age and hardy types in their sixties, seventies, and even eighties. While Americans usually abandon serious participation in sports after graduation from high school or college, most of the German Sport Federation's members are over twenty-one. Sixty thousand German sports clubs field hundreds of thousands of teams at every level of competition, from novice to fully professional. In soccer, for instance, over 90,000 teams are affiliated with the national soccer federation. Among these club-sponsored teams are the professionals organized into regional and national leagues. While these leagues have suffered from corruption and scandal, the bribers and the bribe-takers have not dragged the universities into the mire.

Is it practical to propose such a system for the United States? In one sport—running—private clubs have already developed to the point where they are probably as important as the university-sponsored teams. Millions of Americans of both sexes and all ages are involved in recreational running and in races at every level of competition. Running, of course, is a relatively inexpensive sport; clubs can spring up at almost no cost. Would it be practical to turn the major team sports over to private clubs when colleges and universities have invested billions of dollars in their athletic complexes? The answer is not easy, but the problem may be less formidable than it seems at first glance. Educational institutions would continue to require facilities for physical education and for intramural and recreational sports. Other facilities could be sold or leased to private clubs or even, in some cases, to professional sports franchises. The fact that stadia are *in situ* on the campus is unfortunate but should not blind us to the possibility of legal and administrative transfer from the university to another institution that does not pretend to be involved in higher education. Americans occasionally call for their political leaders to be free of conflicts of interest. Can we ask as much of our educators?

NINE

Black Athletes

Rejection and Acceptance

Of the formal-structural characteristics of modern American sports, equality of opportunity to compete was the last to be realized—if one can say, even now, that it has been. There were instances of exclusion on the basis of social class in colonial times, and the anglophile nineteenth-century elite borrowed the amateur rule from England in order to block, or at least to limit, lower-class participation in modern sports; but social class has not been as high a barrier here as it was in Europe. In the United States, prejudices about race and gender have done more than class biases to hinder the full development of modern sports. Racism and sexism have been important enough to require special treatment in this and the next chapter.

The first notable athlete to represent America in an international sporting event was an ex-slave whose name is usually given as Tom Molineaux. He challenged England's champion pugilist, Tom Cribb, on December 10, 1810, before a crowd estimated at 10,000 persons. The unknown Molineaux lasted thirty-three rounds and might have won the match, had Cribb's seconds not badgered the black athlete with unfounded accusations of foul play. At least one historian, Bernard Darwin, thinks that Molineaux was "jockeyed out of the fight." Molineaux's remarkable feat earned him good food, good ale, and some months of idleness. When he stepped into the ring for a rematch on September 28, 1811, he was in no shape to fight anyone; his already poor physical condition was certainly not improved by his breakfast of "boiled fowl, an apple pie, and a tankard of beer." Pierce Egan, who witnessed the bout at Thiselton Gap in Leicester, thought its excitement exceeded everything in the annals of pugilism:

> Never was the *sporting world* so much interested, and for twenty miles within the seat of action not a bed could be obtained on the preceding night; and by six o'clock the next morning, hundreds were in motion to get a good place near the stage. . . . It is supposed that near 20,000 persons witnessed this tremendous *mill.*

Xenophobia, rather than racism, seems to have motivated the spectators. Egan felt that

> the Black had to contend against a prejudiced multitude; the pugilistic honour of the country was at stake, and . . . MOLINEAUX [was] viewed with jealousy, envy, and disgust: the national laurels to be borne away by a foreigner, the *mere* idea to an English breast was afflicting. . . .

Cribb won in eleven rounds.[1]

The emotions stirred by the fight indicate some of the social forces that have determined the shape of black sports in America and in Europe. For the Englishmen at the Cribb-Molineaux fights, nationalism and racism converged to make the black American an object of "jealousy, envy, and disgust." We have no commentaries from Americans who witnessed the two fights, but we can assume from countless subsequent international athletic encounters that any Americans who were present were also ambivalent. Nationalistic and racist impulses contradicted each other: the first impelled Americans to cheer for Molineaux; the second put them in Cribb's corner. Which impulse was stronger? This question must be asked again and again as one surveys the history of black sports in the United States. The answer at any given moment depends on a constellation of social factors.

Before the question of nationalistic versus racist impulses could be asked, blacks had to be perceived as representative by white Americans as well as by foreigners. In order for that to happen, blacks had to participate directly or indirectly in contests against whites. Molineaux was unquestionably an exception. Afro-Americans were generally barred from organized sports in nineteenth-century America. The enforced servitude of chattel slavery was an obvious bar to participation before Emancipation. As David K. Wiggins has shown in a number of essays, slaves had their recreations and pastimes, including sports, but they rarely interacted with adult whites. Segregationist attitudes and straitened economic circumstance explain the paucity of black athletes in post Civil War America.

Still, the exclusion was never total, and a few exceptional blacks did compete against whites. Black jockeys had ridden their masters' horses in colonial and antebellum times. When a horse named Aristides galloped to victory in the first Kentucky Derby (1875), he was ridden by a black jockey, Oliver Lewis. In fact, all but one of the fifteen jockeys were black. Isaac Murphy, who won the Derby in 1884, 1889, and 1891, was considered the best jockey of his time and might have earned as much as $20,000 a year. The fact that spectators were able to attribute a first-place finish to the speed of the horse rather than to the skill of the jockey may have made it easier for white Americans to accept black jockeys.

There were no black players in the early years of baseball, but, once the game was established as the national pastime, Afro-Americans began to play. Although the National Association of Base Ball Players voted in 1867 to exclude "any club which may be composed of one or more colored persons,"[2] some teams accepted black players. John W. ("Bud") Fowler managed to play for New Castle, Pennsylvania, in 1872. The most famous postbellum black player was Oberlin-educated Moses Fleetwood Walker, who played for Toledo in 1883. When the team entered the American Association in 1884, Walker became the first black major leaguer. In the 1890s, James Francis Gregory, William Henry Lewis, and the marvelously named William Tecumseh Sherman Jackson played baseball and football for Amherst College. Bicycle races were an immensely popular spectator sport in the 1890s, and Marshall W. Taylor pumped his way to fame and fortune. He was the professional world champion in 1899 and the American champion in 1900.

But racism stopped most black athletes in their tracks. Wherever Americans gathered for a game of baseball, Jim Crow called the plays. Although the universalistic logic of modern sports dictates the inclusion of everyone, racism can stymie the egalitarian impulse to field the best possible team. Ironically, exclusionist racism was even more virulent in sports than elsewhere. At play, Americans felt themselves at liberty to indulge in prejudices that economic necessity sometimes moderated in other situations. Adrian Anson of the Chicago White Sox, whom Jules Tygiel calls one of the "prime architects" of baseball's segregationist policies, expressed the sentiments of white America in 1887, when George Stovey was scheduled to pitch for Newark in an exhibition game against the Sox. Anson threatened to take his team from the field if Stovey pitched; Newark's manager acquiesced. That same year Fowler was dismissed from Binghamton's team in the International League, and the last Afro-American was gone from organized baseball by the end of the 1890s.[3]

In antebellum days, black boxers had fought in informal bouts and their masters had bet on them. After Emancipation a number of black fighters won titles in the lighter divisions; among them were featherweight George Dixon, welterweight Joe Walcott, and lightweight Joe Gans. But the great Sam Langford fought at least 250 fights and was never given a chance at the heavyweight championship. Heavyweight boxing's color line was crossed in 1908, when Jack Johnson chased Tommy Burns to Australia and finally taunted him into a fight for the heavyweight championship of the world. Burns sneered foolishly, "All coons are yellow," but he was in error. Johnson humiliated him in the ring and walked off with the title. The first black heavyweight champion was enthusiastically celebrated in the Negro press. Forgetting the work of Booker T. Washington and W. E. B. Du Bois, forgetting also the achievements of other black athletes, the *Richmond Planet* exulted that "no event in forty years has given more genuine satisfaction to the colored people of this country than has the signal victory of Jack Johnson." Although many white racists were upset by Johnson's refutation of the doctrine of white supremacy, they were forced to recognize Johnson as the champion. He had played by the rules and won.[4]

Johnson returned in triumph to the United States, where he set about enjoying his notoriety. He consorted openly with white women, three of whom he married, and he displayed a portrait of the first of them in his Chicago bar. One of his numerous affairs was with a sixteen-year-old white girl. (He managed to insult black people, too. His commentary on his sexual preference was that "I never had a colored girl that didn't two-time me.") His defiance of American folkways set off a frantic search for what was then and ever after known as "the great white hope." Ex-champion Jim Jeffries was persuaded to come out of retirement and racist Americans anticipated a day of sweet satisfaction when Jeffries met Johnson in Reno, Nevada, on the Fourth of July, 1910. As Johnson approached the ring, the band struck up "All Coons Look Alike to Me." The crowd was partisan. Johnson pummeled Jeffries into a bloody mess, and the entire nation was swept by a wave of violence in which mobs of blacks and whites murdered whites and blacks.[5]

Films of the fight were banned throughout the South. Congressman Seaborn A. Roddenberry of Georgia and Senator Furnifold Simmons of North Carolina, two men with suitably Snopesian names, persuaded Congress to outlaw the interstate transportation of fight films. When Johnson married Lucille Cameron, a former prostitute, the enraged Roddenberry addressed the House of Representatives and opined that intermarriage "between whites and blacks is repulsive and averse to every sentiment of pure American spirit."[6] White Americans were generally pleased in 1913, when Johnson was tried and sentenced for violation of the Mann Act (which forbid the transportation of women in interstate sexual commerce). Although the charges against him were falsified, Johnson fled the country. The jury found him guilty; Judge George Carpenter gave him the minimum sentence, in absentia, of a year and a day.

Johnson learned that racism was not simply an American phenomenon. In Paris he was turned away from five hotels before the Terminus offered him a room. Bigots hounded him out of England. His return to the United States after seven years of exile followed a controversial 1915 fight in Havana against Jess Willard. The thirty-seven-year-old Johnson was knocked down by the younger man and counted out by the referee. Immediately after the fight, Johnson remarked that he had no excuses, but he later claimed that he had agreed to take a dive as part of a deal cut with the FBI, which had allegedly promised to allow him to return to the United States if he surrendered his title. As evidence Johnson pointed to the famous photograph which shows him lying on his back, supine before Jess

Willard, with his arms raised. He was, he asserted, shielding his eyes from the Cuban sun. Maybe he was, but the shadow in the photograph does not fall across his eyes, and five years were to elapse between Johnson's quid and the FBI's alleged quo.

In the era of Jack Dempsey and Gene Tunney, the color line was drawn again, not to be definitively erased until Joe Louis won the championship from James Braddock in 1937. In 1938 Louis fought Max Schmeling, who had beaten him two years earlier. Public interest was phenomenal. Seventy thousand fight fans swarmed into Yankee Stadium and 64 percent of the nation's radios were tuned in. For white Americans, the primitive emotions of racism conflicted with the somewhat less primitive emotions generated by nationalism and political ideology. By all accounts, racism proved weaker. Most Americans rejoiced when Louis scored a first-round knockout. The fact that Louis, unlike Johnson, was a reticent man helped gain him acceptance. "A credit to his race" was the phrase mouthed by commentators. His backers, heeding the lesson of Jack Johnson, consciously cultivated the image of the "good Negro." John Roxborough, Julian Black, and Jack Blackburn laid down the law: no photographs in the company of white women, no solitary nightclub visits, no fixed fights, no dirty fights, no gloating over defeated opponents, no politically radical statements. Louis did have affairs with white women. One of them was Sonja Henie, the Norwegian figure skater who became an American film star. But Louis was as discreet as Johnson had been flamboyant—while he decked a number of white challengers, he rocked no boats.[7]

Cassius Clay, who changed his name to Muhammad Ali and then proclaimed himself "the Greatest," behaved in some ways like a resurrected Jack Johnson. He bragged shamelessly and with a poetic flair ("float like a butterfly, sting like a bee"). Although he did not flaunt the red flag of white women, his Black Muslim conversion scandalized many, including Ali's black rival, Floyd Patterson. His refusal to be inducted into the army gave his enemies a pretext for stripping him of his title, but his martyrdom earned him credit among Americans who were opposed to the war in Vietnam. By the time his career had ended, Ali was probably the first black champion to be idolized by whites, perhaps not with the intensity of adoration expressed by blacks, but with an admiration denied Jack Johnson.

In the years between Johnson's dethronement and the arrival of Joe Louis, the most famous black athlete was Jesse Owens. He was certainly not the first great black runner. At St. Louis in 1904, George C. Poag won Olympic medals for his third-place finishes in the 200-meter and the 400-meter hurdles. At the Los Angeles Olympic Games in 1932, against much stiffer competition, Eddie Tolan won gold medals in the 100-meter and 200-meter dashes. Owens's popularity with white Americans was partially attributable to his undeniable athletic ability and his far from militant approach to civil rights, but nationalism was probably the most important factor. Owens and other black athletes were selected by the U.S. Olympic Committee on the basis of their ability to represent America in international competition. Their status apparently made them acceptable to white Americans who still opposed integrated baseball, basketball, or football. Like Joe Louis, Jesse Owens had the good fortune to represent the United States in what was generally perceived as a symbolic contest against fascism. The overwhelming majority of white Americans rejoiced as Owens became the hero of the 1936 "Nazi Olympics," which were supposed to demonstrate the racial superiority of the *Herrenvolk*. Winning gold medals for the 100 meters, the 200 meters, the long jump, and the 400-meter relay, Owens was referred to in the German press as the *Wunderathlet* of the games. His picture, favorably captioned, graced the pages of German magazines. Adolf Hitler's alleged refusal to shake the victor's hand was a journalistic fabrication that added further lustre to Owens's image as a mythic hero. As William J. Baker shrewdly notes, the falseness of the report scarcely mattered: "Like George Washington's cherry tree and Abe Lincoln's log cabin, rail-splitting youth, Owens's snub at the hands of Hitler is the imaginative stuff of hero worship."[8] That Owens can still be seen as the godlike hero of Leni Riefenstahl's documentary masterpiece, *Olympia*, ensures his place in the athletic pantheon.

The integration of baseball also includes a mythic moment, in this case one based on solid historical fact. On April 15, 1947, when Jackie Robinson came up to bat for the Brooklyn Dodgers, an

Afro-American returned to major league baseball. It had taken a long time. In face of their exclusion from organized baseball, at the minor as well as major league levels, Afro-Americans established their own professional teams. The first was the Cuban Giants, created by Frank P. Thompson at Argyle Hotel in Babylon, Long Island, in 1885. Although the Giants (who were, of course, Americans, and not Cubans) were denied admission to the Eastern League, they were able to compete against college teams from Amherst, Penn, Princeton, and Yale. Afro-Americans also organized professional leagues. The Negro National League, which lasted from 1920 to 1931, was founded by Andrew "Rube" Foster, who had played for the Chicago Leland Giants and had formed his own black team, the Chicago American Giants. Robert Peterson wrote of Foster, "As an outstanding pitcher, a colorful and shrewd field manager, and the founder and stern administrator of the first viable Negro league, Foster was the most impressive figure in black baseball history." High praise indeed! In addition to the Chicago American Giants, the NNL had the St. Louis Giants, the Detroit Stars, the Indianapolis ABC's, the Cuban Stars, and the Kansas City Monarchs (which were owned by the only white man in black baseball, J. L. Wilkinson).[9]

Many of the owners in Negro baseball, like many of the white owners of nineteenth-century franchises, were gamblers. In fact, one historian of black baseball, Donn Rogosin, has called NNL meetings "conclaves of the most powerful black gangsters in the nation." William A. ("Gus") Greenlee, for instance, was a bootlegger who became one of Pittsburgh's most important gamblers. Greenlee owned the famous Crawford Grill, a nightclub where black and white entertainers gathered, and was part owner of a musical booking agency. His "main enterprise," according to the historian Rob Ruck, "was the numbers game, a lottery in which bettors wager that the three-digit number they select will be the number that 'hits' that day." Since many numbers players place their hopes on the number that corresponds to the day of the month, Pittsburgh's gamblers were thrown into a panic on August 5, 1930, when the number 805 came up. Most gamblers fled town, but Greenlee and his friend William ("Woogie") Harris paid their debts and became the most trusted—and financially successful—of the city's black gamblers.

That year Greenlee bought a sandlot team, the Crawfords, and set out to eclipse the famed Homestead Grays, owned by Cumberland Posey. The first of his great players was Leroy ("Satchel") Paige, who joined the team in 1931. Raiding the Grays for Oscar Charleston and Josh Gibson, acquiring Cool Papa Bell from Detroit and Judy Johnson from Hilldale, Greenlee put together what may have been, in Ruck's view, "the best baseball team ever assembled for regular season play." The Crawfords defeated the Grays—and every other team in black baseball. Two years after the demise of the original NNL in 1931, Greenlee launched a second NNL, which was subsequently absorbed by the Negro American League in 1948. That league, founded in 1937, staggered on, diminished by the loss of talent to integrated major-league baseball, until 1960.[10]

Black owners wanted to provide first-class *professional* baseball. Despite their underworld connections, they yearned for respectability and for acceptance by white America. Foster's motto was conciliatory: "We have to be ready when the time comes for integration." The Negro press, which provided the only significant coverage of black baseball, warned the players not to drink, dress improperly, use foul language, or gamble. Needless to say, white women were a taboo (although Effie Manley, owner of the Newark franchise, was the white widow of a black owner).

Black fans turned out in large numbers to support Negro baseball, but there was never enough money to create a modern league. Greenlee did well enough economically to invest $100,000 in the first black-owned stadium, but his success was unusual, and even he suffered severe financial reversal. Ruck remarks that Greenlee Field, opened with high hopes in 1932, "never achieved the level of patronage necessary to turn a profit." The black leagues were always makeshift organizations plagued by unstable franchises, ramshackle facilities, imprecise schedules, and insecure finances. Yet, despite their manifold disadvantages, many of the black players developed skills at least equal to those displayed in the majors. While officials of segregated white baseball condescendingly referred to the black teams as "minor league," Rogosin notes that "the Negro league made mincemeat of triple-A teams." They also held their own, and more, in interracial exhibition games. In thirty-two times at bat against white major-league pitchers, Willie Wells hit .412. In fifty-four games, Cool Papa Bell batted .391. Between 1886 and 1948 black teams won 269 games and lost 172 against major league teams. No one knows for sure how Josh Gibson, Cool Papa Bell, Judy Johnson, or the young Satchel Paige might have fared had they been given the opportunity routinely to match their talents with those of the best white players.[11]

The logic of modern sports (and some very vocal black journalists) called clearly for the recruitment of black players who promised to perform better than their white counterparts. White voices, including those of Heywood Broun, Shirley Povich, and Westbrook Pegler, joined with those of black journalists like Wendell Smith of the *Pittsburgh Courier* in demanding equal opportunity in a domain where, theoretically, only performance matters. The entry of the United States into World War II meant that ballplayers were eligible for military conscription, which soon brought about a scarcity of white major leaguers. Starved for good players, relatively unprejudiced entrepreneurs like Bill Veeck and Clark Griffith developed an appetite for Negro stars. Buck Leonard and Josh Gibson were approached by Griffith with hints that they might soon don Washington Senators uniforms. They never did, but wartime rhetoric may have helped the cause of equality in the long run. All but the morally blind saw that Afro-Americans who had served their country in combat deserved the opportunity to participate freely in American sports. The intransigence of Commissioner of Baseball Kenesaw Mountain Landis was a major obstacle to racial justice. In Tygiel's judgment, Landis "brought to baseball a disdain for law and due process characteristic of his judicial career." Landis died in 1944 and was followed by Senator Albert "Happy" Chandler, who told Ric Roberts of the *Pittsburgh Courier*, "If they can fight and die on Okinawa, Guadalcanal, in the South Pacific, they can play ball in America." The owners, however, continued to harbor doubts about democracy. In 1946 they voted secretly, by a margin of 15–1, to maintain the color bar.[12]

The lone dissenter was Branch Rickey. He determined to break what is often referred to without irony as the "gentleman's agreement" on racial exclusion. On April 18, 1946, Jackie Robinson came to bat for the Montreal Royals, a farm team of Rickey's Brooklyn Dodgers. Robinson's first appearance was the occasion for a fan to scream, "Here comes that nigger son of a bitch. Let's give it to him now."[13] It is not clear who gave what to whom, but the Royals demolished the Jersey City Giants 14–1 and Robinson had four hits in five at bats. He also stole two bases and forced two balks.

When Rickey decided to move Robinson to the Dodgers after one year with Montreal, Dixie Walker and a number of other players, not all of them Southerners, protested. Manager Leo Durocher called a midnight meeting, showed up in pajamas and a yellow robe, and laid down the law: "I don't care if a guy is yellow or black, or if he has stripes like a fuckin' zebra. . . . I'm the manager of this team and I say he plays." With some further colorful language, authority upheld ability's rights to equal opportunity. As noted earlier, Robinson played his first major-league game on April 15, 1947. The last embers of revolt among his teammates died away and were replaced by a flame of anger at the racist epithets used against Robinson by opposing players. Years later, in the mid-fifties, Casey Stengel still referred to black players as "niggers" and "jungle bunnies," but even he had to submit to the inevitable. The first black Yankee, Elston Howard, suited up in 1955. The Boston Red Sox remained an all-white team until 1959, nine years after the Boston Celtics made Edward Cooper the first black in the National Basketball Association.[14]

Why did Rickey do it? The historian Jules Tygiel refers to Rickey as a "moralist and mountebank," which barely begins to limn the portrait. The man was a devout Methodist, but the United States had many devout Methodists who believed that God had decided upon racial segregation on the day when Ham spotted his father's nakedness. Rickey differed from such brethren in that he was also a modernizer. "To Rickey baseball represented a science in which one researched, experimented, and refined techniques for maximum results." One example of this experimental attitude was Rickey's innovative development of the farm system during his years as manager of the St. Louis Cardinals. The Cardinals' ownership of minor-league teams assured a steady supply of young players, most of whom Rickey sold to other major-league teams. Materialistic motives also played a role when Rickey signed Robinson and integrated major-league baseball. The Yankees and the Giants had profitable arrangements under which they rented their stadia to Negro teams; the Dodgers did not. Rickey was also insightful enough to realize that black players were certain to draw black spectators. The question was whether or not white boycotters would outnumber the newly attracted black fans. Rickey decided that integration would mean a net gain at the box office, and he was right. Ironically, however, integration destroyed the Negro leagues. J. L. Wilkinson, owner of the Kansas City Monarchs, quit baseball in disgust when blacks abandoned his team in order to ride hundreds of miles to St. Louis and sit in segregated stands and gaze admiringly at black major leaguers.[15]

Why Robinson? His selection by Rickey after a single season with Wilkinson's Kansas City Monarchs embittered many of the older black players whose achievements at the time were far greater. They felt, probably correctly, that they had been passed up because Robinson had played ball with whites at UCLA. The black critics admitted, however, that Robinson had the necessary athletic ability and the equally necessary stoic fortitude to endure the vicious treatment meted out to him by racist players and spectators. It was a different kind of gamble from the one common among baseball owners, but it worked.

Since baseball was still perceived in the 1940s as the "national game," the integration of football seemed less epochal. In 1946 the Los Angeles Rams of the National Football League announced the signing of Kenny Washington and Woody Strode. The Cleveland Browns of the All-America Conference took on Bill Willis and Marion Motley. By the time Arthur Ashe and Althea Gibson became the first black tennis stars, racial discrimination was a minor matter in comparison to the bitter hostility encountered by Robinson. Most Americans cannot recall the names of the first blacks to go on the professional golf circuit. By the time Debi Thomas figure skated her way to a world championship in 1986, she was able to explain to *Sports Illustrated* that she had *never* experienced discrimination. *Sic transit infama mundi*.

When the civil rights revolution came in the 1960s, the central issue in sports was no longer whether or not Afro-Americans had the right to play at the intercollegiate or openly professional level. The main struggle was now over the day-to-day social discrimination suffered by black athletes on college campuses. Athletically gifted blacks recruited by mostly white colleges and universities often heard racial slurs, conscious or unconscious, from the coaches who had cajoled them into matriculating. Harry Edwards was sickened by classmates who called him "coon," "nigger," and "jiggaboo," and then, on Saturday, appealed to him to give his all for dear old San Jose State. By the end of Edwards's first year, "all illusions of California as a super-liberal, interracial promised land had evaporated."[16]

In the 1960s very few black women received athletic scholarships from the eager coaches who were scouring the country for male talent. Black men seeking companionship at predominantly white schools had to search off campus or date white coeds. Some coaches were tolerant. Dee Andros of Oregon State, who seems to have been absolutely hysterical about moustaches, nonetheless defended the right of black football players to date white women: "It takes two to tango." Others were less enlightened. Nothing infuriated racists more than the sight of a black athlete hand in hand with a white cheerleader. Some blacks who defied the taboo were dropped from teams; others were expelled from school. In one case, at the University of Texas at El Paso, Phil Harris became engaged to a blonde "green-eyed Caucasian beauty." He was expelled and she received an unexpected and presumably vindictive failing grade from a professor who had informed her that he disapproved of interracial marriage. At the University of Washington, where one might have expected far more enlightened attitudes, Junior Coffey was told by his coach that dating a white girl was "detrimental" to his future. Although Coffey was the third-best rusher in the nation, he never started again for Washington. These may have been isolated examples, but there were certainly abuses enough to explain Harry Edwards' castigation of the entire system: "The black athlete on the white-dominated college campus . . . is typically exploited, abused, dehumanized, and cast aside in much the same manner as a worn basketball."[17]

That black athletes were "cast aside" can be proven from the dismal figures on their graduation rates. In many football programs, fewer than half of the black players received diplomas. Some universities went for decades without graduating a single black basketball player. While critics acknowledge that many of these athletes were not academically ready for college in the first place, another important fact is often overlooked in the heat of the debate: the graduation rate for academically unqualified white athletes is not much better. Of 206 NCAA Division I athletes who entered college in 1977, only 31 percent of the black and 53 percent of the white athletes had degrees six years later.[18]

While the problem of the analphabetic nongraduate has probably worsened in the last twenty years, for reasons already discussed in Chapter Eight, the prejudice against interracial romance has weakened. On most campuses, racists who once screamed obscene insults at black-white couples have been reduced to scowling and muttering. Overt racism in American sports really has diminished. That the hurdler Edwin Moses has a white wife seems to bother almost no one. A great deal has happened in the eighty years since Jack Johnson nailed his wife's portrait to the wall of his Chicago bar.

Residual Racism

Simply in quantitative terms, black athletes have arrived. In baseball and football they are overrepresented in relation to their share of the population. In basketball, at the collegiate level as well as in the NBA, black dominance is such that even southern universities field mostly black teams. There is, however, still reason to be concerned about racism as a factor that contradicts the logic of modern sport.

There are subtle forms of discrimination that may not even be felt as discriminatory by the perpetrators, the victims, or the observers. In a complicated experiment, Raymond E. Rainville, Al Roberts, and Andrew Sweet played audiotapes of sixteen televised NFL games from all three networks. The exploits of eleven pairs of black and white players of comparable ability (e.g., O. J. Simpson and Larry Csonka) were commented upon in the tapes, but all names, including those of the teams, were disguised. Listeners were then asked to rate the descriptions of the action with an eye to positive and negative comments and physical versus cognitive attributions. The results offered clear evidence of bias: "The announcers are building a positive reputation for white players and a comparatively negative reputation for black players. It is probable that the announcers are not consciously producing this effect." In general, white players are described as intelligent actors, while black players are seen as those acted upon.[19]

Bias of the sort alleged in this study is hard to detect, but all socially aware observers realize that the professional leagues of the United States have very few black franchise owners or managers and that the predominantly white colleges and universities have very few black athletic directors and head coaches. Noting in 1985 that there were no black owners, managers, or coaches in the NFL and only three black managers in the history of major-league baseball, Harry Edwards referred scathingly to the "plantation system" of American sports. Since men and women become owners because they possess the millions of dollars franchises cost, racism is not the only explanation for the absence of black owners, except insofar as racism is the antecedent for the lack of those millions of dollars. Racism, however, is a factor in the exclusion of black former athletes from managing and coaching positions. The dynamics of the situation are more complex than they seem at first glance.[20]

That there are few black catchers in major-league baseball and even fewer black quarterbacks in the NFL has been widely noticed, but few people realize that there is a correlation between the position an athlete plays and the possibility of a post-retirement career as a coach or manager. Sociologists John Loy and Joseph McElvogue have, therefore, studied "stacking" in baseball and football. This approach has important methodological advantages. All the necessary data are available in official team publications, and quantified tests are easy to apply. In a seminal article that has generated dozens of replications, Loy and McElvogue found a statistically signficant correlation between race and playing position in both baseball and football. Dividing positions between "central" and "peripheral," by which they referred not to spatial relationships but rather to the frequency of interactions among the players, Loy and McElvogue demonstrated that black athletes are channeled into peripheral positions. They become, for instance, outfielders in baseball, running backs in football. From these positions black and Hispanic players are less likely to move on, after retirement, to managerial roles. Chi-square tests, which are based on the relationship between expected and observed distributions of nominal variables (like males and females who are Democrats or Republicans), proved that the observed pattern was very improbably random. Once Loy and McElvogue introduced into sports sociology the distinction between central and peripheral positions, other scholars were able to chart the precise path that leads from central position to coach's job. Although only 36 percent of the playing positions in football are defined as central, a 1977 study found that 65 percent of all NCAA Division I head coaches and 49 percent of the assistant coaches had occupied these positions in their college days.[21]

The essay by Loy and McElvogue, originally published in the *International Review of Sport Sociology*, stimulated a great deal of other research. In one variation on their approach, D. Stanley Eitzen and David C. Sanford compared "stacking" in high-school, college, and professional football. The statistical improbability of the distribution of players by race increases as players move from high school to the NFL. In high school, 14 percent of the black players had experience as quarterbacks; in college, only 1.3 percent quarterbacked; in the NFL, the percentage dropped to a paltry 0.6 percent. The Eitzen-Sanford study demonstrated that black football players become defensive linemen because racial discrimination allots them that position, rather than because of some happy match of opportunity and talent.[22]

Since Loy and McElvogue first published their statistics, a number of follow-up studies have attempted to determine whether racial discrimination has increased or diminished. It seems that there has been some increase in the movement of blacks to central positions in college football, but not in the NFL. Research by Marshall Medoff and by David Fabianic unearthed evidence indicating that positional segregation has diminished in baseball and that blacks are no longer underrepresented in central positions. Fabianic maintains that blacks' failure to win managerial positions in baseball can be best explained by the owners' reluctance to choose those blacks who do play in central positions. Medoff argues that economic factors are more important than prejudice; it costs more to train a shortstop or catcher than it does to train a right fielder, and blacks have been less likely than whites to have been coached for central positions. In 1984 Medoff found evidence indicating that the improved economic situation of Afro-Americans generally had led to a higher representation in baseball's central positions. James Curtis and John Loy, however, found that, "if anything, Blacks' proportionate appearance in the peripheral positions of [the] outfield has increased over time." John C. Phillips came to the same conclusion; black major league baseball players occupied 25 percent of the central positions in 1960 and only 15 percent in 1980.[23]

The sports psychologist Barry McPherson has suggested that black athletes are socialized into certain positions because they have black role models in those positions. Sandra C. Castine and Glyn C. Roberts tested this theory on a sample of 129 intercollegiate athletes and found that 60 percent of them had idolized some athlete while still in high school and that 48 percent of them subsequently played the same position as that idol. McPherson offered his hypothesis as an alternative to the Loy-McElvogue interpretation of discriminatory positioning, but it is actually supplemental. Although the emulation of role models cannot account for the original discrimination that placed the role models in *their* peripheral positions, emulation helps perpetuate the system.[24]

Unfortunately, the scholarly debate has gone unnoticed among those most in need of instruction. Appearing on ABC's *Nightline* in April 1987, Dodger vice president for player personnel, Al Campanis, asserted that the absence of black managers can be explained by lack of qualification. Blacks "may not have some of the necessities."[25] Campanis was forced by public pressure to resign his position and the Afro-American sport sociologist Harry Edwards was taken on as a consultant to organized baseball. Edwards may be able to explain the sociological facts to his new employers.

In another approach to the subtler forms of discrimination, a number of economists have employed their favorite instrument, the regression formula, in order to investigate the independent variables that explain the dependent variable of a baseball player's salary. Among the independent variables were race, years in the major leagues, and performance (as measured by batting average, slugging average, earned run average, etc.). Although accurate data on income are not always available, the measurement of performance is relatively easy. The fact that every player comes to bat approximately as often as every other player (except, of course, for pitchers), coupled with the fact that performance at bat is neatly quantified in the batting average, makes baseball a very attractive sport for this kind of approach. (Strictly speaking, the performances of team-sport athletes are not comparable in the sense that the times and distances of track and field competitors are, but the situational differences are assumed to cancel each other out over the length of a career.)

Anthony H. Pascal and Leonard A. Rapping employed a regression formula based on such factors as age, major league experience, and performance; they found that a residual entry barrier inhibited the movement of black players from the minor to the major leagues. Once blacks were in the majors, however, they suffered no pecuniary discrimination: "Black pitchers, black catchers, black infielders, and black outfielders . . . appear to receive compensation commensurate with their demonstrated abilities in the same way that white players do." Gerald W. Scully, however, maintained the opposite. His regression formulae convinced him that black baseball players—who earn, on the average, *higher* salaries than white players—were nonetheless greatly underpaid in terms of their performance. If a black player and a white player both batted .350, the white star earned more money than the black. A black player's superior performance may have brought him a higher salary than that received by his white teammate, but the higher salary was not proportional to the superior performance. Although the differential tended to disappear as the number of years in the league increased, few blacks stayed in the majors long enough to achieve real equity. Scully's results mean that blacks must outperform their white rivals in order to be recruited into the majors; then they must continue to outperform white players for years in order to earn the same salaries. Frequent replications and modifications of the original study show an apparent decline in economic discrimination in baseball, basketball, and football. By the beginning of the

1980s, Robert G. Mogull concluded, "The evidence simply does not support the contention of salary discrimination against blacks."[26]

Quantification and comparison of performance is also easy in track and field, where the domination of black sprinters and hurdlers offers a stark contrast to the superior performance of white distance runners. The problem here is not comparison but explanation. Physiologists have pointed to the fact that, in relation to white athletes, black athletes have a higher proportion of explosive "fast-twitch" muscle fibers and a lower proportion of the "slow-twitch" fibers called upon for endurance. On the average, black Americans seem to have denser bones, less fat, and smaller lung capacities than white Americans—a fact that has been cited as responsible for the relative paucity of black swimmers. In reply to Martin Kane and other proponents of physiological arguments to explain black-white differences in various sports, sociologists have referred to the social factors. Harry Edwards and John C. Phillips have noted that sports in which whites excel—like golf and tennis—tend to require expensive facilities or years of instruction. They are often done in private clubs. Blacks tend to excel in sports taught in the public schools and in sports that entice beginners with the dream of a professional career. The debate about the causes of racial differences in performance is inconclusive and will doubtless continue.[27]

The above-mentioned lure of fame and fortune has had some negative consequences for black Americans. While men and women of good will and democratic convictions are right to demand that Afro-Americans have the opportunity to participate in modern sports at whatever level their inclinations and talents allow, there are risks as well as opportunities. Sports are widely perceived as vehicles for upward social mobility. Marvin Hagler earns more in a single title defense than most Americans earn in a lifetime. Hagler is obviously an exceptional case. Most of the mobility experienced by black athletes is attributable to the fact that their physical skills enabled them to attend college. In fact, their mobility is almost entirely attributable to the advantages of higher education. Sports alone do almost nothing to enhance a person's career—unless that career is in sports. A career in sports is, however, enormously risky. For black athletes who aspire to the NBA or the NFL, prospects are poor. Of high school baseball, basketball, and football players, fewer than one in 10,000 succeeds at the professional level.

Well aware of these odds, some highly successful black athletes have urged young athletes to think twice about their vocational choices. Arthur Ashe, whose skills as a tennis player brought him affluence and renown, has spoken and written eloquently about the distortion of priorities that can occur when black children dream of a career in professional basketball or football. In "An Open Letter to Black Parents," published in the *New York Times* on February 6, 1977, Ashe called for reordered priorities. Urging black youth to buckle down to the books rather than to leap up for the dunk shot, Ashe pointed to the relative risks of a legal versus an athletic career. The odds against the law student who longs for an eventual Supreme Court appointment are heavy, but law students who fail in that ambition are likely, nonetheless, to become lower-court judges or, at least, lawyers with decent (and sometimes indecent) incomes. For black boys enthralled by a fantasy of sports stardom, the probability of the ultimate success of NBA or NFL recruitment is minimal. Unless the unsuccessful aspirant has prepared himself for a career in physical education (which is normally *not* the case), the alternative to success is not just failure but dismal failure. Without a bachelor's degree and without marketable talents, it is all too likely that the high school hotshot will find himself, at the end of his college eligibility, four years older and deeper in debt. He may also find himself addicted to cocaine. Induction into the world of modern sports is a mixed blessing.

TEN

Women's Sports

Emancipating the Leisure Class

In Nathaniel Hawthorne's *Blithedale Romance*, the hero, a rather effeminate poet named Miles Coverdale, falls in love with the frail Priscilla rather than the robust Zenobia. Priscilla's veils attract him more than the thought of her sister's "garb of Eden." Is it significant that Coverdale's heart is won when Priscilla, attempting to run, sprawls weakly on the grass? Can we take this scene as an indication that Hawthorne and his contemporaries idealized female weakness and debility? Was there, as Stephanie Twin has recently alleged, a mid-nineteenth-century "cult of ill health in which women proved their femininity with invalidism"?[1] It is certainly true that the nineteenth century was dominated aesthetically by Romanticism and that one important strain of Romanticism idealized illness and madness as forms of symbolic protest against the vulgar health and shallow sanity of bourgeois society. The alienated artist, however, was as likely to create a sickly hero as a sickly heroine. Thomas Mann's Hans Castorp is as typically romantic as Giacomo Puccini's Mimi, and neither can be taken to represent the dominant ideal of bourgeois society.

While some feminist historians have suggested that men encouraged female frailty in order to consolidate the power of patriarchal society, it seems improbable that many nineteenth-century husbands were so insecure in their patriarchal roles that they needed the additional reassurance of physically debilitated wives and daughters. As Deborah Gorham notes in *The Victorian Girl and the Feminine Ideal* (1982), "Those who gave advice to the middle classes . . . were aware that . . . middle-class girls would grow up with tasks too difficult and too essential to permit chronic invalidism."[2] Eve healthy was a better helpmate than Eve bedridden with a nervous breakdown. It is also unlikely that medical professionals were insincere in their repeated statements of concern about "nervousness" and other maladies brought on by the stress of modern life. As early as the mid-nineteenth century, reformers like Diocletian Lewis and Catharine Beecher were worried about the sorry state of women's health and eager to promote some kind of moderate exercise as a tonic. There is no reason to assume that their advice was less popular than S. Weir Mitchell's infamous "rest cure" (which undoubtedly *did*, by its sensual and intellectual deprivations, produce physical and psychic disaster). In reply to recent feminist accusations that women's health suffered at the hands of the male-dominated medical profession, Edward Shorter has argued in his *History of Women's Bodies* (1982) that the nineteenth century brought dramatic improvements in women's health, which had been wretchedly poor, and that these improvements were directly attributable to advances in medical research and to the nineteenth-century husband's heightened concern for his wife's wellbeing.

The worry about women's health did not mean that middle-class women were encouraged to participate in sports. Catharine Beecher responded to the miseries of sedentary women and warned in her popular *Treatise on Domestic Economy* (1841) that lack of exercise produced "softness, debility, and unfitness." To remedy the situation, she advised in her *Letters to the People on Health and Happiness* (1855) that "every man, woman, and child . . . ought to spend one or two hours every day in *vigorous* exercise of *all* the *muscles*,"[3] but her concerns were hygienic rather than athletic. She deemed housework the best form of exercise. For a woman with servants, calisthenics were her recommended substitute. By no stretch of the imagination can she be said to have been an enthusiast for women's sports.

Lydia Maria Child included an appeal for girls' sports in *The Little Girls' Own Book* (1847):

> Walking and other out-of-door exercises cannot be too much recommended to young people. Even skating, driving hoop and other boyish sports may be practised to great advantage by little girls provided they can be pursued within the enclosure of a garden or court; in the street, of course, they would be highly improper. It is true, such games are rather violent, and sometimes noisy, but they tend to form a vigorous constitution; and girls who are habitually lady-like, will never allow themselves to be rude and vulgar, even in play.

Her views were a not unusual mix of prudish caution and brave determination.[4]

Catharine Beecher's view was more typical. Until very recently, modern sports have been considered a masculine domain. Young boys were encouraged to run, jump, throw, climb, and wrestle while tomboys were merely tolerated. With the onset of puberty, boys were expected to display physical prowess as a symbol of virility and dominance; girls were left to develop the domestic skills and the physical wiles attractive to potential husbands. In English books and magazines, which strongly influenced the anglophile American middle class, sports were "forcefully and graphically depicted as the 'natural' province of males; hence, sport contributed substantially to establishing and maintaining ideologies about the proper sphere of women." On both sides of the Atlantic, the Cult of Domesticity and the Doctrine of Separate Spheres kept Victorian women in the home rather than on the playing field. The virtues of strenuous athletic competition were extolled as a means to prepare the male animal for the breadwinner's struggle, but the female of the species was destined to comfort and to nurture. While slugging a baseball and sliding into second base were thought to be a useful preparation for life in industry and commerce, there was no apparent connection between ball games and childcare.[5]

Arguments against female participation in sports were based on aesthetic ideals as well as on conceptions of woman's "natural" role as wife and mother. Of course, the aesthetic ideals were related to conceptions of social role in that Darwinists considered a woman's beauty as an important weapon in the struggle for survival, i.e., the capture of a husband. Athleticism was thought by many to diminish a woman's physical attractiveness and to hamper her in the race to matrimony.

Conventional Victorians, English and American, feared that the athletic girl fortunate enough to catch a husband was liable to have damaged her reproductive organs or even to have been rendered permanently infertile. Although Arabella Kenealy held a medical degree and might have been expected to challenge conventional wisdom, she wrote to condemn the physically active female. Her 1899 essay on "Woman as an Athlete," published in both *Living Age* and *Nineteenth Century*, described the foolish athleticism of a young woman named Clara. Once unable to walk two miles without fatigue, Clara later played tennis and field hockey and toured the countryside on her bicycle. While a hasty judgment might be positive, Kenealy asks her readers to ponder the fact that Clara had lost her gentleness, warmth, and sparkle:

> In her evening gown she shows evidence of joints which had been adroitly hidden beneath tissues of soft flesh, and already her modiste has been put to the necessity of puffings and pleatings where Nature had planned the tenderest and most dainty of devices. Her movements are muscular and less womanly. . . . Her voice is louder, her tones are assertive.

Behind Kenealy's critique lay the mechanical theory of fixed force: Clara wasted her portion of energy for pulmonary and muscular development and jeopardized her brain and her reproductive organs. Nature allegedly groans at the sight of athletic women because "Nature knows . . . it is the birthright of babies Clara and her sister athletes are squandering." The riders of bicycles and swingers of tennis rackets also risk madness and early graves: "Athletes die proverbially young. Lunatics and other diseased persons frequently exhibit muscular strength which seems almost superhuman."[6] An outraged rejoinder from L. O. Chant appeared in the two journals that had published Kenealy's article. *She* thought that the most beautiful male and female bodies were those of Barnum and Bailey acrobats.

Kenealy's and Chant's can be dismissed as unrepresentative extremist voices, but Luther Gulick was—as we have seen—an influential leader in American physical education. His stand against women's sports was influenced by popular Darwinism. Primitive man was "a hunter and a fighter." Primitive woman was not: "Boyhood and manhood have . . . for ages long been both tested and produced by athletic sports. . . . The case is very different for women. They were not predominantly hunters or fighters. They cared for the home." Exercise is necessary, but "serious, public competition" is not. Dudley A. Sargent, director of Harvard's Hemenway Gymnasium and a prestigious physical educator, discounted the common fear that all sports masculinized, but even he deprecated female boxers, wrestlers, and ballplayers.[7]

As Sargent's defense of "feminine" sports suggests, the effective demands for women's inclusion in *sports* (as opposed to mere physical education) came from the elite. While most members of the middle class remained committed to the Cult of Domesticity and most lower-class women were too overwhelmed with physical labor inside and outside the home to have the time or energy for sports, the seeds of change were sown in the exclusive women's colleges of New York and New England.

Vassar College constructed a gymnasium for its students in 1865. The college catalog informed the students that a "suitable portion of each day is set aside for physical exercise and every young lady is required to observe it as one of her college duties." Students at Vassar, like those at Mount Holyoke before them, were drilled in the calisthenic system designed by Diocletian Lewis at the Normal Institute for Physical Education in Boston. Between 1875 and 1900, Vassar women were introduced to archery, baseball, basketball, rowing, tennis, and track. The prestige accruing to athletic accomplishments can be seen in a comment in *Century* magazine: "A pink V on a Vassar girl's sweater," wrote Alice Fallows, "means she has broken a [school] record." Although she was writing for *Popular Science Monthly*, Sophia Foster Richardson relied upon classical references to legitimate Vassar's baseball and basketball games: "The daughters of Sparta were handsome and more attractive than the more delicately nurtured Athenians." Wellesley, which had a program similar to Vassar's, required athletic participation from 1906; Bryn Mawr followed a year later. Within a few months after the invention of basketball at Springfield, Massachusetts, Senda Berenson adapted the game for the students at nearby Smith College. Not everyone was pleased by Smith's athletic program. Writing in *Godey's Lady's Magazine* in 1895, Winifred Ayres complained of a student who had gone overboard for the outdoor life. Not only was she tanned, but her "arms were bare also, and the muscles were so developed they appeared in lumpy protuberances, just as those of the professional athletes are wont to do." The female educators of the elite women's colleges, undeterred by such criticism, defied convention and proclaimed an ideal of physical activity that flew in the face of Gilded Age shibboleths about ladylike decorum. Vassar's Harriet Isabel Ballintine announced boldly,

> If refinement and quietness are but the results of weakness and inactivity, and a pronounced manner must necessarily be the outcome of a more vigorous life, we must be willing to sacrifice the former feminine attributes for the more precious possession of good health.

When she wrote these words in 1898, Ballintine was still opposed to intercollegiate competition and the quest for records. She soon altered her opinions, however, and decided that some women were rugged enough for a more strenuous approach to sports.[8]

In some ways, the most appropriate model of the upper-class sportswoman was the British-born Constance Applebee, who introduced field hockey to girls attending Harvard's 1895 summer school. A club for Vassar students was formed that year at Poughkeepsie. Applebee, who lived to be over one hundred years old, taught at Bryn Mawr from 1904 to 1928. She was presumably gratified in 1920, when the sport's kilted enthusiasts sailed for England as "the first American team of women in any sport to engage in international competition." Sending the team overseas was Applebee's defiant response to the refusal of the International Olympic Committee to allow women's field hockey at the 1920 Olympic Games in Antwerp.[9]

Upper-class receptivity to women's sports is nicely documented in *The Book of Sport*, which appeared in 1901. This lavishly illustrated volume, which only the wealthy were able to purchase, ignored lower-class pastimes like baseball and concentrated on the sports of the leisure class. Photographs of well-dressed women graced the book's chapters on women's golf and tennis. Similar photographs appeared in *Outing*, a kind of nineteenth-century *Sports Illustrated*. The journal included articles on baseball, football, and track and field, but there was a pronounced emphasis on upper-class recreation.

The editors of *Outing* clearly felt that women ought to be involved in sports. In the 1880s and 1890s Margaret Bisland wrote a series of articles advocating a variety of women's sports. She scorned the timid souls who advised that light boats were best for women's "meagre muscles," and she reassured her readers that excessive muscularity was not a real danger of rowing: "By some happy provision of kind Nature, no matter if the woman's biceps grow as hard as iron and her wrists as firm as steel, the member remains as softly rounded, as tenderly curved, as though no greater strain than the weight of jeweled ornaments had been laid upon [it]." In a 1902 *Outing* article subtitled "The Athletic Girl Not Unfeminine," Christine Terhune Herrick waxed lyrical about "the joys of the track with its competition and chance to make or break a school record." Modern readers will be astonished to see that *Outing* also published photographs and drawings of nudes in order to illustrate Elizabeth Dryden's article, "How Athletics May Develop Style in Women."[10]

"The Country Club," which Robert Dunn published in the *Outing* issue for November 1905, emphasizes the fact that women were not excluded from country-club sports. At a time when it was almost as unusual for a woman to watch as to play a game of baseball, the wives and daughters of the wealthy played golf and tennis. (The latter game was brought to the United States from Bermuda in 1874 by Mary Ewing Outerbridge, a charter member of the Ladies' Club for Outdoor Sports.) The country-club environment protected members from the urban masses by social as well as geographical distance. Shielded from vulgar eyes by fences and hedges, women who had participated in sports while at Mount Holyoke, Smith, Vassar, and Wellesley were able to ride, swim, row, swing their golf clubs and their tennis rackets, and bend their bows in graceful emulation of Diana (whom Augustus Saint-Gaudens sculpted and placed atop Madison Square Garden).[11] Elizabeth Cynthia Barney's 1894 *Fortnightly Review* article, "The American Sportswoman," proclaimed the arrival of a new kind of woman. In the immediate post Civil War years, the American girl "was supposed to live on candy and novels, and too often sink into a nervous invalid before she was thirty," but the passing of a mere "generation has sufficed to effect a complete change." The modern American sportswoman was a creature of "strong, active physique, erect carriage and energetic spirit." She was "aglow with the ruddy color of physical health and energy." She was also, quite emphatically, a member of the leisure class. Barney dwelled admiringly on the exclusive sports clubs of the elite; she was, for instance, enthusiastic about the national ladies' tennis championships held in Philadelphia:

> The Philadelphia Country Club ranks with the foremost in tone and social standing, and every thing that it does is in the best style. Consequently the tournaments . . . are social functions of the highest class, and none enter their names but those of assured social position. As a matter of fact, all our first lady tennis players belong to the best families.

As the historian Donald J. Mrozek notes in commenting on this tournament, "Matches were determined by invitation only, in a way that openly violated the supposedly democratic quality of modern sport."[12]

It is undeniably true that money mattered and that golf and tennis were attractive to the country-club set because they required costly lessons, expensive equipment, or extensive tracts of land; i.e., because they were exclusive. But it is also true that many of the most favored sports were popular because they were considered appropriate for both men and women. Since none of the popular country-club games allowed for physical contact and most were played in modest (and cumbersome) dress, men and women were free to play in mixed groups. In sports, the robber barons demanded social, not sexual, segregation.[13]

It is impossible to say just how serious upper-class women were about athletic competition. A Marxist historian, Jennifer Hargreaves, has belittled the middle-class approach to sports by maintaining that it was on a par with "playing the piano, singing, drawing and painting, reciting poetry and doing needlework." No doubt there were tight-laced corseted ladies who dawdled at croquet and breathlessly murmured lines from Tennyson, but the evidence suggests dedication as well as dilettantism. (For that matter, there were women who were serious about the piano, too.) After all, the first national championships for female athletes were inaugurated in the sports most favored by women of the leisure class. The archers gathered in 1879, twenty in number. In 1887 the Philadelphia Cricket Club sponsored the first national tournament for women tennis-players. Eight years later, one hundred women met to vie for the golfers' trophy. In 1900 Margaret Abbot of the Chicago Golf Club came home from Paris with the first Olympic medal won by an American woman.[14]

From a somewhat different feminist perspective, Patricia Vertinsky has described the new physical freedom of the 1890s as essentially conservative. Women were encouraged by male medical professionals "to hone their bodies to a machine-like efficiency through modest and sociable sport and exercise in order that they might better secure the biological future of the race." There is certainly an element of truth in this sharply worded assertion. No historian can deny that male (and female) reformers were motivated by a concern for health, hygiene, and prospective motherhood. It is, however, reductionist to conclude from the evidence that this was the only motive. One might also ask if bearing a healthy child with "machine-like efficiency" is not preferable—for those women who want children—to dying in the middle of prolonged and difficult delivery. If the advocates of women's sports had been as conservative as historians like Hargreaves and Vertinsky say they were, then truly conservative voices, like Arabella Kenealy's, would not have cried out at the allegedly extreme behavior of sport-obsessed women.[15]

The Search for an Alternative Model

Any expectations that the female athlete was about to take her place next to the male were destined for disappointment. In the popular imagination, the 1920s were the Jazz Age, the years when flappers bobbed their hair, donned their shorts, grabbed their tennis rackets, played three furious sets against F. Scott Fitzgerald, and danced all night. In reality, the development of women's sports paralleled the history of American feminism, which lost most of its impetus after the achievement of suffrage in 1920. The ensuing decade was a period of stagnation in women's sports.

In a 1929 *School and Society* article entitled "Olympics for Girls?" Frank R. Rogers answered his own question with a resounding negative: "Intense forms of physical and psychic conflicts tend to destroy girls' physical and psychic charm and adaptability for motherhood." The female physical educators who listened to such voices constituted a receptive audience.[16]

Of course, there *were* women like Helen Wills Moody and Alice Marble in tennis and Mildred ("Babe") Didrikson in track and field, women who paid no attention whatsoever to the admonitions of men like Rogers, women whose spectacular performances earned them national and even international reputations; but these women received little encouragement from the colleges and universities. Women's sports were sponsored by industrial leagues or by the Amateur Athletic Union, rather than in the educational institutions that had once nurtured them. The female physical educators who had fought for athletic emancipation in the 1890s and the early twentieth century were replaced by a more timid generation that thwarted and frustrated the efforts of the liberal minority who wanted women's full participation in modern sports. The women who controlled physical education at the elite colleges were appalled by the evident corruption in men's intercollegiate athletics. Idealistically, they determined to provide an alternative for women. The result was the "play day," at which, typically, young women from different schools were assigned to mixed teams; for instance, a single basketball team might include students from Mount Holyoke, Wellesley, and Smith. Fun and games were followed by tea and cookies. Competitiveness was not prized.

When the Amateur Athletic Union sent a team of female swimmers to Paris in 1922, female members of the American Physical Education Association were "incensed and withdrew from any cooperative ventures with the AAU." The female physical educators then institutionalized their conception of women's sports in the Women's Division of the National Amateur Athletic Federation, founded in 1923. This organization, which eventually merged with the Division for Girls' and Women's Sports of the American Association for Health, Physical Education, and Recreation, looked askance at intercollegiate competition and adamantly opposed state and national championships for women. Rejecting the tendencies of men's sports, the platform of the Women's Division advocated "competition that stresses enjoyment of sport and development of good sportsmanship and character rather than those types that emphasize the breaking of records and the winning of championships for the enjoyment of spectators or for the athletic reputation or commercial advantage of institutions and organizations." Women's colleges were urged not to sell tickets to sporting events lest the taint of Mammon, which had certainly afflicted men's sports, be visited upon them. After the introduction of women's track and field at the 1928 Olympics, the Women's Division petitioned the International Olympic Committee not to repeat the "experiment" in 1932. The dominant view of the 1920s and 1930s was summed up by Agnes Wayman: "What is sauce for the gander, is *not* sauce for the goose."[17]

In 1942 the Women's Division, along with the AAU, the YWCA, the YWHA, and seven other national groups, opposed competition at the district or county levels. The 100-yard dash was also discouraged as too strenuous for female athletes. In 1956 the Division of Girls' and Women's Sports (as the organization was then known) continued to urge that extramural competition "not lead to county, state, district or national championships." In 1957 the DGWS called once again for "sports days" instead of intercollegiate encounters. Varsity sports were finally accepted in 1963, national championships in 1967. The Canute-like effort to halt the tide of modern sports finally ended.[18]

The Liberation of the Female Athlete?

As the second wave of feminism swirled through the United States in the 1960s and 1970s, old attitudes were washed away and women's sports were transformed. Assertive women demanded that tournament sponsors offer equal prizes for men and women. The tennis star Billie Jean King led a boycott of the 1970 Pacific Southwest Championships because the men's prize was $12,500 and the women's only $1,500. When the United States Lawn Tennis Association resisted the demand for equality, King helped Gladys Heldman organize the Virginia Slims Circuit, financed by the Phillip Morris Company. Within three years the women's circuit encompassed twenty-two cities and offered prize money of $775,000. (The men played in twenty-four cities for $1,280,000.) In 1973 the U.S. Open equalized its awards for men's and women's singles. In that same year King played her notorious match against Bobby Riggs, with over 30,000 spectators in the stadium and some 40,000,000 TV viewers. Her win over the fifty-five-year-old "clown prince of tennis" was a travesty of modern sports, but it was said to have been an occasion for Bella Abzug to make book "with a half-dozen congressmen on the floor of the House of Representatives," and it was probably a victory of sorts for feminism.[19]

The women who eventually defeated Billie Jean King on the tennis court carried on her struggle for equal rights. Chris Evert Lloyd and Martina Navratilova became activists in the Women's Tennis Association (after initial hesitation on the part of the former). The fact that Navratilova has admitted to bisexuality has not made her a heroine to the Moral Majority, but neither has the admission destroyed her career.

In the 1970s female physical educators created a new institutional base in the form of the Association for Intercollegiate Athletics for Women (1971). Split at first between those who wanted full participation in modern sports and those who argued for a separate path, if not for a separate sphere, the AIAW initially opposed national championships and athletic scholarships. Both positions were subsequently abandoned. Long before the organization was absorbed by the NCAA, at the start of the 1980s, the majority of AIAW members had overcome their reluctance about modern sports. Inevitably, once the AIAW gave its full endorsement to intercollegiate athletics, it was wracked internally by the same controversies that have marked the history of men's sports. Women accused each other of recruiting violations and other forms of skullduggery. Although AIAW rules prohibited personal visits for recruitment, many coaches admitted that they found such visits indispensable. Marianne Stanley of Old Dominion asked, "What good are rules if you can't enforce them?" That winter, Old Dominion was accused of flagrant violation of the AIAW's recruitment rules.[20]

If the AIAW failed to provide a viable alternative to men's sports, it did encourage wider female participation. In 1971–72 fewer than 30,000 women were engaged in varsity sports; a decade later, nearly 150,000 competed. The increase at the high school level was even more spectacular. In the 1970s the number of girls involved in interscholastic sports rose almost sevenfold, from under 300,000 to over 2,000,000. The number of boys on high school teams increased by only about 20 percent so that there were approximately twelve times as many boys as girls engaged in interscholastic sports when the decade began, and only twice as many when it ended.

The boom in women's sports has been accompanied by a mini-revolution in sports journalism. Traditionally, women's sports have been shamefully neglected in the press and on TV. During *Sports Illustrated*'s first twenty-five years, female athletes appeared on only fifty-five of the magazine's 1,250 covers. In the mid-1970s the *Los Angeles Times* and the *Washington Post* pictured female athletes in a mere 8 percent of their sports-page photographs. In a thirteen-month period from August 1972 to September 1973, a minuscule 0.2 percent of NBC's live sports coverage was devoted to women's events. Grete Waitz set a world's record in the 1979 New York Marathon and was not mentioned once in more than two hours of live coverage. Tennis was the only sport whose female stars appeared regularly on network TV. Feminists have protested this scanty coverage, and the media have gotten the message; they have made an effort to redress the traditional imbalance. ABC hired Ellie Riger as the first female sports producer, and CBS Sports hired Jane Chastain as a commentator (only to replace her with a wholly inexperienced former Miss America). *Sports Illustrated* has increased its reporting on women's sports and has attempted to avoid sexual stereotypes. Indeed, some of the magazine's writers seem determined to forge new stereotypes. Barbara McDermott wrote of the Belgian judo champion Ingrid Berghmans, "If some still believe women don't have the right to sweat and win without apology—or sport pumped-up, Nautilus-constructed biceps just like the big boys

—she's impressive evidence to the contrary. . . . Ingrid . . . is as much today's female as she is the modern athlete. Big, blonde and beautiful. . . ." On the other hand, the magazine continues to run its annual "swimsuit issue" with not a pumped-up biceps in sight.[21]

Swimsuits aside, frailty is now out of favor. The young Marilyn Monroe worked out in secret; Jane Fonda, well into middle age, has gone public. Kodak now runs magazine and TV advertisements showing a girl smiling at her well developed biceps. "The winsome Breck Girl might have once been an ideal," exulted Janice Kaplan, "but now shampoo ads featured Chris Evert and . . . Dorothy Hamill." A magazine, *Strength Training for Beauty*, is now devoted entirely to the proposition that muscular women are not only strong but also beautiful. Since aesthetic ideals are intensely subjective (for which we should be grateful) and vary widely within pluralistic modern societies, no one can prove that the sinewy female in her running shorts is more or less beautiful than the bosomy debutante in her evening gown. Despite the belief that women seriously involved in sports still suffer from stigmatization and role conflict, most recent psychological and sociological studies show that female athletes experience little of either and that they are perceived positively both by men and by other women. Looking at forty-four female powerlifters, who are the antithesis of china-doll femininity and ought to suffer role conflict if any female athletes do, Maria T. Allison and Beverly Butler concluded that the problem had been greatly exaggerated. Only 9.1 percent of the lifters admitted to having experienced role conflict.[22]

Although it may still be a part of folk wisdom that girls and women participate in sports to compensate for low self-esteem, several studies have shown, to the contrary, that female athletes have a more positive self-image than non-athletes do. The comment of one pentathlete, Jane Frederick, cannot be taken as representative, but it deserves quotation: "Men go cuckoo for me. . . . As long as I love my body, everyone else does, too." Do men really go "cuckoo" over female athletes? What does the American public now think about the combination of once discrepant social roles? Robert C. Woodford and Wilbur J. Scott interviewed 350 Oklahoma City residents to discover their reactions to six provocative statements, including the following: "Women are likely to develop unsightly muscles if they exercise regularly" and "A woman cannot be both a good athlete and a truly feminine person." Only 27.2 percent of the sample agreed with the first statement, only 10.8 percent with the second. As one might have expected, the older and less educated respondents were much more likely to agree with the negative stereotypes. In this, as in other studies, men were found to be more positively disposed toward female athletes than were women. While widespread admiration for female gymnasts, figure skaters, and swimmers does not necessarily signal enthusiasm for boxers, shot putters, and powerlifters, there is a growing tendency for men (and, to a lesser extent, women) to say that whatever a woman does is feminine. There is certainly a greater acceptance of female athletes in the United States than in Europe, where French and German intellectuals continue to titter about Jane Fonda, Lisa Lyon, and all those ugly muscles.[23]

Undeniably, economic motives play a role in the increased interest in and support for women's sports. Healthy profits can be made from the new vogue for athletic bodies. Tennis camps and aerobics classes cost money. Sports and fitness magazines are full of glossy advertisements for digital chronometers, exercise machines, tennis racquets, surfboards, running shoes, Goretex training suits, food supplements, and workout manuals. In the articles, lovely young females grimace as they set records or work on their biceps femoris. In the advertisements, lovely young females smile as they wield chromium-plated weights or bound about in iridescent leotards. Observing that cosmetics manufacturers have zeroed in on the fitness market, two feminist scholars complain that even Billie Jean King's magazine, *Women's Sports*, appeals mainly to the "cosmopolitan, affluent, upwardly mobile young, white, heterosexual woman." Further evidence of this trend appeared in 1978, when Phillip Morris dropped the Virginia Slims Circuit and Avon Products rushed in to pick up the tab.[24]

Economic motives also influence the kinds of women's sports that will appear on television. Commercial TV depends on advertisers, and advertisers prefer to invest their money in sports that attract affluent viewers: golf and tennis, rather than softball and track and field. These same advertisers are also likely to sponsor golf and tennis tournaments. For golfers and tennis players, endorsements have become an important source of extra income. "If I play well," said Chris Evert Lloyd, "my dresses will sell well." For the networks, women's sports are a relatively inexpensive form of programming. For the viewers, the sight of Martina Navratilova and Nancy Lopez is an incentive to go and do likewise, preferably with the latest in racquets, clubs, shorts, and shoes.[25]

It is doubtful that sports participation was an important consideration in the legislative battles that culminated in the passage of Title IX of the Education Act of 1972, but the increases in participation in women's interscholastic and intercollegiate sports have certainly been abetted by legal changes. Title IX made discrimination on the basis of gender illegal in all institutions receiving federal support: "No person . . . shall, on the basis of sex, be excluded from participation in, be denied the benefits of, or be subjected to discrimination under any educational programs or activities receiving federal financial assistance." That the inequalities between men's and women's programs were gross is undeniable. The Syracuse, New York, school board's 1969 budget for extracurricular sports allocated $90,000 to the boys' teams and $200 to the girls'; when money grew tight, the board eliminated the girls' budget. At the University of New Mexico, the 1970–71 budget for men's sports was $527,000 and for women's sports $9,150. In comparison to the University of Washington's budget, New Mexico's was wildly feminist: in Seattle in 1973–74, the men received $2,582,000 and the women $18,000. In response to moral and legal pressure, Washington increased the women's 1974–75 budget to $200,000.

That Title IX has made a difference can also be seen in the before-and-after legal judgments. When Susan Hollander of Hamden, Connecticut, sued her school board for the right to run with the boys' cross-country team because there was no girls' team, John Clark FitzGerald of New Haven Superior Court ruled that

> our younger male population has not become so decadent that boys will experience a thrill in defeating girls in running contests. . . . It could well be that many boys would feel compelled

> to forgo entering track events if they were required to compete with girls. . . . With boys vying with girls . . . the challenge to win and the glory of achievement, at least for many boys, would lose incentive and become nullified. Athletic competition builds character in our boys. We do not need that kind of character in our girls.[26]

In *Gregorio* v. *Board of Education of Asbury Park* (1971), which was also decided before the passage of Title IX, the Superior Court of New Jersey ruled that girls had no right to join the boys' tennis team merely because there was no girls' team. After the new law came into effect, the U.S. Court of Appeals for the 6th District of Michigan ruled, in *Morris* v. *Michigan Board of Education* (1973), that girls had the right to try out for the boys' tennis team even when there was also a girls' team. The drive toward equality was partially blocked, however, when the Supreme Court decided, in *Grove City College* v. *Bell* (1984), that illegal discrimination within a single department was not grounds for action against an entire college or university. If the geologists refuse to hire women, they are liable to lose their own federal grants, but their colleagues in physical education will continue to be funded.

Although Title IX has forced changes, it has not wrought miracles. Walter Byers of the NCAA lobbied hard against Title IX because it spelled "the possible doom of intercollegiate sports." As the bill approached a final vote, the NCAA fought for Senator John Tower's amendment, which would have exempted the "revenue-producing" sports, most of which turn out to be men's sports. The lobbying failed, but most athletic departments are controlled by men and many continue to resist full implementation of the law.[27]

Debates continue on the meaning of equality. The radical view is that parity must be calculated on the basis of the male/female ratio of the entire student body; if 52 percent of the *students* are women, female athletes should receive 52 percent of the funding. The more moderate view, accepted by the Department of Education, is that the males and females actually participating in sports form the relevant population: if 30 percent of the *athletes* are female, women's sports should receive 30 percent of the money. Having failed to prevent the enactment of Title IX, the NCAA has been less than Draconian in its enforcement efforts. In the spring of 1984, the organization ruled that a school's failure to equalize the number of male and female teams would be punished by a ban on national competition—for the women's teams. One suspects that some NCAA members are poor losers.

Debates continue about the opportunity for women to play on men's teams. Many male athletes still feel that their masculinity is undermined by women who outperform them. When Jan Merrill, a middle-distance runner, ran against eight men in a two-mile race in 1979, she came in fifth, which so unnerved Fitchburg College coach Jim Sheehan that he cried out, "I'd die before I would ever be beaten by a woman." Of the Auburn University student whom Becky Birchmore defeated while a member of the University of Georgia men's tennis team, Coach Dan Magill lamented, "It ruined him. I really wish I hadn't done it." Ellen Cornish of Frederick, Maryland, had no chance to ruin the lives of the boys from Thomas Johnson High School; she was dragged from the track before she broke the tape.[28]

Even if one feels that male athletes who are defeated by female athletes will have to live with their fates, other questions remain to be answered. Federal law is currently interpreted to mean that girls whose high schools have no girls' tennis team have the right to play on the boys' team, but this may not be the best solution. Most of the girls who play on boys' teams are liable to perform at a level below that of their male teammates. Does this cause the girls psychological damage? And what is the equitable solution to the dilemma of boys who want to join the girls' team because their school has no boys' team in their chosen sport? This may seem like a foolish question, but National Public Radio for August 31, 1986, broadcast a report from Annapolis High School, where two boys have requested to be allowed to join the girls' field hockey team.

On average, men are taller and heavier than women, have faster reaction times, more acute vision, better spatial perception, and greater muscular strength. Women, on the other hand, are more flexible than men and surpass men at very long distance running and swimming. With these physiological facts in mind, Jane English has suggested that we "should develop a variety of sports in which a variety of physical types can expect to excel." If the sports in which women outperform men were as salient in the public's imagination as the sports in which men have the physical advantage, then women would more likely be perceived as men's physical equals. Through their superiority in these "alternative sports" women would have an opportunity to gain in self-respect, which English describes as a "basic benefit" of sports which should be available to all women. Whether such sports can realistically be expected to attain the prestige and popularity of baseball, basketball, football, ice hockey, and other male-dominated sports is, however, questionable.[29]

Some feminists have stressed the cultural factors behind the physical differentials and have concluded that women do not need alternate sports because women have the undeveloped physical potential to equal men's performances in the modern sports now dominated by male athletes. These feminists are correct to assert that socialization, rather than genetic endowment, explains why the average American woman attains her maximum strength at the age of twelve and a half while the strength of the average man continues to increase into his twenties, but it is unlikely that cultural factors can account for *all* the observed gender differences in strength and in sports performance. In official contests (as opposed to recreational situations) a commitment to equality dictates that, as a general rule, men be matched against men and women against women. The ideal legal solution therefore takes into account physical differences when these differences are relevant to athletic performance.[30]

Finally, ethical questions arise for which there are now no satisfactory legal answers. Can those who condemn boxing as brutal and dangerous welcome the entry of women into the ring? Should we rejoice that some women now have the chance to suffer the brain damage that is the boxer's occupational hazard? One might respond that boxing should be made illegal for both sexes, but other questions remain. Is the development of female bodybuilding an indication that women are determined to be strong and independent, as proponents say? Or is it a humiliating sign that they merely wish to imitate men? What is the moralist to make of the use of anabolic steroids by women who seek greater muscle mass than can be obtained by Nautilus workouts alone? Putting the question more generally, *are* there physical and psychological differences between males and females that might allow women to create humane alternatives to some of the distortions and abuses of modern sports?

ELEVEN

The Destruction of the Body

Excess in the Name of Excellence

Aside from satisfying innate or culturally induced psychological needs through competition, sports provide opportunities for the mastery of physical skills, for a sense of self-realization. Some scholars refer to "flow" or "peak experience," to moments so intense that one feels no division between mind and body or between self and environment. A tragic irony of modern sports is that they sometimes lead not to the enhancement but to the destruction of the physical self. Even without the obsessive compulsion to win the contest no matter what the consequences to oneself or one's opponent, there is the equally obsessive quest for records. If the first obsession appears most frequently in the highly organized world of "big-time" sports, whether allegedly amateur or openly professional, the second occurs at all levels (e.g., when a runner staggers forward to a new "personal best" despite an injured achilles tendon or a torn cartilage in the knee).

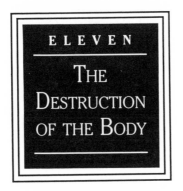

The destruction of the body through sports is not exactly new. At the sacred games of the ancient Greeks, seekers of glory in the pankration (which combined the techniques of boxing and wrestling) sometimes died of the injuries incurred. Death was a familiar event in the Roman arena and a frequent occurrence in early medieval tournaments. In the legendary decades of English bare-knuckle pugilism, from the mid-eighteenth century to the early nineteenth, blood flowed freely and battered bodies were accepted as symbols of masculinity. Following Norbert Elias, with whom he has sometimes collaborated, Eric Dunning has marshaled considerable evidence to prove that legitimate sports violence (i.e., that committed within the rules of the game) has declined over the past several hundred years.

The last two or three decades, however, seem to have brought an upsurge in the level of physical destruction. Sports medicine has become a thriving specialty. Motor sports are the most obviously dangerous; certainly the fiery deaths of the speedways are the most spectacular indications that sports are not always good for one's health. When accidents happen, motorcyclists are even less likely than automobile drivers to survive. Parachutists, too, accept a certain amount of risk.

That many boxers have been killed in the ring and that many others have suffered serious brain damage from repeated concussions is no secret either. In fact, since 1945 more than 350 boxers have been killed in the ring or have died as an immediate consequence of injuries incurred there. Recent articles in the *Journal of the American Medical Association* offer a clear—or should one say shadowed?—picture of what happens when the brain is jarred by blows to the head. Fight fans have long suspected what medical investigators now know. (The terms "punchy" and "punch drunk" are a part of the English language.) Since the sport requires each fighter to do physical damage to the other, injuries are unavoidable. Masochism cannot be dismissed as a motive for the boxers. The pugilists of Regency England prided themselves on their "bottom" and American fighters still boast of their indomitable "heart." As was the case with nineteenth-century German fencers, scars offer proof of virility.[1]

The counterpart of masochism in the ring is sadism in the stands. Sadism is unquestionably one of the attractions for the fans. No doubt there are others, such as the demonstration of swiftness and agility, but the ambience of the boxing ring cannot help but remind one of the gladiatorial games. Why else are the venues called "arenas"? The sight of blood invariably evokes shouts of enthusiasm. If no team of sociologists has actually quantified the relationship between bloodied boxers and the "roar of the crowd," the reason is that the relationship is too obvious for even the most correlation-crazed empirical investigator.

The mayhem wrought by football is almost as obvious as that committed under the guise of "the manly art of self-defense." Jerry Kramer, who played for the Green Bay Packers under Vince ("winning is the only thing") Lombardi, introduced *Instant Replay* (1968) with a brief account of the twenty-two operations required to keep his body on the line. No wonder he scribbled into his diary, "I ache beyond description." Players consider it a point of pride to "play hurt," that is, to continue the game despite injury. They are also proud of their ability to inflict injury. Oakland Raider safety Jack Tatum entitled his autobiography *They Call Me Assassin* (1979). "My idea of a good hit," he boasts, "is when the victim wakes up on the sidelines with the train whistles blowing in his head and wondering who he is and what ran over him." One of Tatum's victims, Darryl Stingley of the New England Patriots, was permanently paralyzed.[2]

Although Peter Gent, a former offensive end for the Dallas Cowboys, drew upon his own experiences for the novel *North Dallas Forty* (1974), one must recognize the exaggerations of the genre. The effect of the novel, and of the film made from it, is nonetheless appalling. Gent's hero, Phillip Elliott, lives a life of nearly constant pain: "Trying to blow a breathing hole through my shattered nose resulted in lots of blood but not much relief. My nose had been broken several times and the cartilage was now lodged at peculiar angles across the nasal passages. It made breathing difficult and uncomfortable. . . . Getting arthritic joints, torn muscles, and traumatized ligaments warm took at least an hour." The players constitute a "brotherhood of mutiliation."[3]

For those who prefer the statistical to the narrative mode, a few data should suffice. During the 1978 season, after thirteen weeks, 186 players were incapacitated and placed on the "injured reserve list." This was 14.9 percent of the total NFL. Eight years later, the NFL reached midseason with 286 players on the injured reserve list. The percentage of players incurring injuries severe enough to cause them to miss at least one game a season is over 100 percent; this means not that every NFL player is injured at least once each season, but that those who are not injured are more than offset by those who are injured several times. The average length of a playing career has dropped to 3.2 years, which is not long enough to qualify a player for inclusion in the league's pension plan. Artificial turf, which increases the rate of injury by roughly half, is now the norm in both the NFL and NCAA Division I football, although a 1974 study conducted by Stanford University "found that in 17 out of 17 categories, natural grass was safer to play on than . . . artificial surfaces." In the calculations of franchise owners and of NCAA athletic directors, the economic benefits of artificial turf apparently outweigh the risks run by the players. (Soccer coaches can display the same insensitivity to the human costs of the game. When San Diego Sockers' team physician Jay Malkoff insisted that a player had a fractured cheekbone, the coach insisted that he did not. The doctor finally made his point by telling the coach, "Find yourself another doctor.")[4]

Injuries are obviously incurred at the high school and college levels too. One study cited by John Underwood determined that thirty-two players become paraplegics every year. The damage is often done when young players emulate NFL stars by attempting to "spear" their opponents, i.e., to block or tackle with their helmets. Their necks cannot take the impact, and the result is crippling. Although the NCAA outlawed this technique in 1970, Southern Methodist University's defensive coach, Steve Sidwell, remarked eight years later that the custom was "more prevalent than ever." Joe Paterno of Pennsylvania State said, "You see it all the time. . . . What is worse, you see it as the third or fourth hit on a play."[5]

That boxers and football players endure physical torment in their pursuit of what Paul Weiss calls "excellence of the body" is no surprise, but runners suffer, too. Injuries are simply a part of the experience for almost everyone involved, whether it is the beginning jogger with his or her mile a day or the world-class marathoner. "Runner's knee" is as widely known as "tennis elbow," and *Runner's World* scarcely puts out an issue without an article on the avoidance or treatment of various common injuries. The magazine's medical advice contains a reiterated theme: don't try to continue your run when pain has reduced you to hobbling; don't try to return to the track before the torn muscle or strained tendon has had time to heal. There are also helpful suggestions about what to do during the pyschologically unbearable weeks of recovery: one can take up cycling (which puts less strain on the joints) or tread water in a pool (which gives even more of a workout with even less risk of aggravating the injury). One bit of advice is seldom offered: quit.

Although the problem has not been very much discussed, some runners are psychologically similar to anorexics. They do not appear emaciated because they run too much; they run in order to avoid imagined obesity or to prevent menstruation. For most runners the cardiovascular benefits probably outweigh the skeletal deficits, but the running mania is clearly emblematic of something more than the desire for glowing health.

Modern gymnastics were developed by German educators at the end of the eighteenth century. At private boys' schools Johann Bernhardt Basedow, Christian Gotthilf Salzmann, and Johann Christian Friedrich GutsMuths involved their aristocratic and upper-middle-class pupils in a wide variety of sports and exercises. In the early nineteenth century Friedrich Ludwig Jahn stimulated the formation of independent gymnastics clubs; later Adolf Spiess organized (and deadened) gymnastics and made physical exercise and drill a part of the curriculum at state-run schools. Nineteenth-century French and Swedish reformers had their own versions of gymnastics, and there were interminable controversies over the physical benefits of the various systems.

The irony, of course, is that gymnastics, which began as an antidote to the poison of a too sedentary life, has become a modern sport that frequently cripples its champions. Gymnastics has undergone what the Germans call "sportification" (*Versportlichung*). Competition, which was generally frowned upon by nineteenth-century proponents of gymnastics, has become a central element, and gymnastics contests now have very different physical consequences from calisthenics or mass displays of suppleness. The drive to surpass others in quantified achievement has encouraged gymnasts to adopt increasingly dangerous moves and to demand more and more of their joints and sinews. The men who leap and tumble through the floor exercises and the women who fly around the uneven parallel bars symbolize a modern physical ideal, but their beautiful bodies are often wracked by pain. In addition to accidents, which cannot be entirely eliminated and which are more and more likely as gymnasts press toward the limits of the humanly possible, there is constant strain as the body is forced to take unnatural positions and to undergo unbearable stress. Can any gymnastics buff forget the pictures of Olga Korbut in the shape of a pretzel? That *most* gymnasts suffer from back injuries is no surprise. Female gymnasts are expected to smile, but the pain sometimes distorts their faces into a grimace.

Then there are the bodybuilders. Unlike the weight lifters, whose goal is to heave aloft as much iron as humanly possible, the bodybuilders' enterprise is aesthetic. For men, success consists of developing the greatest possible muscle mass with the most sharply delineated muscular "definition." In women's bodybuilding there is a basic ambivalence between those who idealize the firm but still "feminine" physique (e.g., Lisa Lyon) and those who want the female body to look as "masculine" as possible (e.g., Beverly Francis). Bodybuilders are part of a more or less deviant subculture in that their ideal body image is at odds with that of most of the population.

If one admits that the ideal body is a cultural artifact and that there are no absolute standards for its attainment, then one has no right to disown the bodybuilders' achievements as "grotesque." But there is more to the problem than meets the eye. A modicum of aerobics and a light workout with the dumbbells, like a "reasonable" amount of jogging, is surely beneficial to one's health; however, the logic of modern sports seems to entail excess. Injuries occur, but they are not the worst problem. Drugs are.

Aside from "recreational drugs," which are discussed in the next section of this chapter, drugs in sports have two main functions: they enhance performance and they deaden pain.

The drug problem is not new. The Welsh cyclist Arthur Linton is said to have used strychnine to enhance his performance in the 1886 Bordeaux-to-Paris race. His French rivals are thought to have favored caffeine. The word "doping" seems to have entered the English language in 1889, a mere six years after the first use of the word "record" in the sense of an unsurpassed quantified sporting achievement. The first Olympian to die from drugs was a cyclist, Denmark's Knut Jensen, who collapsed at the 1960 games in Rome. He had taken amphetamines and nicotinyl tartrate and was able, therefore, to break through the physiological barriers that normally prevent us from utterly exhausting ourselves. The death of twenty-nine-year-old Thomas Simpson on July 13, 1967, during the ascent of Mount Ventoux (part of the cyclists' Tour de France) seems to have been the event that shocked some sports administrators into recognizing that drugs had become a major problem. Amphetamines were found in Simpson's jersey pockets and in his luggage. The International Olympic Committee established its first commission on drugs. Five years later, in 1972, a German expert estimated that 25 percent of the world's top athletes were doped in one form or another.[6]

As long as any given drug is forbidden, it will be impossible to know how widely it is used. Rumors fly. That illegal performance-enhancing drugs are common in track and field seems undeniable. At the 1983 Pan-American Games in Caracas, for instance, eleven weightlifters, a cyclist, a fencer, a sprinter, and a shotputter were disqualified for using prohibited drugs. At this point, twelve American athletes who had not yet competed departed for the United States. None admitted to steroid use, but it was difficult to imagine that athletes of their calibre suffered simply from homesickness.[7]

As the statistics from Caracas suggest, anabolic steroids, which were first marketed in 1958 when Ciba pharmaceuticals began selling Dianabol, have been the curse of those sports that require great strength. Everyone knows that steroids are effective in the sense that they, in combination with heavy exercise, produce huge gains in muscle mass. Everyone also knows (or ought to know) that the side effects of steroid use are severe. The body's hormonal system is destabilized. The prostate can swell, the testicles can shrink, and men can become sterile. Some medical authorities see a link between steroid use and liver cancer. Women who use steroids experience physical masculinization; their voices deepen, their shoulders broaden, they often grow facial hair, they can suffer severe muscular pain. Looking back upon her experiences as a drug-assisted powerlifter, Tam Thompson commented, "I've been off the drugs for almost two years now, but I still have to shave every day."[8] Men and women can also experience moments of murderous rage.

The International Olympic Committee banned steroids in 1975 and disqualified eight athletes at the 1976 games in Montreal. Unfortunately, tests cannot detect steroids that are taken for years and then discontinued some weeks before the contest. Since steroids are assumed to improve the prospects for winning gold medals in international contests, the protestations of national sports bureaucracies must be taken with a grain of salt. When elite athletes, like East Germany's Ilona Slupianek, are caught and disqualified, their national federations usually manage to have them reinstated in time for the next Olympics. Slupianek won the gold medal in the shotput at the European Championships in Prague in 1978, lost the medal when she failed the drug test, and replaced it with the gold medal that she won in the Olympic Games in Moscow two years later. The attitude of East German sport officials can be surmised from the fact that Slupianek was elected sportswoman of the year. By 1981, Finland's javelin champion was moved to assert that "at least 80% of top sportsmen are slaves of hormone products."[9]

No one knows how many football players use anabolic steroids in order to develop the size and strength thought to be necessary for NFL survival. When the National Collegiate Athletic Association initiated drug testing as a prerequisite for participating in a post-season football game, twenty-one players failed the anabolic-steroid test and were banned from playing.

In weight lifting and in bodybuilding, which has now become an internationally organized sport, steroids are pandemic. Three Canadian weight lifters were arrested in 1983 when they checked in at the Montreal airport with 22,000 anabolic steroid tablets in their luggage. In a recent article Alan M. Klein described bodybuilding as a drug culture riddled by cynicism and hypocrisy. Steroids are "virtually universal" among male competitors and are frequently used by females. The bodybuilders who compete in national and world championships write articles in which they condemn the use of drugs, but there is evidence that their advice is insincere. "One well known pro read his own advice column aloud in the gym in mocking tones. As he read his quote on banning steroids, he and the others gathered around him rolled with laughter."[10]

Many bodybuilders employ other physically destructive techniques. Since success depends not on strength (as it does for weight lifters) but on appearance, many contestants prepare for the major competitions by fasting and taking diuretics in order to minimize subcutaneous fat, expel fluids, and achieve the absolute maximum in muscular definition. Appearances deceive: "When we walk onstage we are closer to death than we are to life."[11] Some women have described their state as close to total collapse. As they flex and smile, they fight back nausea and dizzy spells.

It is not always easy to distinguish performance enhancers from painkillers. An anodyne that enables an athlete to overcome otherwise unbearable pain is obviously a performance enhancer. Still, the distinction is useful.

Few of us are Spartan enough to spurn aspirin or to undergo operations without anesthetics. On the other hand, few of us are foolish enough, in our daily lives, to anesthetize ourselves in order to continue an activity and worsen an injury. That, of course, is exactly what now happens in modern sports. As two British scholars have noted, "While there is still much to be discovered about how we perceive pain, its crucial *protective* function should be recognized." Peter Gent's novel, *North Dallas Forty*, provides vivid examples of the routine reckless disregard of this very protective function of pain. His fictional team suffers from a medley of injuries and ailments but continues to play because it is regularly supplied with codeine, novocaine, demerol, and dexadryn. The first-person narrator describes a teammate's halftime rehabilitation:

> Alan Claridge lay face down on the table while the doctor probed and prodded his right hamstring. Finding the knot, the doctor held his thumb on it and reached for a syringe. He drove the needle deep into Claridge's leg, moved it around, and emptied the syringe into the muscle. Repeating the procedure twice more, he deadened a large portion of the hamstring. If Claridge reinjured the leg in the second half, he wouldn't know until it was too late, but with luck he would finish the game with little problem.

Claridge's luck runs out. A second-half tackle sidelines him forever.[12]

Gent's style is not likely to win him any prizes, but his verisimilitude is what matters. The scenes of physical carnage (and orgiastic sexuality) are similar to those described by other novelists and to those attested to by Arnold J. Mandell, a psychiatrist who worked with the San Diego Chargers. Mandell was enthusiastic about his assignment with the team. He began his stint as a fan and left it persuaded that NFL football "breaks ribs, ruins knees, twists lives." Drugs, both those given to enhance performance and those taken to deaden pain, were a major problem. Mandell quotes a player who insisted, "Doc, I'm not about to go out one-on-one against a guy who's grunting and drooling and coming at me with big dilated pupils unless I'm in the same condition." Anodynes were as essential as "uppers." When asked *why* he prescribed them, Mandell screamed at his interrogator, "You shyster motherfucker! Were *you* there? Did *you* see those men in pain?" When he offered to do a drug clinic at a team physicans' meeting in 1973, NFL Commissioner Alvin ("Pete") Rozelle canceled it because of "bad public relations." At that time the NFL objected to urine tests as "an invasion of privacy." For his candor Mandell was disowned by the NFL, placed on professional probation for five years, and deprived of his right to prescribe drugs. Small wonder that he called his book *The Nightmare Season* (1974).[13]

Mandell's dilemma is routinely confronted by team physicians. Managers and coaches, consciously or unconsciously, press them to declare the players fit to play. Furthermore, the players themselves dread forced retirement. David Meggyesy's *Out of Their League* (1970), a comprehensive indictment of intercollegiate and openly professional football, includes an account of the steroids, amphetamines, and barbiturates allegedly common throughout the NFL. "Most NFL trainers," wrote the former player, "do more dealing in these drugs than the average junky." Culpability is not limited to managers, coaches, and trainers. Football players tend also to take a masochistic pride in their stoic ability to continue despite pain. In their words, they can "play hurt." William Nack summed up their attitude: "Sitting out with an injury is like being socially ostracized." If novocaine can bring them off the bench and into the game, they are ready to accept the possibility that novocaine might also doom them to a wheelchair.[14]

The Cocaine Culture

Another important distinction must be made in the discussion of modern sports and modern drugs. There is a difference between performance enhancers and painkillers; there is a further difference between both of these categories and a third kind of drug, which is used "recreationally." Cyclists have taken amphetamines in order to cycle faster; weight lifters have taken steroids in order to hoist more; football players have been shot full of novocaine and cortisone in order that they might return to the fray. But nothing about the inner logic of modern sports impels athletes to use heroin or cocaine. Rather, social factors account for the "recreational" drug usage that has afflicted professional team sports.

The problem in major league baseball is serious; as early as 1983 four players for the Kansas City Royals received prison sentences for drug abuse. In NFL football the situation is catastrophic. In 1982 Don Reese and John Underwood published a *Sports Illustrated* article entitled "I'm Not Worth a Damn," the story of Reese's "descent down the ladder of success." While a member of the Miami Dolphins, Reese began to use cocaine and then to deal in it. Betrayed by a contact, arrested, tried, convicted, and sentenced to a year in jail, Reese discovered that conviction for a felony was no bar to a new NFL contract. After serving his sentence, he went to the New Orleans Saints, where "players snorted coke in the locker room before games and again at halftime." (This custom most definitely did not enhance the team's performance—the Saints lost fourteen games in a row.) From his roommates Reese learned to freebase cocaine: "I was in a stupor much of the time. I had no conception of night and day." He was eventually suspended from the team—not for drug abuse, but for fighting during practice. Sent to the San Diego Chargers, Reese found that his new teammates were part of the same subculture. He continued to use cocaine. When injury ended his playing career and his NFL paychecks, he ran into debt with dealers and was threatened with death. "I reached the point where I really *wanted* to die. To kill myself. One night in Miami I went into the streets looking for enough heroin to do the job." In desperation, Reese fled to a hospital and begged for help. He told Underwood that neither the NFL nor the Players Association wanted to take the problem seriously. Once *Sports Illustrated* published the story, Ed Garvey, the executive director of the NFL Players Association, dismissed it as "sensationalism"; nevertheless, Reese's New Orleans teammate Chuck Muncie asserted that 60 percent of the Saints used drugs, and Carl Eller, a former Minnesota Viking player and an NFL consultant on drugs, estimated that 15 percent of all players were problem cocaine users. While the controversy raged, a former New Orleans player, Mike Strachan, was indicted for selling cocaine.[15]

Within the next five years the problem of drug addiction among football players had become too severe for denial. On June 27, 1986, Cleveland Browns' safety Don Rogers was killed by cocaine. In a single week later that summer, from July 28 to August 3, in five separate courts, five NFL or United States Football League players were charged, indicted, convicted, or sentenced for the use, possession, or sale of cocaine. They had played for the Bengals, Chargers, Chiefs, Colts, Federals, Raiders, Rams, Redskins, Saints, and Seahawks. The owners now call for the urine tests that they had formerly condemned as an invasion of privacy, but the players continue to resist.[16]

The white plague of cocaine has spread to intercollegiate sports as well. In June 1986 University of Maryland basketball star Leonard Bias was picked to play for the Boston Celtics. It was the fulfillment of his dream, but the dream was short lived. Bias and two of his teammates celebrated with cocaine, and Bias died of an overdose. When Maryland's basketball program was investigated, it was discovered that Bias had failed or withdrawn from five courses that spring. In fact, the entire basketball team had a Grade Point Average of 1.48 (i.e., closer to D than C). It was also discovered that 20 percent of the entire student body admitted to having used cocaine at least once.[17]

Gary McLain scored eight points in Villanova's upset victory over favored Georgetown in the 1985 national basketball championships. Having played many of his games while high on cocaine, McLain saw no reason to change his habits when Ronald Reagan invited the winning team to be honored at the White House: "President Reagan was welcoming my teammates and me at the White House and giving his little speech about how inspirational our victory was. And the cocaine had me floating in my own private world." After the words of presidential praise, coach Rollie Massimino, who had questioned McLain about rumors of cocaine use but who had never tested him, explained to the press how he warned his players against drugs. The plague, however, continues to spread.[18]

Why have athletes allowed themselves to be victimized by drugs? Most discussions of the problem emphasize the fact that talented athletes are accustomed to special treatment. There is a great deal of truth to this observation. From childhood the athlete's achievements on the field have been rewarded by favors off the field. Transgressions in high school and college are forgiven. Plagiarism is no problem. ("All is forgiven.") Drunkenness and assault are minor matters. ("Don't do it again.") Traffic violations are merely what one expects from men and women in stressful situations. ("They have to let off a little steam.") Like film stars and rock singers, talented athletes expect to be praised for their achievements and can grow accustomed to all sorts of shameless flattery. Sycophants abound. In a culture that tends to measure success by the twin yardsticks of income and public recognition, teenaged millionaire athletes are among the most fawned upon media celebrities. Small wonder that young men and women who are treated like demigods begin to see themselves as something special. Commenting on his first week at Villanova, Gary McLain describes his own sense of the athlete's privileged status: "We skipped the orientation sessions the first night at school, figuring only the geeks would walk around with orientation counselors. We were on the basketball team. We didn't have to do that stuff. We just hung out." Once they actually began to play for the university, McLain and his teammates received "unrealistic worship." Ordinary mortals might become addicts, the lionized athlete tells himself. *He* will have the universal safe conduct of his fame.[19]

There is more to the drug problem than the moral weakness of flattered youth. Neither journalists nor scholars are especially eager to investigate the possibility that cocaine use seems to be more common among black athletes than among whites. The reluctance to comment on the racial variable is understandable. Racism has blighted American society since 1619, and no decent person wants to encourage racist responses to social problems. Drugs, including cocaine, are bought and sold by socially mobile middle-class whites as well as by ghetto-bound blacks, but there seems little reason to doubt the correctness of a recent *New York Times* report documenting a higher incidence of drug abuse, especially in the form of "crack," among the impoverished inner-city minority population.[20] The Afro-American athlete is statistically more likely than his white teammate to have been born into a subculture where drugs are commonplace, where dealers are real "sports," where avoidance of drugs is considered a sign of effeminacy. If college attendance on an athletic scholarship meant a real education (which, of course, it sometimes does), black athletes might develop a greater awareness of what drug dependence can do, but many of them are encouraged to waste their four years of educational opportunity. When they finally learn what damage drugs can do, it is too late. Gary McLain was lucky; Leonard Bias was not.

The irony could hardly be greater. The search for "excellence of the body" can culminate in the body's destruction. The most physically gifted Americans are among those most likely to be ravaged by drugs. They are pathetic examples of athletes dying young.

TWELVE

The Rejection of Modern Sports

Searching for Alternatives

While most Americans seem wholly committed to the quantified ecstasy of twentieth-century play and fully at home in the surrealistic domed stadia of spectator sports, some have remained faithful to more traditional recreations. Anglers angle as they did in Izaak Walton's day, and hunters hunt with bows and arrows as well as with high-powered telescopic rifles. While children are taught to play baseball as if they were major leaguers, many middle-aged Americans have rediscovered the less competitive summertime pleasures of slow-pitch softball (with or without a sixpack of beer). For men and women disillusioned with the packaged pastimes of modernity there is the lure of the mountains. Indeed, one might almost say, with only a modicum of whimsy, that mountaineering was invented as an escape from the hectic pace of modern society. Rock climbing, which can be considered as a version of mountaineering, is "the exact antithesis of the American preoccupation with spectator sports."[1] In the early seventeenth century, when the scientific revolution symbolized by the name of Sir Isaac Newton had just begun, mountains were still considered to be aesthetic blemishes, rough distortions of our Earth's otherwise perfect sphere, obstacles to trade and commerce, dangerous places inimical to all civilized endeavor. By the end of the eighteenth century, as English society was transformed by the Industrial Revolution that modern science and technology had made possible, as "Merrie England" became a land of "dark Satanic mills," mountains were seen in a different light. In the words of Marjorie Nicolson, mountain gloom became mountain glory. Childe Harold's pilgrimage took him through the Alps, and a flock of Anglican ministers set out after him.

Some of the early climbers were naturalists whose initial motivations were primarily scientific. Their investigations may have begun routinely, but many of them were overcome by awe when they began to realize the true ages of geological formations. They responded with what Charles Rosen has referred to as a "Romantic sense of the complexity of time in landscape." Romantic response without the antecedent scientific fieldwork is associated with the name of Jean-Jacques Rousseau. His *Confessions*, written in the 1760s, contain some powerfully vivid descriptions of mountain scenery and some uncanny evocations of the giddy joys of vertigo. Rousseau's *Nouvelle Héloïse* (1760) popularized the new attitudes. In the early years of the next century, these Romantic attitudes were assumed to be—what else?—natural.[2]

A twenty-four-year-old Swiss climber, Jean-Jacques Balmat, who may well have been named for Rousseau, ascended Mont Blanc on August 8, 1786; Johann Rudolf and Hieronymous Meyer conquered the Jungfrau on August 3, 1811. Mountain climbing as a sport can conveniently be dated from 1857, when Edward Whymper founded the Alpine Club of London. Victorian gentlemen began to raise their eyes to the mountains, from whence came their recreation. The Swiss, puzzled at first by such arduous and risky play, learned to cope with and to feed, shelter, and guide a yearly invasion of earnest English nature-lovers. (That rail connections between Paris and Geneva had been finished in 1856 abetted the invasion.) The English were soon joined by other temporary fugitives from modernity. By the time Whymper successfully scaled the Matterhorn in 1865, Austria had its Alpenverein, Switzerland its Alpenklub, and Italy its Club Alpino Italiano. The Club Alpin Français and the Deutscher Alpenverein were founded shortly after Whymper published his influential *Scrambles amongst the Alps in the Years 1860–1869* (1871).[3]

Whatever his or her nationality, the mountain climber was likely to come from the professional middle class. Ministers were strongly represented among the early climbers, perhaps because they thought mountains evidenced divinity better than did less rugged landscape. They were followed by the natural scientists, engineers, technicians, doctors, lawyers, and other city dwellers who first invented the modern world and then departed to experience primeval sublimity and to test their mettle against the elements. It was not long before the test became a contest, first against Nature, whose "impossible" summits were conquered one by one, and then against other climbers who had arrived later, taken longer, or risked less with their ascents. It was surely inevitable that the tallest mountain of all posed the greatest challenge. Mount Everest frustrated innumerable climbers before Sir Edmund Hillary reached its summit on May 29, 1953. Everest continues to exact its tribute in human lives as climbers now compete to make the ascent with less and less equipment.

From what they wrote of their motivations we can infer that nineteenth-century climbers were like twentieth-century mountaineers. They sought to encounter an environment more or less untouched by urban-industrial society, to bind themselves to a select company of chosen others in the "fellowship of the rope," to shudder with a *frisson* of risk, and to achieve a sense of mastery over Nature and Self, to experience the wholistic phenomenon that Mihaly Csikszentmihalyi refers to as "flow."

There can be no doubt about the first motive. As civilization encroaches ever more destructively upon wilderness, wilderness seems all the more what Henry David Thoreau called it: "the salvation of the world." If Canadians respond like Americans (which they probably do in a sport as international as mountaineering), we can learn from a careful study of 266 members of the Alpine Club of Canada. A sociological research team found that enjoyment of "wilderness, fresh air and nature" was by far the most important motive cited by the club members. "The fellowship of the rope" is a more problematic motive, if only because most mountaineers seem to be introverted men and women. Two climbers, the belayer and the leader, are tied together, in Richard G. Mitchell's words, "in one of life's most intimate and fateful embraces," but the relationship itself seems rarely to be the motive for the climb. Gregarious outdoor types congregate at ski lodges, rather than on the slopes of Kilimanjaro. Although only 1 percent of the Canadian sample acknowledged risk as a motive, mortal danger—controlled and calculated, but nonetheless omnipresent—is what chiefly distinguishes mountain climbing from tamer outdoors activities like hiking, backpacking, and orienteering. While climbers are among the least reckless people around, they savor the danger that sets their avocation apart from the diurnal round and also from less dangerous sports.

"The urge for risk in sports," writes George Leonard, "runs counter to the tendency in modern industrial society to reduce or eliminate risk from every aspect of life." The most succinct statement is from Showell Styles, who wrote, "The thing is useless, like poetry, and dangerous, like lovemaking." Mastery as a motive has appeared strongly in German research, where climbers testify that they have, at least for a moment, overcome the "fragmentation and disharmony" of daily life in order to engage themselves in an action that requires total concentration and rewards the actor with a sense of wholeness, power, and, in a truly literal sense, superiority. This sense of absorption in the task is part of what Mihaly Csikszentmihalyi, in his influential *Beyond Boredom and Anxiety* (1977), has described as "flow." In this experience, which is almost mystical, the climber transcends individuality and becomes one with the All.[4]

Mountain climbing originally had few of the characteristics of modern sports. It was an essentially secular pastime (although the emotions involved in a state of "flow" are clearly akin to those experienced by religious mystics), and it was potentially egalitarian in that climbers seldom had to clamber over ascriptive barriers to participation. The pristine form of the sport was not especially marked by specialization, rationalization, bureaucratization, or quantification. There was, of course, the honor of the first ascent, but such an achievement is only an approximation of the modern quantified athletic record, which is by definition an unsurpassed but theoretically surpassable achievement. It was precisely because mountain climbing was *not* modern that Whymper risked his life, and four of his companions lost theirs, on the Matterhorn.

There is, however, mountain climbing—and there is mountain climbing. Not all forms have remained pristinely antimodern. In fact, one can detect more than a trace of incipient modernization. Specialization has developed. A major expedition like Hillary's possesses an immense cast of characters who play highly specialized ized roles:

> the labor of perhaps hundreds of lowland porters, scores of high-altitude porters, and a dozen or more climbers combine to make possible the summit bid of perhaps a single pair of climbers. All this activity may be directed with military-like precision through daily radio orders to all climbers and other personnel, issued from the expedition leader in his or her headquarters at base camp.

There is rationalization. Some purists climb with no equipment at all beyond a pair of sturdy boots; others attack the peak with a panoply of technical gear. Hillary's Mount Everest expedition required 7.5 tons of equipment transported by ship, train, truck, and porters. Guidebooks are also necessary equipment containing a great deal of exact information. Steve Roper's *Climber's Guide to the High Sierras* (1976) is very explicit: "Venusian Blind Arete. . . . Climb the lefthand snowfield for 150–200 feet until a snow-covered ledge leads horizontally left about 350 feet to the left side of the base of the 200-foot-high sweeping slab." These instructions are for a single phase of the ascent. Rationalization transforms the mountaineer's equipment, which is increasingly efficient, and his or her techniques, which are increasingly sophisticated. When Whymper ascended the Matterhorn, he carried "a then modern ice axe of wrought iron and hickory which weighed 4 pounds and he slept in a tent of his own design that weighed 'only' 23 pounds. Today's climber has available such exotic tools as ice axes of titanium and aluminum that weigh 19 ounces and two-person tents of Mylar and polyester fabric with aircraft aluminum tubing that weigh a gossamer 28 ounces."

There is bureaucratization. Serious climbers are members of national mountaineering organizations that are, in turn, organized into the Union Internationale des Associations d'Alpinisme (UIAA). One of the many functions of the UIAA is to test the synthetic-fiber lines that have replaced the nineteenth century's hemp or manila ropes. Another function is to rate the mountains, in a display of the characteristically modern tendency to quantify sports (along with everything else). Repugnant as it may seem to the Byronic soul, ascents are now numbered and their difficulties are expressed in mathematical terms. The ascent of Venusian Blind Arete, plotted in the guidebook mentioned a moment ago, is rated III 5.5 by one of the several systems now in use. Mitchell notes that a "climber who has led one or more established routes rated 5.11 is accorded more prestige than another climber who has only followed 5.2 routes."[5]

The truly modern reader of the *American Alpine Journal* also calculates the Index of Inequality devised by Lawrence C. Hamilton to ascertain whether some climbers claim many first ascents and others few—or, on the contrary, whether the sport has become so popular and egalitarian that many climbers share the glory of first ascents. (The Index of Inequality is determined by the formula $Vx = V/V+1$, where V is the standard deviation divided by the mean number of claimed first ascents.) With the quantification of mountaineering in mind, we can then grasp the significance of Mitchell's observation that the occupational choices of mountain climbers demonstrate "an interesting and significant bias in favor of the applied physical sciences." If 46 percent of the Southern California Sierra Club's Mountaineering Training Committee are active in the applied physical sciences, we can conjecture that they seek a wilderness environment unlike what they experience in their daily routines and, simultaneously, that they bring to that avocational environment the very same cast of mind that characterizes their professional lives. And then there is the obsession with records. One can smile condescendingly at the singleminded "peak-baggers" who struggle up and down mountains in order to log more ascents than the Joneses, but there are also men and women who risk (and sometimes lose) their lives in the race to the summit. How many died while hoping to be the very first atop Mount Everest? How many have died since? In short, the archetypically Romantic sport of mountain climbing has become a most ambiguous instance of the escape from modernity.[6]

There is, however, another way out of what Max Weber pessimistically referred to as the "iron cage" of modern bureaucratic organization. Eugen Herrigel's seminal essay, *Zen in the Art of Archery*, tells of Herrigel's discovery of a form of archery utterly unlike what he had known in Europe. From Roger Ascham's *Toxophilus* (1549) to Horace Alfred Ford's *The Theory and Practice of Archery* (1856),

European and American archery went one way; Japanese archery went another. The stages traversed in the replacement of earthen butts and wooden birds with the archery target's concentric circles of quantified fields beautifully exemplifies the path taken by European archery. The Japanese, who may have invented the modern target before the Europeans did, trod the path with a wholly different frame of mind. "Under the rubric of archery," wrote Herrigel, "the Japanese understands a religious experience [*kultisches Geschehen*] rather than a sport." When Herrigel impatiently complained to his master that the master's accuracy was the result of practice, the skeptic was invited to tea. Herrigel's host then shot twice into the dark. The second arrow split the first, which was lodged in the center of the target. Eventually the pupil learned his lesson. "And all—bow, arrow, target and self—flow into one another so that I can no longer separate them. And even the need to separate them disappears." The arrow "shoots itself," and the goal is attained not by arduously practicing a set of rationalized techniques but by abandoning the self in mystic transcendence.[7]

Americans, too, have recently shown an intense interest in what Michael Murphy, a founder of the Esalen Institute, calls "the psychic side of sports." Books like Murphy's *Golf in the Kingdom* (1972) have tantalized conventional believers in modern sports with tales of Shivas Irons, who is a golfer, a Celtic shaman, and an expert in altered states of consciousness. Not many Americans have taken to Zen archery or golf "in the kingdom," but they have converted in droves to Asian martial arts that have also been influenced by Zen Buddhism. Classes in judo and aikido are taught in small towns as well as in urban centers; their adepts outnumber boxers and are probably more numerous than wrestlers. For some, the martial arts represent an alternative to modern sport. For George Leonard, an admirer of Michael Murphy, aikido and other imports from the East are instances of "the psychic side of sports" and, simultaneously, exemplars of what might be thought of as postmodern sports. Such at least are the implications of Leonard's book, *The Ultimate Athlete* (1975).

Leonard is not quite ready to concede that modern sports are a lost cause. He writes lyrically of O. J. Simpson, who dances in tune with the universal flow of energy. He admires the exploits of Alphonse Juilland, a runner who held the 100-meter record for fifty-year-olds. Nonetheless, the emphasis of *The Ultimate Athlete* is on feats scarcely imagined in the West. If Leonard can be believed, participants in aikido enter new ontological dimensions and achieve harmony with immense sources of energy. Leonard, for instance, describes the vain attempts of bullishly muscular Americans to bend an apparently frail but mysteriously "energized" arm. In another of Leonard's examples, his 110-pound daughter "moved her *ki* energy downward so effectively that a weight lifter was unable to budge her."

Leonard tells remarkable anecdotes about an aikido master named Morihei Uyeshiba. "On one occasion, completely surrounded by men with knives, Uyeshiba reputedly disappeared and reappeared at the same instant, looking down at his attackers from the top of the flight of stairs." At the age of seventy-eight Uyeshiba "invited four of the toughest judokas . . . to attack him. A large group of distinguished Japanese witnesses gathered at the edge of the mat. Uyeshiba seated himself, cross-legged, in the center and was blindfolded. He meditated for some two minutes, after which the judokas . . . attacked one after another, at full force, from behind. Uyeshiba threw his attackers easily. They landed on their backs, looking bewildered." What happens in aikido? Leonard translated Japanese religion into European philosophy: "The attacker dances Thanatos. The defender, accepting and blending with the attack, dances Eros. And in the harmonious merging of the two, Cosmos may be achieved—two limited human bodies emulating the joining of mountain streams, the swing of distant stars." Such mysticism is obviously not everyone's cup of tea, but the fascination of Asian martial arts is clearly more than a fad and is certainly related to a sense that modern sports have led us astray.[8]

Once again, however, the situation is more complex than it seems at first glance. The martial arts as they were practiced in Japan are a way of life. The words *judo* and *aikido*, like the word *kendo*, are compounds based on *do*: the path. Although they can all be used for self-defense, that is only a small part of their larger purpose, which is to create a harmonious unity of mind and body at one with nature.

The first Europeans and Americans to adopt judo were attracted to traditional elements of Japanese culture. Many of the first generation of judokas were fascinated by Buddhism, made an effort to learn the Japanese language, and were certainly serious about the rituals of the sport. Today judo is an Olympic discipline and has undergone what I have referred to, borrowing from German theorists, as *Versportlichung* (sportification). Serious interest in Buddhism or in the Japanese language has all but disappeared. Rituals are hurried through or completely ignored. Many of the second generation of European and American judo experts approach judo the way boxers and wrestlers approach their sports. The emphasis is not on a way of life, but on the path to the championship. If a technique works, use it. True, there are still a few seekers of wisdom who immerse themselves in the spirit of judo or aikido, but the juggernaut of modern sports rolls on.

THE CRITIQUE OF MODERN SPORTS

In addition to the implicit criticism of modern sports contained in the search for premodern or postmodern alternatives, there is explicit criticism. There have always been voices raised to protest the American commitment to sports at the expense of other activities. The satirical novelist Ludwig Lewisohn, for instance, lumped athletes together with fundamentalist preachers and traveling royalty. There are occasional professors (dwindling in numbers) who fear that the groves of academe are about to be decimated to make room for yet another practice field.

In the late 1960s and early 1970s, in the heady days of the civil rights and antiwar movements, criticism of modern sports rose to a crescendo. Harry Edwards wrote *The Revolt of the Black Athlete* (1969), and Jack Scott authored *The Athletic Revolution* (1971). Concerned sports sociologists, many of them influenced by Marxist theory, founded two radical periodicals: *Arena Newsletter* and the *Journal of Sport and Social Issues*. Billie Jean King inaugurated a magazine to further the cause of women's sports. Although many varsity athletes were conspicuous in the role of prowar campus "hard hats," some black athletes protested exploitive sports programs and coaches who were insensitive to their players' psychological needs. Harry Edwards attempted to lead black athletes in a boycott of the 1968 Olympics, and two runners, John Carlos and Tommy Smith, demonstrated their anger by raising gloved fists during the victory ceremony at Mexico City.

The critiques and the protests were less radical than they seemed. Whether their revolt took verbal or behavioral forms, activists like Edwards and Scott acted in conformity with the inner logic of modern sports. Common to nearly all of the American protest was the axiomatic assumption that equality of opportunity to participate in sports is a fundamental human right. Excluded groups demanded inclusion. Blacks and women wanted their "piece of the pie." Few critics asked, "What kind of pie?" Hardly anyone this side of the Atlantic wondered, "Is this pie really good for you?"

The geographical qualification is important because, in France and in West (but not East) Germany, a wave of neo-Marxist criticism threatened to wash away the entire theoretical basis of modern sports. While Edwards, Scott, and a number of other Americans blasted away at the discriminatory aspects of modern sports, the French and the Germans undermined the whole enterprise. The Europeans wanted to eliminate the very processes that the Americans sought to perfect. The American critics, even the Marxists, carried banners reading SPORT FOR ALL and the European posters read A BAS LE SPORT! and WEG MIT DEM SPORT!

The neo-Marxist argument is that sports are—in Ulrike Prokop's succinct dismissal—"the capitalistically deformed form of play." It may be useful to summarize the central thesis of the neo-Marxist critique of sports. Beginning with the notion that modern sports are the progeny of industrial capitalism, the neo-Marxists definitely *do* want to throw out the baby with the bathwater. Unlike contemporary Marxists, who castigate "capitalist" sports and simultaneously celebrate "socialist" sports, neo-Marxists, especially those under the spell of Theodor Adorno and Herbert Marcuse, are wholly negative about modern sports *wherever* they appear. At the level of description (as opposed to judgment), the neo-Marxist analysis of modern sports is fully congruent with mine. They have said little about the secularism and equality of opportunity of modern sports because their conception of spontaneous play assumes and affirms both characteristics. Specialization, however, they condemn as akin to dismemberment. Rationalization they describe as "Taylorism" or the manipulative scientific management of what is better left to flower on its own. Bureaucratic organization is deplored as totally repressive. Quantification is even worse: "In all human relationships, in all sectors of social life," writes Jean-Marie Brohm, "capitalism begets quantification." Men and women are reduced to abstractions. The quest for records, in this neo-Marxist analysis, is simply an extreme case of the achievement principle that permeates capitalistic society. In short, modern sports are structurally identical with modern industrial production. In the view of Ulrike Prokop, Jean-Marie Brohm, Bero Rigauer, and other European neo-Marxists, the domain of sports simply reproduces the class-dominated exploitative world of alienated labor. The result is not the liberation and self-fulfillment proclaimed by "bourgeois-idealist" physical educators, but a new form of imprisonment. In the illusory belief that he is free, the athlete locks the door of his cell.[9]

There is a great deal more to the neo-Marxist critique, and there are many ways to respond to the criticisms leveled against modern sports. Some of the accusations are credible; indeed, I have not attempted to conceal my distress at what I take to be the distortions of modern sports. But the neo-Marxist indictment is too relentlessly accusatory and too unready to admit that modern sports can emancipate as well as enslave. Rather than rehearse my previous criticisms of their critique, I shall limit myself here to one psychological and one sociological remark. In the first place, condescension about the alleged "false consciousness" of the masses is not enough to refute the proposition that participation in modern sports is essentially voluntary and that the actual physical experience is felt by most participants to be different from, and preferable to, what most of them experience at work. In the second place, the fact that participation is positively correlated with income, educational attainment, social status, and the privileges of male gender makes a mockery of the argument that athletic participation is tantamount to dehumanization. The insistence that modern sports alienate and dehumanize requires us to believe that the advantaged members of society have inexplicably chosen to immolate themselves on the sacrificial altar of modern sports.[10]

What matters in the present context is not the debate but the fact that most Americans have totally ignored the controversy. Paul Hoch's excoriation of American sports, *Rip Off the Big Game* (1972), is not taken seriously—which is understandable, in view of the hysterical overkill that can refer to nineteenth-century British schoolboy sports as a mechanism for sublimating heterosexuality into "white (racist) male (sexist) British (nationalist) ruling class (elitist) chauvinism."[11] The translations of Jean-Marie Brohm's *Sport: A Prison of Measured Time* (1978) and Bero Rigauer's *Sport and Work* (1981) have been ignored except by a handful of sports sociologists. Feminist Joan Hundley has adapted Brohm, Hoch, and Rigauer to a critique of "patriarchy" in sports, but most American critics of modern sports have been reformists content to urge equal opportunity for blacks to be figure skaters, for women to work out with weights, and for all the Little Leaguers to come up to bat. The more fundamental challenges to modern sports have tended to be behavioral; the weary tennis whiz becomes a mountain climber, the burned-out swimmer takes up aikido. These relatively thoughtless responses probably represent a traditional American bias for pragmatism and against "mere theory." The antitheoretical bias is unfortunate. Until we realize what modern sports are all about, it will be impossible for us to distinguish clearly between use and abuse, between the bounty made available to the millions and the distortions created by obsession and excess.

THIRTEEN

The Future of American Sports

Prediction, like hang-gliding, is risky fun, but it seems fairly safe to predict that American sports will continue along the paths already taken over the last three centuries. No more than the modernization of American society has the transformation of American sports been inevitable, ubiquitous, and linear, but the communications satellite and the computer are here to stay, and sports promise (or threaten) to become, in a formal-structural sense, ever more specialized, rationalized, bureaucratized, and quantified. Thanks to the communications satellite, global spectatorship is commonplace. It is easier to watch a track meet in Oslo than to make your own popcorn. Thanks to the computer, we can hear about the baseball player's "stats" before he's reached second base.

Is it still necessary to argue that satellites and computers and other symbols of technological progress are but the material embodiments of culture, the outward and visible signs of *mentalité*? The conviction that every child ought to be involved in some kind of adult-organized athletic program from the age of six through college graduation is as much a product of the scientific revolution as is the fact that astronomers now have more prestige than astrologers. Full employment is our proclaimed economic policy; sports for all is the ludic parallel. The demand that black and female athletes should have equal opportunity to participate and to realize the financial benefits of stellar performance is part of a larger conviction that discrimination on the basis of race or gender is anachronistic (which is, of course, not to assert that such discrimination has vanished). In short, we can expect to see further modernization in the ways that we characteristically approach our sports.

What might that mean? Attentive readers should not find it difficult to imagine extrapolations of the trend. Since it is impossible for people of normal size to compete against seven-foot players who loom over them like Gulliver over the Lilliputians, a concern for equality within the rules of the game should lead basketball down the path long since taken by boxing, wrestling, and weight lifting. The only rational solution to the radical inequality that mars contemporary basketball is the institution of height divisions. We don't ask 125-pound men to box against 250-pound behemoths, and we shouldn't send 5′6″ basketball players out on the court to suffer the tortures of Tantalus. If we continue to respond to the inner logic of modern sports, we can also expect to see baseball go the way of football, i.e., to intensify the specialization already present in the game and to divide the players into fielders and batters, into offensive and defensive teams with wholly separate personnel. The invention of the designated hitter is a step in that direction. If we take the next steps, then scouts of the twenty-first century will not have to enter into their personal computers the haunting phrase, "Good hit, no field."

Scientific research into the physics, chemistry, physiology, biomechanics, and psychology of sports will continue. The investment in research guarantees a steady harvest of improved equipment, facilities, and techniques. American sports seem destined to become as rationalized as East German sports. Preparations for the Olympic Games have already begun to resemble a NASA countdown. The last few years have also seen an acceleration in the rationalization of sports administration. The few sports still resistant to bureaucratization will probably succumb so that their officials can enjoy the manifold benefits and suffer the equally manifold annoyances of modern organization. Quantification will become even more pervasive than it is now, difficult as that may be to imagine. The mathematical probabilities of the game may some day persuade baseball managers that their best hitters should bat first. Sportscasters will babble statistics that are ever new and ever less significant. Finally, unless the United States undergoes some tumultuous upheaval on the order of China's "Cultural Revolution," the obsessive quest for world, national, state, local, school, and personal records will continue ad infinitum.

The fact that most American sports are likely to become increasingly modern in their formal-structural characteristics quite definitely does *not* mean that all Americans will favor such sports, or that those who do will completely eschew other leisure-time possibilities. Many Americans have fled the exigencies of employment in the multinational corporation, moving instead to farms in Vermont and craft shops in California. Many Americans have sought and will continue to seek alternatives to modern sports. They will jog (but not record their times, distances, and rates of recovery). They will take up judo (but not to compete against other judokas). They will climb mountains (but not with oxygen masks). They will play frisbie (but not to score points). The number of these Americans alienated from the system of modern sports will probably increase, but they are likely to remain a minority. At any rate, I cannot imagine the United States experiencing a cultural revolution of the magnitude required to shake the nation loose from the spell cast by modern sports.

If we adjust our sociological lens to a more empirical focus, we can speculate about some possible consequences of the commitment to modernity. It is likely that American children will continue to be socialized into adult-organized sports and that some parents and coaches will still urge kids in Pop Warner Football to behave like their heroes in the National Football League. Sports psychologists will warn against the psychic consequences of excessive competition, and medical specialists will decry the traumatic results of premature specialization. Concerned parents will rescue their offspring from coaches who use the children as vehicles for adult ego gratification. Those who call for the abolition of adult-sponsored children's sports will be frustrated, but the millions of children who compete will probably be no worse off than those of us who were left by our parents to find our own fun in vacant lots and miscellaneous mischief.

I am much more pessimistic about the chances for reform in intercollegiate athletics. Reformers can take heart that Jan Kemp won her case against the University of Georgia; she recovered the teaching position that she had lost after protesting the violation of academic ethics by administrators too eager to aggrandize Georgia's football fame. Kemp's victory, however salutary and however welcome, was less significant than the University of Georgia's success in its suit against the National Collegiate Athletic Association. The Supreme Court's majority convinced itself that it had struck a blow for amateur athletics, but the judgment in *Board of Regents of the University of Oklahoma* v. *NCAA* actually liberated schools like Georgia and Oklahoma to make their own deals with the networks. It is impossible to believe that the opportunity to harvest larger sums of money will be accompanied by a stricter observance of the NCAA's rules for recruiting and subsidizing "student-athletes." It is far more likely that intercollegiate athletics will become increasingly professionalized at the top while many of the weaker schools (weaker in athletics, that is) drop out of the competition. In time, we may see an end to hypocrisy, i.e., the admission that it is difficult, if not impossible, to compete in "big-time" college sports and still obtain a decent education. If the sham ends, the universities will be free to amuse the public by sponsoring openly professional sports.

Sports have always involved the quest for physical excellence. Given the logic of modern sports, which use any technique that promises to make us stronger, faster, more agile, less tired, we cannot expect the athletic elite to renounce the use of any means that promise to enhance performance. We are left with two options. The first is to abandon the campaign against drug taking and to accept it as we have accepted other practices that can and do damage the body. If we do take this step, then program directors and individual athletes will be forced to choose whether or not to use amphetamines and anabolic steroids. If one does, others will feel impelled to do likewise; the psychological and economic pressures are extreme. The second option is to introduce a more elaborate system of tests, controls, and sanctions. The International Olympic Committee has moved in this direction, and there are signs that the NFL and other openly professional leagues are ready to follow. While the prospect of drug tests for high school athletes is a melancholy one, we will probably see it, sooner or later. One hopes, perhaps naively, that children's sports will remain relatively drug free and that common sense will persuade the recreational runner and the weekend tennis player to enhance their performances with dextrose instead of dexydrin. Since active participation is positively correlated with "passive" participation, i.e., spectatorship, we are all but certain to see the continued boom in spectator sports. It is hard to imagine that the seasons will grow longer—not even the NBA can play basketball thirteen months a year—but it is likely that the leagues will continue to expand and be joined by new leagues in new sports with new television contracts. Expansion is not simply linear—the North American Soccer League collapsed, and ventures like openly professional women's basketball proved premature—but the public's appetite for spectator sports is difficult to sate. The diehard fan can now watch televised sports twenty-four hours a day. Dips in the Nielsen ratings are probably temporary. As long as network and channel television offer millions and even billions of dollars for the rights to televise sporting events, owners will make fat profits and athletes will demand fabulous salaries. Economic resources are, however, finite. Just as the Pentagon has had to live with a decrease in the rate of its budgetary increase, athletes may have to tighten their belts.

Much of what I have said is pessimistic, but there are consolations, too. There is every reason to expect a continued boom in participation in recreational sports of all kinds as the hours of leisure increase and ascriptive barriers are dismantled. All data show a continuous increase in participation. What was once the luxury of the elite has long since become the necessity of the middle class. Those once excluded from participation by race and gender are now, by and large, welcome. Poverty drastically diminishes the opportunities to participate in modern sports, but we can at least hope that the secular trend will be to alleviate economic misery and to allow participation for all. On the assumption that most people can be moderate, or only mildly obsessed, about acquiring physical skills and testing them in competition, the rise in participation is a boon.

American participation, mainly in team sports, has traditionally peaked during childhood and adolescence. Except for Little League Baseball and its analogs, sports have been institutionalized within the educational system. This has begun to change as runners have organized thousands of independent clubs and as commercial entrepreneurs have rushed to build tennis courts and fitness centers. As Americans become accustomed to and restive within the bonds of interdependence characteristic of modern society, we are likely to feel that we have had enough of teamwork and cooperation. In our play we will become more likely to seek individual excellence. As Ronald Reagan reminded us at Los Angeles in 1984, Americans have traditionally gone out collectively to "win one for the Gipper"; however, "personal best" may well become the motto of the future.

How should reasonable men and women feel about the trends and tendencies I have attempted to describe? Ambivalent. After flourishing in the heyday of the New Criticism, the term "ambivalence" has fallen into disrepute. This is unfortunate. How else can we respond to a phenomenon as complex as American sports? It is impossible unambiguously to solve the Benthamite calculus of pleasure and pain. We can do no better than to ponder Robert Frost's poignant claim that he was one who had a "lover's quarrel with the world."

Notes

PREFACE

1. Joseph Strutt, *Sports and Pastimes of the People of England*, 2d ed. (London: Thomas Tegg, 1838), pp. xvii–xviii.

CHAPTER 1

1. Max Weber, *Wirtschaft und Gesellschaft*, ed. Johannes Winckelmann, 2 vols. (Cologne: Kiepenheuer und Witsch, 1964), 1:15.

2. Allen Guttmann, *From Ritual to Record* (New York: Columbia University Press, 1978), pp. 54–55.

3. Richard D. Brown, *Modernization: The Transformation of American Life 1600–1865* (New York: Hill and Wang, 1976), p. 19.

4. Peter N. Stearns, "Modernization and Social History," *Journal of Social History* 14, no. 2 (Winter 1980): 189.

5. Ibid., p. 196.

CHAPTER 2

1. Stewart Culin, *Games of the North American Indians* (Washington, D.C.: U.S. Government Printing Office, 1907), p. 31.

2. Robert Gerald Glassford, *Application of a Theory of Games to the Transitional Eskimo Culture* (New York: Arno Press, 1976); Alyce Cheska, "Native American Games as Strategies of Societal Maintenance," in *Forms of Play of Native North Americans*, ed. Edward Norbeck and Claire R. Farrer (St. Paul, Minn.: West Publishing, 1979), pp. 227–47.

3. Michael A. Salter, "Meteorological Play-Forms of the Eastern Woodlands," in *Studies in the Anthropology of Play*, ed. Phillip Stevens, Jr. (West Point: Leisure Press, 1974), 16–28; Michael A. Salter, "Play in Ritual," *Stadion* 3, no. 2 (1977): 240.

4. James Mooney, "The Cherokee Ball Play," *Play, Games, and Sports in Cultural Contexts*, ed. Janet C. Harris and Roberta J. Park (Champaign, Ill.: Human Kinetics, 1983), p. 264.

5. George Catlin, *Letters and Notes on the Manners, Customs, and Conditions of the North American Indians*, 2 vols. (1844; rpt. New York: Dover, 1973), 2:125; Kendall Blanchard, *The Mississippi Choctaws at Play* (Urbana: University of Illinois Press, 1981), p. 30.

6. Mooney, "The Cherokee Ball Play," pp. 268–69.

7. Catlin, *North American Indians*, 2:126; Mooney, "The Cherokee Ball Play," p. 281; Horatio Cushman quoted in Blanchard, *Mississippi Choctaws at Play*, p. 37; Creek informant quoted by Mary R. Haas, "Creek Intertown Relations," *American Anthropologist* 42, no. 3 (July–September 1940): 483.

8. Stewart Culin quoted in Blanchard, *Mississippi Choctaws at Play*, p. 166; Kendall Blanchard, "Stickball and the American Southwest," in Norbeck and Farrer, eds., *Forms of Play of Native Americans*, p. 173.

9. Morris Opler, "The Jicarilla Apache Ceremonial Relay Race," *American Anthropologist* 46 (January–March 1944): 78, n. 13.

10. Ibid., p. 77.

11. Desmond Morris, *The Soccer Tribe* (London: Jonathan Cape, 1981), pp. 8, 10; Geoffrey Winningham and Al Reinert, *The Rites of Fall* (Austin: University of Texas Press, 1979), p. 158.

CHAPTER 3

1. Thomas Babington Macaulay, *History of England*, 6 vols., ed. C. H. Firth (London: Macmillan, 1913–15), 1:142; Vernon Louis Parrington, *Main Currents in American Thought*, 3 vols. (New York: Harcourt, Brace, 1927–30), 1:116–17.

2. Dennis Brailsford, *Sport and Society: Elizabeth to Anne* (London: Routledge and Kegan Paul, 1969), p. 141; Deobold B. Van Dalen and Bruce L. Bennett, *A World History of Physical Education*, 2d ed. (Englewood Cliffs: Prentice-Hall, 1971), p. 146; Foster Rhea Dulles, *America Learns to Play* (New York: D. Appleton-Century, 1940), pp. 5–6, 20.

3. Hans Peter Wagner, "Literary Evidence of Sport in Colonial New England," *Stadion* 2, no. 2 (1976): 245; Hans Peter Wagner, *Puritan Attitudes toward Recreation in Early Seventeenth-Century New England* (Frankfurt: Peter Lang, 1982), pp. 19, 158; Christian Graf von Krockow, *Sport und Industriegesellschaft* (Munich: Piper, 1972), p. 31; Gerhard Schneider, *Puritanismus und Leibesuebungen* (Schorndorf: Karl Hofmann, 1968), pp. 100, 127; Erich Geldbach, *Sport und Protestantismus* (Wuppertal: Brockhaus, 1975), p. 46.

4. Philip Stubbes, *Anatomy of Abuses*, ed. Frederick J. Furnivall (London: N. Truebner, 1877–79), p. 184; Thomas Elyot quoted in Brailsford, p. 20;

"Sabbath Days" quoted in Joachim K. Ruehl, *Die "Olympischen Spiele" Robert Dovers* (Heidelberg: Carl Winter, 1975), p. 64; Stubbes, *Anatomy of Abuses*, p. 178; Edward Burghall quoted in Joachim K. Ruehl, "Religion and Amusements in Sixteenth- and Seventeenth-Century England," *British Journal of Sport History* 1, no. 2 (September 1984): 144.

5. L. A. Govett, *The King's Book of Sports* (London: Eliott Stock, 1890), pp. 37–39.

6. Parliament quoted in Ruehl, *Olympische Spiele*, p. 68.

7. Court of Assistants quoted in Nancy L. Struna, "Puritans and Sport," *Journal of Sport History* 4, no. 1 (Spring 1977): 4.

8. William Bradford, *Of Plimouth Plantation*, ed. Samuel Eliot Morison (New York: Alfred A. Knopf, 1952), p. 97.

9. Thomas Morton, *New-England Canaan*, ed. Charles Francis Adams (Boston: Prince Society, 1883), p. 256; Bradford, *Of Plimouth Plantation*, pp. 205–6.

10. Samuel Sewall, *Diary*, ed. M. Halsey Thomas, 2 vols. (New York: Farrar, Straus and Giroux, 1973), 2:795–96.

11. John Downame, William Perkins, Edward Elton, and William Prynne quoted in Schneider, *Puritanismus und Leibesuebungen*, pp. 67, 69, 81–82, 85; Richard Baxter, *Practical Works*, 4 vols. (London: Thomas Parkhurst, Jonathan Robinson, and John Lawrence, 1707), 1:366.

12. Increase Mather quoted in Struna, "Puritans and Sport," p. 9; Cotton Mather quoted in Peter Wagner, "Puritan Attitudes toward Physical Recreation in 17th Century New England," *Journal of Sport History* 3, no. 2 (Summer 1976): 144.

13. Baxter, *Practical Works*, 1:366; Cotton Mather, Jeremiah Dummer, William Perkins, and Thomas Gouge quoted in Peter Wagner, "Literary Evidence," pp. 94–96, 238.

14. Brailsford, *Sport and Society*, p. 141; John Downame quoted in Struna, "Puritans and Sport," p. 3.

CHAPTER 4

1. Nancy L. Struna, "The Formalizing of Sport and the Formation of the Elite: The Chesapeake Gentry, 1650–1720," *Journal of Sport History* 13, no. 3 (Winter 1986): 227.

2. Elliott J. Gorn, "'Gouge and Bite, Pull Hair and Scratch': The Social Significance of Fighting in the Southern Backcountry," *American Historical Review* 90, no. 1 (February 1985): 23; Philip Vickers Fithian, *Journal and Letters*, ed. Hunter Dickinson Farish (Williamsburg: Colonial Williamsburg,

1943), pp. 240–41; Elkanah Watson, *Men and Times of the Revolution*, 2d ed., ed. Winslow C. Watson (New York: D. Appleton, 1861), pp. 71–72.

3. Hugh Jones quoted in John Dizikes, *Sportsmen and Gamesmen* (Boston: Houghton Mifflin, 1981), p. 316 n. 22.

4. Clifford Geertz, *The Interpretation of Cultures* (New York: Basic Books, 1973), p. 417.

5. Rhys Isaac, *The Transformation of Colonial Virginia, 1740–1790* (Chapel Hill: University of North Carolina Press, 1982), p. 103; John Brickell and *North Carolina Journal* quoted in B. W. C. Roberts, "Cockfighting," *North Carolina Historical Review* 42 (Summer 1965): 305, 311.

6. Isaac, *Transformation of Colonial Virginia*, pp. 101–2; Fithian, *Journal and Letters*, pp. 121, 128; François Jean Beauvoir, Marquis de Chastellux, *Travels in North America in the Years 1780, 1781, and 1782*, trans. and ed. Howard C. Rice, Jr. (Chapel Hill: University of North Carolina Press, 1963), pp. 386–87.

7. Watson, *Men and Times*, pp. 300–301.

8. Rollin G. Osterweis, *Romanticism and Nationalism in the Old South* (New Haven: Yale University Press, 1949), p. 4.

9. Andrew Jackson quoted in Dizikes, *Sportsmen and Gamesmen*, p. 10; Drew Gilpin Faust, *James Henry Hammond and the Old South* (Baton Rouge: Louisiana State University Press, 1982), p. 159; John B. Irving quoted ibid.

10. John Bernard, *Retrospections of America, 1797–1811* (New York: Harper and Brothers, 1887), p. 154; Thomas Anburey, *Travels through the Interior Parts of America*, 2 vols. (Boston: Houghton Mifflin, 1923), 2: 229; Fithian, *Journal and Letters*, p. 32.

11. Anburey, *Travels*, 2:228; Bernard, *Retrospections*, pp. 155–56.

12. Thomas Ashe, *Travels in America Performed in 1806*, 3 vols. (London: John Abraham, 1808), 1:227, 229.

13. Frederick Law Olmsted, *The Cotton Kingdom*, ed. Arthur Meier Schlesinger (New York: Alfred A. Knopf, 1953), p. 414.

14. John Randolph quoted in Dizikes, *Sportsmen and Gamesmen*, pp. 34–35.

15. Melvin L. Adelman, *A Sporting Time: New York City and the Rise of Modern Athletics, 1820–70* (Urbana: University of Illinois Press, 1986), pp. 5, 56, 62; Dale A. Somers, *The Rise of Sports in New Orleans, 1850–1900* (Baton Rouge: Louisiana State University Press, 1972), pp. 34–35.

16. T. H. Breen, "Horses and Gentlemen: The Cult of Gambling among the Gentry of Virginia," *William and Mary Quarterly* 34, no. 2 (April 1977): 239, 247.

17. Adelman, *A Sporting Time*, p. 31.

18. Somers, *Rise of Sports*, p. 24.

19. Josiah Quincy quoted in Bertram Wyatt-Brown, *Southern Honor* (New York: Oxford University Press, 1982), p. 344; Richard D. Brown, *Modernization: The Transformation of American Life, 1600–1865* (New York: Hill and Wang, 1976), p. 141.

CHAPTER 5

1. Albert G. Spalding, *America's National Game* (New York: American Sports Publishing, 1911), pp. 3–4.

2. Irwin Shaw, *Voices of a Summer Day* (New York: Delacorte Press, 1965), p. 12; Thomas Wolfe quoted in Tristram P. Coffin, *The Old Ball Game* (New York: Herder and Herder, 1971), p. 183.

3. Mark Twain quoted by Harry Clay Palmer, "The Around the World Tour," in *Athletic Sports in America, England and Australia*, ed. Harry Clay Palmer (Philadelphia: Hubbard Brothers, 1889), p. 447.

4. Keith Sandiford, "Cricket and the Victorian Society," *Journal of Social History* 17, no. 2 (Winter 1980): 310.

5. C. L. R. James, *Beyond a Boundary* (1963; rpt. New York: Pantheon, 1983), pp. 351–52.

6. Rudolf Kircher, *Fair Play: Sport, Spiel und Geist in England* (Frankfurt: Frankfurter Societaets-Druckerei, 1927); Hans Indorf, *Fair Play und der "englische Sportgeist"* (Hamburg: Friedrichsen und de Gruyter, 1938).

7. Ken Sobol, *Babe Ruth and the American Dream* (New York: Random House, 1974), p. 37.

8. Graig Nettles and Ramon Aviles quoted in Steve Wulf, "Tricks of the Trade," *Sports Illustrated* 54 (April 13, 1981): 104, 108; ibid., pp. 98, 108.

9. Abraham Cahan, *Yekl* (New York: D. Appleton, 1896), pp. 4, 10.

10. Hugh Fullerton quoted in Steven A. Riess, *Touching Base: Professional Baseball and American Culture in the Progressive Era* (Westport, Conn.: Greenwood Press, 1980), p. 25.

11. Harold Seymour, *Baseball: The Early Years* (New York: Oxford University Press, 1960), p. 175.

12. Eric Rolfe Greenberg, *The Celebrant* (New York: Everest House, 1983); Robert Mayer, *The Grace of Shortstops* (Garden City, N.Y.: Doubleday, 1984).

13. Steven Hardy, *How Boston Played* (Boston: Northeastern University Press, 1982), p. 189.

14. Riess, *Touching Base*, pp. 61, 66, 76.

15. Ibid., pp. 71–72.

16. James B. Dworkin, “Balancing the Rights of Professional Athletes and Team Owners: The Proper Role of Government,” in *Government and Sport*, ed. Arthur T. Johnson and James H. Frey (Totowa, N.J.: Rowman and Allanheld, 1985), p. 25.

17. Thomas N. Daymont, “The Effects of Monopsonistic Procedures on Equality of Competition in Professional Sport Leagues,” *International Review of Sport Sociology* 10, no. 2 (1975): 83–97.

18. Steven A. Rivkin, “Sports Leagues and the Antitrust Laws,” in *Government and the Sports Business*, ed. Roger G. Noll (Washington, D.C.: Brookings Institution, 1974), p. 408.

CHAPTER 6

1. James Naismith, “Basket Ball,” *American Physical Education Review* 19, no. 5 (May 1914): 339–40.

2. Charles Kingsley quoted in Bruce Haley, *The Healthy Body and Victorian Culture* (Cambridge, Mass.: Harvard University Press, 1978), pp. 109–10, 119.

3. Naismith, “Basket Ball,” p. 349.

4. Paul Gallico, *Farewell to Sport* (New York: Alfred A. Knopf, 1938), p. 325.

5. Charles Rosen, *Scandals of ’51, How the Gamblers Almost Killed College Basketball* (New York: Holt, Rinehart and Winston, 1978), pp. 15, 29.

6. Neil D. Isaacs, *All the Moves: A History of College Basketball* (Philadelphia: J. B. Lippincott, 1975), pp. 105–6, 108.

7. Everett Case quoted in William H. Beezley, “The 1961 Scandal at North Carolina State and the End of the Dixie Classic,” *Arena* 7, no. 3 (November 1983): 39; John Underwood, “The Biggest Game in Town,” *Sports Illustrated* 64 (March 10, 1986): 54.

8. Douglas S. Looney, “Big Trouble at Tulane,” *Sports Illustrated* 62 (April 8, 1985): 36–39; Franz Lidz, “Scorecard: The Tulane Scandal,” *Sports Illustrated* 62 (April 15, 1985): 17; Douglas S. Looney, “ ‘All I Want Is to Be Happy,’ ” *Sports Illustrated* 62 (April 22, 1985): 36–43; Franz Lidz, “Scorecard: The Tulane Point-Shaving Case,” *Sports Illustrated* 63 (August 26, 1985): 25–26; Jaime Diaz, “A Quick Start for the Hot Rod,” *Sports Illustrated* 65 (November 10, 1986): 47, 61.

9. H. Roy Kaplan, “Sports, Gambling and Television,” *Arena Review* 7, no. 1 (February 1983): 5; James H. Frey, “Gambling, Sports, and Public Policy,” in *Government and Sport*, ed. Arthur T. Johnson and James H. Frey (Totowa, N.J.: Rowman and Allanheld, 1985), pp. 193, 209; Martin McGurrin,

Vicki Abt, and James Smith, "Play and Pathology," in *The Masks of Play*, ed. Brian Sutton-Smith and Diana Kelly-Byrne (New York: Leisure Press, 1984), pp. 98–105.

CHAPTER 7

1. Brian Sutton-Smith and B. G. Rosenberg, "Sixty Years of Historical Change in Game Preferences of American Children," *Journal of American Folklore* 74 (1961): 17–46.

2. Jack W. Berryman, "From the Cradle to the Playing Field: America's Emphasis on Highly Organized Competitive Sports for Preadolescent Boys," *Journal of Sport History* 2, no. 2 (Fall 1975): 112.

3. Stephen Hardy, *How Boston Played* (Boston: Northeastern University Press, 1982), p. 87.

4. Dominick Cavallo, *Muscles and Morals: Organized Playgrounds and Urban Reform, 1880–1920* (Philadelphia: University of Pennsylvania Press, 1981), p. 2.

5. Stanley Aronowitz, foreword to Cary Goodman, *Choosing Sides: Playground and Street Life on the Lower East Side* (New York: Schocken Books, 1979), p. x.

6. Joseph Lee's youthful informant is quoted in Hardy, *How Boston Played*, p. 99.

7. Hall is quoted in Cavallo, *Muscles and Morals*, p. 59.

8. Quoted in Goodman, *Choosing Sides*, p. 109.

9. Quoted in Cavallo, *Muscles and Morals*, p. 91.

10. Curtis is quoted ibid., p. 85; Cavallo quote, ibid., p. 99.

11. Goodman, *Choosing Sides*, pp. xxiv, 3, 68–69, 94, 106.

12. Ibid., pp. 131–32.

13. Play Committee quoted in Hardy, *How Boston Played*, p. 104.

14. Stewart Culin quoted in Bernard Mergen, *Play and Playthings* (Westport, Conn.: Greenwood Press, 1982), p. 52.

15. Berryman, "From the Cradle to the Playing Fields," p. 115; Edward C. Devereux, "Backyard versus Little League Baseball: The Impoverishment of Children's Games," in *Social Problems in Athletics*, ed. Daniel M. Landers (Urbana: University of Illinois Press, 1976), p. 46.

16. Terry Orlick cited in John Underwood, *Spoiled Sport* (Boston: Little, Brown, 1984), p.169; Geoffrey G. Watson, "Family Organization and Little League Baseball," *International Journal of Sport Sociology* 9, no. 2 (1974): 5–31.

17. Ernest Havemann, "Down Will Come Baby, Cycle and All," *Sports Illustrated* 39 (August 13, 1973): 49.

18. John Underwood "Taking the Fun Out of a Game," *Sports Illustrated* 43 (November 17, 1975): 96.

19. Ibid., p. 95; Geoffrey G. Watson, "Games, Socialization and Parental Values," *International Review of Sport Sociology* 12, no. 1 (1977): 17–48.

20. Jonathan J. Brower, "Little League Baseballism," in *Joy and Sadness in Children's Sports*, ed. Rainer Martens (Champaign, Ill.: Human Kinetics, 1978), p. 45; Larry Csonka quoted in Underwood, "Taking the Fun Out of a Game," p. 89.

21. Underwood, "Taking the Fun Out of a Game," p. 90.

22. Edmund W. Vaz, *The Professionalization of Young Hockey Players* (Lincoln: University of Nebraska Press, 1982), pp. 8–9, 29, 99, 105.

23. Ibid., p. 16; Michael D. Smith, "Social Learning and Violence in Minor League Hockey," in *Psychological Perspectives in Youth Sports*, ed. Frank Smoll and Ronald E. Smith (Washington, D.C.: Hemisphere Publishing, 1978), p. 100; John Underwood, *The Death of an American Game* (Boston: Little, Brown, 1979), p. 70.

24. Smith, "Social Learning and Violence," p. 102.

25. Harry Webb, "Professionalization of Attitudes toward Play among Adolescents," in *Aspects of Contemporary Sport Sociology*, ed. Gerald S. Kenyon (Chicago: Athletic Institute, 1969), pp. 161–78; Vaz, *Professionalization*, p. 183.

26. Richard Woodley, "How to Win the Soap Box Derby," *Harper's* 249 (August 1974): 62–69.

27. Robert Cupp quoted in Underwood, "Taking the Fun Out of a Game," pp. 95–96; Gene Bovello quoted in Michael Jay Kaufman and Joseph Popper, "Pee Wee Pill Poppers," *Sport* 63 (December 1976): 151; anonymous coach quoted in Underwood, "Taking the Fun Out of a Game," p. 92.

28. Hartmut Gabler, *Leistungsmotivation im Hochleistungssport* (Schorndorf: Karl Hofmann, 1972).

29. Vaz, *Professionalization*, p. 179; Underwood, "Taking the Fun Out of a Game," p. 88.

30. R. C. Townsend, "The Competitive Male as Loser," *Beyond Sex Roles*, ed. Alice G. Sargent (St. Paul, Minn.: West Publishing, 1977), pp. 228–42; Emery W. Seymour, "Comparative Study of Certain Behavior Characteristics of Participant and Non-Participant Boys in Little League Baseball," *Research Quarterly* 27, no. 3 (October 1956): 338–46; Elvera Skubic, "Emotional Responses of Boys to Little League and Middle League Competitive Baseball," *Research Quarterly* 26, no. 3 (October 1955): 342–52.

31. Paul E. Dubois, "The Effect of Participation in Sport on the Value Orientations of Young Athletes," *Sociology of Sport Journal* 3, no.1 (March 1986): 29–42; Smith, "Social Learning and Values," p. 104.

32. Page B. Walley, George M. Graham, and Rex Forehand, "Assessment and Treatment of Adult Observer Verbalizations at Youth League Baseball Games," *Journal of Sport Psychology* 4, no. 3 (1982): 254–66; Ronald E. Smith, Frank L. Smoll, and Bill Curtis, "Coaching Behaviors in Little League Baseball," in Smoll and Smith, eds., *Psychological Perspectives in Youth Sports*, p. 183.

33. Quoted in Martin Ralbovsky, *Destiny's Darlings* (New York: Hawthorne Books, 1974), pp. 39, 50, 48, 106, 218–19.

34. Ibid., pp. 58, 112, 244.

CHAPTER 8

1. John J. MacAloon, "Olympic Games and the Theory of Spectacle in Modern Societies," in *Rite, Drama, Festival, Spectacle*, ed. John J. MacAloon (Philadelphia: ISHI, 1984), pp. 241–80; Edwin H. Cady, *The Big Game* (Knoxville: University of Tennessee Press, 1978), p. 75.

2. Theodore Roosevelt, *The Strenuous Life* (New York: Century, 1901), p. 156; Donald J. Mrozek, *Sport and American Mentality, 1880–1910* (Knoxville: University of Tennessee Press, 1983), p. 46.

3. Wilbur Bowen, "The Evolution of Athletic Evils," *American Physical Education Review* 14 (1909): 155; Howard J. Savage et al., *College Athletics* (New York: Carnegie Foundation, 1929), pp. xv, viii, xii.

4. Robert M. Hutchins quoted in Hal A. Lawson and Alan G. Ingham, "Conflicting Ideologies Concerning the University and Intercollegiate Athletics: Harper and Hutchins at Chicago, 1892–1940," *Journal of Sport History* 7, no. 3 (Winter 1980): 56; Herman Hickman, "The College Football Crisis," *Sports Illustrated* 5 (August 6, 1956): 7; Bobby Knight quoted in Ray Kennedy, "427: A Case in Point," *Sports Illustrated* 40 (June 10, 1974): 88; John Underwood, "The Writing Is on the Wall," *Sports Illustrated* 52 (May 19, 1980): 43.

5. Trustee quoted by Edwald B. Nyquist, "The Immorality of Big-Time Intercollegiate Athletics," in *Sport and Higher Education*, ed. Donald Chu, Jeffrey O. Segrave, and Beverly J. Becker (Champaign, Ill.: Human Kinetics, 1985), p. 107; Willie Morris, *The Courting of Marcus Dupree* (Garden City, N.Y.: Doubleday, 1983), p. 333.

6. John Underwood, *Spoiled Sport* (Boston: Little, Brown, 1984), p. 41.

7. Ibid., p. 192; Jim Benagh, *Making It to Number 1* (New York: Dodd, Mead, 1976), pp. 140–41.

8. Lee Sigelman and Robert Carter, "Win One for the Giver? Alumni Giving and Big-Time College Sports," *Social Science Quarterly* 60 (September 1979): 284–94; James H. Frey, "The Place of Athletics in the Educational Priorities of University . . . Alumni," *Review of Sport and Leisure* 6, no. 1 (Summer 1981): 57; Kenneth Denlinger and Leonard Shapiro, *Athletes for Sale* (New York: Thomas Y. Crowell, 1975), p. 30.

9. Benagh, *Making It*, p. 15; John Durso, *The Sports Factory* (New York: Quadrangle Books, 1975), pp. 27–28; Jerry Kirshenbaum, "Scorecard: Such Standards," *Sports Illustrated* 62 (February 18, 1985): 9; Morris, *Marcus Dupree*, pp. 349, 444.

10. Billy Harris quoted in Underwood, *Spoiled Sport*, p. 205; Peter Monaghan, "7 Athletes Suspended in Slush-Fund Case at Texas Christian U," *Chronicle of Higher Education* (October 2, 1985): 1; Robert Sullivan, "The High Price of an All-America," *Sports Illustrated* 63 (October 14, 1985): 19; Douglas Looney, "Deception in the Heart of Texas," *Sports Illustrated* 63 (September 30, 1985): 30; Craig Neff and Robert Sullivan, "Scorecard: Death Threat for SMU?" *Sports Illustrated* 65 (November 24, 1986): 17; SMU petition quoted in Bruce Selcraig, "The SMU Faculty Says Enough Is Enough," *Sports Illustrated* 65 (December 1, 1986): 9; David Berst quoted in *New York Times*, March 8, 1987.

11. Roy Cave, "A Ruse Flushes Some Eager Recruiters," *Sports Illustrated* 14 (May 29, 1961): 20–23.

12. Dan Winters quoted in Jerry Kirshenbaum, "Majoring in Sports at Arizona," *Sports Illustrated* 55 (October 26, 1981): 17; John Papanek, "Now New Mexico Feels the Heat," *Sports Illustrated* 51 (December 10, 1979); Robert H. Boyle, "A Scandal That Just Gets Worse and Worse," *Sports Illustrated* 52 (June 9, 1980): 22–25; Manny Goldstein and Phillip D. Baiamonte quoted in John Papanek, "Scorecard: A Mockery of Justice," *Sports Illustrated* 55 (July 20, 1981): 7; anonymous student quoted in Jerry Kirshenbaum, "Scorecard: Inside a Trojan Horse," *Sports Illustrated* 52 (March 31, 1980): 7; Underwood, *Spoiled Sport*, p. 198.

13. William Nack, "This Case Was One for the Books," *Sports Illustrated* 64 (February 24, 1986): 34–42; *Academe* 72, no. 4 (July August 1986): cover.

14. Robert Vare, *Buckeye* (New York: Harper's Magazine Press, 1974), pp. 117–18.

15. James F. Rooney, Jr., *The Recruiting Game* (Lincoln: University of Nebraska Press, 1980), p. 160.

16. James Michener, *Sports in America* (New York: Random House, 1976), p. 217.

17. John C. Weistart, "College Sports Reform: Where Are the Faculty?" *Academe* 73, no. 4 (July–August 1987): 12.

CHAPTER 9

1. Bernard Darwin, *John Gully and His Times* (New York: Harper and Brothers, 1935), p. 38; *The Sporting Magazine* (October 1811) cited in Carl B. Cone, ed., *Hounds in the Morning* (Lexington: University Press of Kentucky, 1981), p. 156; Pierce Egan, *Boxiana*, 5 vols. (London: Sherwood, Neely and Jones, 1829), 1:367, 409.

2. National Association quoted in Robert W. Peterson, *Only the Ball Was White* (Englewood Cliffs, N.J.: Prentice-Hall, 1970), pp. 16–17.

3. Jules Tygiel, *Baseball's Great Experiment* (New York: Oxford University Press, 1983), p. 14.

4. Tommy Burns quoted in Randy Roberts, *Papa Jack* (New York: Free Press, 1983), p. 53; *Richmond Planet* quoted in Al-Tony Gilmore, *Bad Nigger!: The National Impact of Jack Johnson* (Port Washington: Kennikat Press, 1975), p. 32.

5. Jack Johnson quoted in Roberts, *Papa Jack*, p. 75.

6. Seaborn Roddenberry quoted in Gilmore, *Bad Nigger!*, p. 108.

7. Anthony O. Edmunds, "The Second Louis-Schmeling Fight," *Journal of Popular Culture* 7 (Summer 1973): 43; Dominic J. Copeci, Jr., and Martha Wilkerson, "Multifarious Hero," *Journal of Sport History* 10, no. 3 (Winter 1983): 5–25; Joe Louis, Edna Rust, and Art Rust, Jr., *Joe Louis: My Life* (New York: Harcourt Brace Jovanovich, 1978), pp. 81–82.

8. William J. Baker, *Jesse Owens: An American Life* (New York: Free Press, 1986), p. 4.

9. Peterson, *Only the Ball Was White*, pp. 103–4.

10. Donn Rogosin, *Invisible Men* (New York: Atheneum, 1983), pp. 17, 107; Rob Ruck, *Sandlot Seasons: Sport in Black Pittsburgh* (Urbana: University of Illinois Press, 1987), p. 156.

11. Ibid, p. 163; Art Rust, Jr., *"Get That Nigger Off the Field!"* (New York: Delacorte, 1976), pp. 62–63; John Holway, *Voices from the Great Black Baseball Leagues* (New York: Dodd, Mead, 1975), pp. 108, xvi–xvii.

12. Tygiel, *Baseball's Great Experiment*, p. 31; Albert Chandler, quoted in Rogosin, *Invisible Men*, p. 199. Tygiel (p. 43) gives a slightly different version of Chandler's remark.

13. Quoted in Tygiel, *Baseball's Great Experiment*, p. 122.

14. Leo Durocher and Casey Stengel quoted in ibid., pp. 170, 294.

15. Ibid., pp. 48–49.

16. Harry Edwards, *The Revolt of the Black Athlete* (New York: Free Press, 1969), p. 12; Harry Edwards, *The Struggle That Must Be* (New York: Macmillan, 1980), p. 112.

17. Dee Andros quoted in John Underwood, "Shave Off That Thing!" *Sports Illustrated* 31 (September 1, 1969): 23; Jack Olsen, *The Black Athlete* (New York: Time, Inc., 1968), p. 136; Paul Hoch, *Rip Off the Big Game* (Garden City: Doubleday-Anchor, 1972), p. 188; Edwards, *Revolt of the Black Athlete*, p. 20.

18. Don Sabo, "Sport, Patriarchy, and Male Identity," *Arena Review* 9, no. 2 (November 1985): 6.

19. Raymond E. Rainville, Al Roberts, and Andrew Sweet, "Recognition of Covert Racial Prejudice," *Journalism Quarterly* 55, no. 2 (1978): 24.

20. Harry Edwards, "Beyond Symptoms," *Journal of Sport and Social Issues* 9, no. 2 (Summer/Fall 1985): 9.

21. John W. Loy, Jr., and Joseph F. McElvogue (wrongly given as "Elvogue"), "Racial Segregation in American Sport," *International Review of Sport Sociology* 5 (1970): 5–23; John D. Massengale and Steven R. Farrington, "The Influence of Playing Position Centrality on the Careers of College Football Coaches," *Review of Sport and Leisure* 2 (June 1977): 107–15.

22. D. Stanley Eitzen and David C. Sanford, "The Segregation of Blacks by Playing Position in Football," *Social Science Quarterly* 55 (March 1977): 948–59; see also John Schneider and D. Stanley Eitzen, "Racial Discrimination in American Sports," *Journal of Sport Behavior* 2, no. 3 (August 1979): 136–42; Wilbert M. Leonard II, "Stacking and Performance Differentials of Whites, Blacks, and Latins in Professional Baseball," *Review of Sport and Leisure* 2 (June 1977): 77–106.

23. M. H. Medoff, "Positional Segregation and Professional Baseball," *International Review of Sport Sociology* 12 (1977): 49–54; David Fabianic, "Minority Management in Professional Baseball," *Sport Sociology Journal* 1, no. 2 (1984): 163–71; M. H. Medoff, "Positional Segregation and the Economic Hypothesis," *Sport Sociology Journal* 3, no. 4 (December 1986): 297–304. James E. Curtis and John W. Loy, "Positional Segregation in Professional Baseball," *International Review of Sport Sociology* 13, no. 4 (1978): 5–23; Jerry Freischlag and Brent Strom, "Dimensions of Racial Discrimination in Organized Baseball," *Review of Sport and Leisure* 3, no. 2 (Winter 1978): 42–53; John C. Phillips, "Race and Career Opportunities in Major League Baseball," *Journal of Sport and Social Issues* 7, no. 2 (Summer/Fall 1983): 1–17.

24. Sandra C. Castine and Glyn C. Roberts, "Modeling in the Socialization Process of the Black Athlete," *International Review of Sport Sociology* 9, nos. 3–4 (1974): 67; Barry D. McPherson, "The Segregation by Playing Position Hypothesis in Sports," *Social Science Quarterly* 55 (March 1975): 960–66.

25. Quoted by Peter Gammons, "Scorecard: The Campanis Affair," *Sports Illustrated* 66 (April 20, 1987): 31.

26. Anthony H. Pascal and Leonard A. Rapping, "The Economics of Racial Discrimination in Organized Baseball," in *Racial Discrimination in American Life*, ed. Anthony H. Pascal (Lexington, Mass.: D. C. Heath, 1972), p. 137; Gerald W. Scully, "Discrimination: The Case of Baseball," *Government and the Sport Business*, ed. Roger G. Noll (Washington, D.C.: Brookings Institution, 1974), pp. 221–73; Robert G. Mogull, "Racial Discrimination in Professional Sports," *Arena Review* 5, no. 2 (September 1981): 14.

27. Martin Kane, "An Assessment of 'Black Is Best,'" *Sports Illustrated* 34 (January 18, 1971): 72–83; Harry Edwards, "The Sources of the Black Athlete's Superiority," *Black Scholar* 3 (November 1971): 32–41; John C. Phillips, "Toward an Explanation of Racial Variation in Top-Level Sports Participation," *International Review of Sport Sociology* 2, no. 3 (1976): 39–53.

CHAPTER 10

1. Stephanie L. Twin, ed., *Out of the Bleachers* (New York: McGraw-Hill, 1979), p. xviii.

2. Deborah Gorham, *The Victorian Girl and the Feminine Ideal* (Bloomington: Indiana University Press, 1982), p. 93.

3. Catharine Beecher, *A Treatise on Domestic Economy* (Boston: Marsh, Capen, Lyon, and Webb, 1841), p. 49; Beecher, *Letters to People on Health and Happiness* (New York: Harper and Brothers, 1855), p. 187.

4. Lydia M. Child quoted in Gorham, *The Victorian Girl*, p. 71.

5. Roberta J. Park, "Sport, Gender and Society in a Transatlantic Victorian Perspective," *British Journal of Sport History* 2, no. 1 (May 1985): 5–6.

6. Arabella Kenealy quoted in Twin, *Out of the Bleachers*, pp. 44–45, 48.

7. Luther Gulick, "Athletics Do Not Test Womanliness," *American Physical Education Review* 11 (September 1906): 158–59; Dudley A. Sargent, "Are Athletics Making Girls Masculine?" *Ladies Home Journal* 29 (March 1912): 11, 71–73.

8. Vassar catalog, quoted in Margery A. Bulger, "American Sportswomen of the 19th Century," *Journal of Popular Culture* 16, no. 2 (1981): 11; Alice

Katharine Fallows, "Athletics for College Girls," *Century* 66, no. 1 (May 1903): 61; Sophia Foster Richardson, "Tendencies in Athletics for Women in Colleges and Universities," *Popular Science Monthly* 50 (February 1897): 519; Winifred Ayres quoted in Karen Kenney, "The Realm of Sports and the Athletic Woman: 1850–1900," in *Her Story in Sport*, ed. Reet Howell (West Point: Leisure Press, 1982), p. 109; Harriet Isabel Ballantine, "Out-of-Door Sports for College Women," *American Physical Education Review* 3 (March 1898): 42; Harriet Isabel Ballantine, "The Value of Athletics to College Girls," *American Physical Education Review* 6, no. 2 (June 1901): 151–53.

9. Ellen W. Gerber, "Chronicle of Participation," in Ellen W. Gerber et al., *The American Woman in Sport* (Lexington, Mass.: Addison-Wesley, 1974), p. 102.

10. Margaret Bisland, "Rowing as a Recreation for Women," *Outing* 14 (September 1889): 423; Bisland, "Bowling for Women," *Outing* 16 (April 1890): 36; Christine Terhune Herrick, "Women in Athletics: The Athletic Girl Not Unfeminine," *Outing* 40 (September 1902): 719; Elizabeth Dryden, "How Athletics May Develop Style in Women," *Outing* 42 (July 1903): 412–18.

11. Robert Dunn, "The Country Club," *Outing* 47 (November 1905): 160–73.

12. Elizabeth Cynthia Barney, "The American Sportswoman," *Fortnightly Review* 52 (August 1894): 263–67; Donald J. Mrozek, *Sport and American Mentality, 1880–1910* (Knoxville: University of Tennessee Press, 1983), p. 116.

13. John A. Lucas and Ronald A. Smith, *Saga of American Sport* (Philadelphia: Lea and Febiger, 1978), pp. 158–62.

14. Jennifer A. Hargreaves, "Playing Like Gentlemen While Behaving Like Ladies," *British Journal of Sport History* 2, no. 1 (May 1985): 43.

15. Patricia Vertinsky, "God, Science and the Market Place," *Canadian Journal of History of Sport* 17, no. 1 (May 1986): 39.

16. Frank R. Rogers, "Olympics for Girls?" *School and Society* 30 (August 1929): 194.

17. Judy Jensen, "Women's Collegiate Athletics," *Arena Review* 3, no. 2 (May 1979): 15; Alice A. Sefton, *The Women's Division National Amateur Athletic Federation* (Palo Alto, Cal.: Stanford University Press, 1941), pp. 8, 82–84; Agnes Wayman quoted in Ellen W. Gerber, "The Controlled Development of Collegiate Sports for Women, 1923–1936," *Journal of Sport History* 2, no. 1 (Spring 1975): 20.

18. Gerber, "Chronicle of Participation," p. 75.

19. Grace Lichtenstein, *A Long Way, Baby* (New York: Morrow, 1979), p. 24.

20. Kent Hannon, "Too Far, Too Fast," *Sports Illustrated* 48 (March 20, 1978): 38.

21. Mary A. Boutilier and Lucinda SanGiovanni, *The Sporting Woman* (Champaign, Ill.: Human Kinetics, 1983), pp. 187, 192, 197–98; Barbara McDermott, "Handle at Your Own Risk," *Sports Illustrated* 63 (November 11, 1985): 54.

22. Janice Kaplan, *Women and Sports* (New York: Viking, 1979), p. 6; for positive views, see Cyd Atkins, Claire Morse, and Richard Zweigenhaft, "The Stereotype and Recognition of Female Athletes," *Journal of Psychology* 100 (1978): 27–31; Elden E. Snyder and Elmer Spreitzer, "Change and Variation in the Social Acceptance of Female Participation in Sports," *Journal of Sport Behavior* 6, no. 1 (March 1983): 3–8; J. Anthrop and Maria T. Allison, "Role Conflict and High School Female Athletes," *Research Quarterly* 54, no. 2 (1974): 104–11; Maria T. Allison and Beverly Butler, "Role Conflict and the Elite Female Athlete," *International Review of Sport Sociology* 19, no. 2 (1984): 157–66; for the contrary view, see Gaylene P. Douctre, Glenna A. Harris, and Kathryn E. Watson, "An Analysis of the Self-Image Differences of Male and Female Athletes," *Journal of Sport Behavior* 6, no. 2 (July 1983): 77–83.

23. On body image, see Elden E. Snyder and Joseph E. Kivlin, "Women Athletes and Aspects of Psychological Well-Being and Body Image," *Research Quarterly* 46 (May 1975): 191–99; Linda Ho and Jon E. Walker, "Female Athletes and NonAthletes: Similarities and Differences in Self Perception," *Journal of Sport Behavior* 5, no. 1 (March 1982): 12–27; George H. Sage and Sheryl Loudermilk, "The Female Athlete and Role Conflict," *Research Quarterly* 50 (March 1979): 88–96; Jane Frederick quoted in Kaplan, *Women and Sports*, p. 77; Robert C. Woodford and Wilbur J. Scott, "Attitudes toward the Participation of Women in Intercollegiate Sports," *Studies in the Sociology of Sport*, ed. Aidan O. Dunleavy et al. (Fort Worth: Texas Christian University Press, 1982), p. 209; Howard L. Nixon, Philip J. Maresca, and Marcy A. Silverman, "Sex Differences in College Students' Acceptance of Females in Sport," *Adolescence* 14 (1979): 755–64.

24. Boutilier and SanGiovanni, *The Sporting Woman*, p. 217.

25. Chris Evert Lloyd quoted in Lichtenstein, *A Long Way*, p. 88.

26. John Clark FitzGerald quoted in Bil Gilbert and Nancy Williamson, "Sport Is Unfair to Women," *Sports Illustrated* 38 (May 28, 1973): 95.

27. Walter Byers quoted in Linda Jean Carpenter, "The Impact of Title IX on Women's Intercollegiate Sports," in *Government and Sport*, ed. Arthur T. Johnson and James H. Frey (Totowa, N.J.: Rowman and Allanheld, 1985), p. 63.

28. Jim Sheehan quoted in Anita Verschoth, "She's His Fair Lady," *Sports*

Illustrated 50 (February 26, 1979): 35; Dan Magill quoted in Bil Gilbert and Nancy Williamson, "Programmed to Be Losers," *Sports Illustrated* 38 (June 11, 1973): 62.

29. Jane English, "Sex Equality in Sports," *Philosophy and Public Affairs* 7, no. 3 (Spring 1978): 275, 277.

30. Jackie Hudson, "Physical Parameters . . . ," in *Women and Sport*, ed. Carole A. Oglesby (Philadelphia: Lea and Febiger, 1978), pp. 19–57; Ann Crittenden Scott, "Closing the Muscle Gap," *Ms*. 3 (September 1974): 49–50, 54, 89; E. A. E. Ferris, "Attitudes to Women in Sport," in *The Female Athlete*, ed. J. Borms, M. Hebbelinck, and A. Venerando (Basel: Karger, 1981), pp. 12–29.

CHAPTER 11

1. R. J. Ross, M. Cole, and J. S. Thompson, "Boxers—Computed Tomography, EEG, and Neurological Evaluation," *Journal of the American Medical Association* 249 (January 14, 1983): 211–13; "Council on Scientific Affairs Report," ibid., pp. 254–57; see also Robert J. McCunney and Pearl K. Russo, "Brain Injuries in Boxers," *Physician and Sports Medicine* 12 (May 1984): 53–64.

2. Jerry Kramer, *Instant Replay* (New York: World Publishing, 1968), p. 24; Jack Tatum quoted in Robert L. Simon, *Sports and Social Values* (Englewood Cliffs, N.J.: Prentice-Hall, 1985), p. 53.

3. Peter Gent, *North Dallas Forty* (New York: William Morrow, 1973), pp. 43–44, 140.

4. John Underwood, *The Death of an American Game* (Boston: Little, Brown, 1979), pp. 95–97; John Underwood, "Just an Awful Toll," *Sports Illustrated* 63 (August 12, 1985): 49; Paul Zimmerman, "The Agony Must End," *Sports Illustrated* 65 (November 10, 1986): 17; Jay Malkoff quoted in William Nack, "Playing Hurt—the Doctors' Dilemma," *Sports Illustrated* 50 (June 11, 1979): 36.

5. Steve Sidwell and Joe Paterno quoted in Underwood, *Death of an American Game*, p. 114.

6. Helmut Acker, "Im Sog der Chemie," in *Rekorde aus der Retorte*, ed. Helmut Acker (Stuttgart: Deutsche Verlags-Anstalt, 1972), pp. 7–13; Ludwig Prokop, "Zur Geschichte des Dopings," ibid., pp. 22–30; Tom Donohoe and Neil Johnson, *Foul Play: Drug Abuse in Sports* (Oxford: Basil Blackwell, 1986), pp. 3–9.

7. Craig Neff, "Caracas: Scandal and Warning," *Sports Illustrated* 58 (September 5, 1983): 18–23.

8. Thompson quoted in Terry Todd, "Anabolic Steroids," *Journal of Sport History* 14, no. 1 (Spring 1987): 88.

9. Finnish champion,quoted in Tom Donohoe and Neil Johnson, *Foul Play*, p. 107.

10. Alan M. Klein, "Pumping Irony," *Sociology of Sport Journal* 3, no. 2 (June 1986): 122–23.

11. Ibid., p. 124.

12. Donohoe and Johnson, *Foul Play*, pp. 94–95; Gent, *North Dallas Forty*, p. 252.

13. Arnold J. Mandell, *The Nightmare Season* (New York: Random House, 1976), pp. 195–98; Underwood, *Death of an American Game*, pp. 76, 78.

14. David Meggyesy, *Out of Their League* (Berkeley, Calif.: Ramparts, 1970), p. 83; Nack, "Playing Hurt," p. 36.

15. Don Reese and John Underwood, "I'm Not Worth a Damn," *Sports Illustrated* 56 (June 14, 1982) 66–82; John Underwood, *Spoiled Sport* (Boston: Little, Brown, 1984), pp. 26–35. Jerry Kirshenbaum, "Scorecard: The Painful, Essential Process of Getting Don Reese's Message," *Sports Illustrated* 57 (July 5, 1982): 13, 16.

16. Roger Jackson, "For the Record," *Sports Illustrated* 65 (August 11, 1986): 77.

17. Craig Neff and Bruce Selcraig, "One Shock Wave after Another," *Sports Illustrated* 65 (November 10, 1986): 76–92.

18. Gary McLain, "A Bad Trip," *Sports Illustrated* 66 (March 26, 1987), quoted from front cover.

19. Ibid., pp. 48, 50.

20. *New York Times*, August 30, 1987.

CHAPTER 12

1. John J. MacAloon and Mihaly Csikszentmihalyi, "Deep Play and the Flow Experience in Rock Climbing," in Mihaly Csikszentmihalyi's *Beyond Boredom and Anxiety* (San Francisco: Jossey-Bass, 1975), p. 362.

2. Charles Rosen, "Now, Voyager," *New York Review of Books* 33, no. 17 (November 6, 1985): 58.

3. Aloys Dreyer and Ernst Enzensperger, "Geschichte der Touristik und Alpinistik," *Geschichte des Sports*, ed. G. A. E. Bogeng (Leipzig: E. A. Seemann, 1926), pp. 238–84.

4. Robert D. Bratton, George Kinnear, Gary Koroluk, "Why Man Climbs Mountains," *International Review of Sport Sociology* 14, no. 2 (1979): 30;

Richard G. Mitchell, *Mountain Experience* (Chicago: University of Chicago Press, 1983), p. 12; George Leonard, *The Ultimate Athlete* (New York: Avon Books, 1977), p. 243; Showell Styles quoted in Mitchell, p. 155; Ulrich Aufmuth, "Risikosport und Identitaetsproblematik," *Sportwissenschaft* 13, no. 3 (1983): 255.

5. Mitchell, *Mountain Experience*, pp. 16, 24, 90; Steve Roper quoted ibid., p. 7.

6. Lawrence C. Hamilton, "The Changing Face of American Mountaineering," *Review of Sport and Leisure* 6, no. 1 (Summer 1981): 20–22; Mitchell, *The Mountain Experience*, p. 185.

7. Eugen Herrigel, *Zen in der Kunst des Bogenschiessens* (Tübingen: Otto-Wilhelm Barth, 1975), pp. 12, 77.

8. Leonard, *The Ultimate Athlete*, pp. 62, 266, 283.

9. Ulrike Prokop, *Soziologie der Olympischen Spiele* (Munich: Hanser Verlag, 1971), p. 21; Jean-Marie Brohm, "Sociologie politique du sport," *Sport, culture et répression* (Paris: François Maspero, 1972), p. 23.

10. For my criticisms, see Allen Guttmann, *From Ritual to Record* (New York: Columbia University Press, 1978), pp. 69–89, and my introduction to Bero Rigauer, *Sport and Work* (New York: Columbia University Press, 1981), pp. vii–xxxiv.

11. Paul Hoch, *Rip Off the Big Game* (Garden City, N.Y.: Doubleday-Anchor, 1972), p. 202.

Bibliographical Essay

Fifteen years ago, when I began to do intensive research in sports studies, I encountered numerous well-founded laments to the effect that little had been accomplished in this neglected field. Today scholars are liable to be overwhelmed by the avalanche of published scholarship. What follows is highly selective. To keep this essay within reasonable bounds, I have omitted unpublished dissertations, mentioned only the most important articles, and concentrated on monographs. For a book-length bibliography, the reader should consult Robert J. Higgs, *Sports: A Reference Guide* (Westport, Conn.: Greenwood Press, 1982).

Theoretical frameworks for the study of sports as an aspect of social and cultural history can be found in Allen Guttmann, *From Ritual to Record: The Nature of Modern Sport* (New York: Columbia University Press, 1978); Richard D. Mandell, *Sport: A Cultural History* (New York: Columbia University Press, 1984); and Richard Gruneau, *Class, Sports, and Social Development* (Amherst: University of Massachusetts Press, 1983). Gruneau's work, influenced by the Marxist tradition, offers an avowedly materialist interpretation of sports history. Mandell and I have both been influenced by the brilliant and prolific German scholar Henning Eichberg. Of Eichberg's books, none of which, unfortunately, has been translated into English, the most generally relevant are *Der Weg des Sports in die industrielle Zivilisation* (Baden-Baden: Nomos Verlag, 1973) and *Spannung, Leistung, Geschwindigkeit* (Stuttgart: Klett-Cotta, 1978). Eichberg's books draw upon the work of Norbert Elias and Eric Dunning, whose important theoretical essays on sports have been collected as *Quest for Excitement* (Oxford: Basil Blackwell, 1986). Another important book is Jacques Ullmann's *De la Gymnastique grec aux sports modernes*, 2d ed. (Paris: Vrin, 1971). All of these works offer paradigms with which to describe and account for the transformation from premodern to modern forms of sport. Two good surveys of various approaches to sports history are Benjamin G. Rader, "Modern Sports: In Search of Interpretations," *Journal of Social History* 13 (Winter 1979): 307–21; and Nancy L. Struna, "In 'Glorious Disarray': The Literature of American Sports History," *Research Quarterly* 56, no. 2 (1985): 151–60.

There are at least a dozen reasonably comprehensive general histories of American sports, some good, some bad. In *America's Sporting Heritage, 1850–1950* (Lexington, Mass.: Addison-Wesley, 1974), John R. Betts sought more or less successfully to locate sports within the historical context. Since Betts died before the book was completed, it contains a plethora of unsifted data, but the book is well worth the effort it takes to read it. Among more recent efforts, the most useful are John Lucas and Ronald A. Smith, *The Saga of American Sports* (Philadelphia: Lea and Febiger, 1978); Betty Spears and Richard Swanson, *A History of Sport and Physical Activity in the United States* (Dubuque, Iowa: William C. Brown, 1978); Paula Welch and Harold A. Lerch, *History of American Physical Education and Sport* (Springfield, Ill.: Charles C. Thomas, 1981); Benjamin Rader, *American Sports* (Englewood Cliffs, N.J.: Prentice-Hall, 1983). *The American Sporting Experience*, ed. by Steven A. Riess (West Point, N.Y.: Leisure Press, 1984), is an excellent collection of primary and secondary sources. Although it is less comprehensive, *Sport in America*, ed. by Donald Spivey (Westport, Conn.: Greenwood Press, 1985), also has some good chapters. Its two-page bibliographical essay is inaccurate and unreliable. Articles on American sports appear regularly in the *Canadian Journal of History of Sport* and the *Journal of Sport History*. The latter also publishes abstracts of past and present articles appearing in other journals.

On pre-Columbian sports, Stewart Culin's *Games of the North American Indians* (Washington, D.C.: U.S. Government Printing Office, 1907) remains the most comprehensive source. James Mooney's classic 1890 essay on Cherokee stickball is reprinted in Culin and also in Janet C. Harris and Roberta J. Park, eds., *Play, Games, and Sports in Cultural Contexts* (Champaign, Ill.: Human Kinetics, 1983), an anthology that includes a number of important anthropological essays. The anthropological approach, which has obvious advantages for the study of sports in preliterate cultures, is also well represented in Kendall Blanchard and Alyce Cheska, *The Anthropology of Sport* (South Hadley, Mass.: Bergin and Garvey, 1985). Kendall Blanchard's *The Mississippi Choctaws at Play* (Urbana: University of Illinois Press, 1981) and Robert Gerald Glassford's *Application of a Theory of Games to the Transitional Eskimo Culture* (New York: Arno Press, 1976) are extensive and sophisticated anthropological analyses of cultures in transition from premodern to modern sports. Elizabeth Atwood Lawrence's anthropological study, *Rodeo* (Knoxville: University of Tennessee Press, 1982), is very good; Kristine Fredrickson's history of the sport, *American Rodeo* (College Station: Texas A and M University Press, 1985), is not.

On the immediate English background of American colonial sport, Dennis Brailsford's *Sport and Society: Elizabeth to Anne* (London: Routledge and Kegan Paul, 1969) and Robert W. Malcolmson's *Popular Recreations in English Society: 1700–1850* (Cambridge: Cambridge University Press, 1973) are still standard works. Aside from Nancy L. Struna's "Puritans and Sport,"

Journal of Sport History 4, no. 1 (Spring 1977): 1–33, the best work on the sports and other recreations of the American Puritans has been done by the German scholar Hans Peter Wagner, who wisely took American monolingualism to heart and published in English. His essays in various journals were incorporated in *Puritan Attitudes toward Recreation in Early Seventeenth-Century New England* (Frankfurt: Peter Lang, 1982).

One of the few essays to discuss sports in the "middle colonies" is J. Thomas Jable's "Pennsylvania's Blue Laws: A Quaker Experiment in the Suppression of Sport and Amusements, 1682–1740," *Journal of Sport History* 1, no. 2 (November 1974): 107–21.

The sports of the colonial and antebellum South have received more attention. Jane Carson's *Colonial Virginians at Play* (Charlottesville: University of Virginia Press, 1965) is a useful chronicle. T. H. Breen's "Horses and Gentlemen: The Cult of Gambling among the Gentry of Virginia," *William and Mary Quarterly* 34, no. 2 (April 1977): 239–57, attempts to do for Virginia what Clifford Geertz did for Bali in his famous essay, "Deep Play: Notes on the Balinese Cockfight." The section on horse races and cockfights in Rhys Isaac's *The Transformation of Virginia, 1740–1790* (Chapel Hill: University of North Carolina Press, 1982) is also theoretically important. For the Chesapeake Bay area, the best study is Nancy L. Struna's "The Formalizing of Sport and the Formation of an Elite: The Chesapeake Gentry, 1650–1720," *Journal of Sport History* 13, no. 3 (Winter 1986): 212–34. Sports are rarely mentioned, but some information on the recreations of the slaves is to be found in David K. Wiggins, "Good Times on the Old Plantation: Popular Recreations of the Black Slaves in the Antebellum South, 1810–60," *Journal of Sport History* 4, no. 3 (Fall 1977): 260–84. Although it emphasizes fights in earnest rather than sports, a recent essay by Elliott Gorn is especially stimulating: " 'Gouge and Bite, Pull Hair and Scratch': The Social Significance of Fighting in the Southern Backcountry," *American Historical Review* 90, no. 1 (February 1985): 18–43.

Articles appear regularly in *Pennsylvania History* and other state historical journals, but relatively few monographs have been written on early nineteenth-century sports in the North. The early chapters of Melvin Adelman's *A Sporting Time: New York City and the Rise of Modern Athletics, 1820–70* (Urbana: University of Illinois Press, 1986) are excellent. Lewis Fielding has published several good essays on northern and southern sports during the Civil War: "War and Trifles: Sport in the Shadows of Civil War Army Life," *Journal of Sport History* 4, no. 2 (Summer 1977); and "Sport: the Meter-Stick of the Civil War Soldier," *Canadian Journal for History of Sport* 9, no. 1 (May 1978): 1–18. For the later years of the nineteenth century, the situation is very different. Adelman's book continues to 1870.

Stephen A. Hardy's *How Boston Played: Sport, Recreation, and Community, 1865–1915* (Boston: Northeastern University Press, 1982) offers excellent social history (and includes unusually well-chosen illustrations). *Sport and American Mentality, 1889–1920* (Knoxville: University of Tennessee Press, 1983), by Donald Mrozek, is admirably wide in its scope and bold in its interpretations. For southern sports in the postwar period, there is Dale A. Somers, *The Rise of Sports in New Orleans, 1850–1900* (Baton Rouge: Louisiana State University Press, 1972).

Every sport has its historians, some professional, most amateur. When I include physical educators and journalists under the latter rubic, I do not mean to imply that their ventures into historiography have been entirely in vain. It is, however, a sad truth that most popular sports histories have been uncritical and inaccurate and that most sports biographies have been exercises in hagiography or public relations rather than scholarly assessments.

Like novelists and poets, professional and amateur historians alike have concentrated on "the national game." For antiquarian baseball buffs there is even a *Baseball Research Journal.* There are two excellent multivolume histories: Harold Seymour's *Baseball*, 2 vols. to date (New York: Oxford University Press, 1960), and David Quentin Voigt's *American Baseball*, the first of two volumes which were published by the University of Oklahoma Press (1966, 1970), with the third volume published by the Pennsylvania State University Press (1986). Leverett T. Smith, Jr., *The American Dream and the National Game* (Bowling Green: Bowling Green University Popular Press, 1975), written from an American Studies perspective, skillfully places baseball in its cultural context. The origins of the game are well told in Harold Peterson's *The Man Who Invented Baseball* (New York: Scribner's, 1973). Peter Levine's *A. G. Spaulding and the Rise of Baseball* (New York: Oxford University Press, 1985) is a model of the man-in-his-times approach. Steven A. Riess's *Touching Base: Professional Baseball and American Culture in the Progressive Era* (Westport, Conn.: Greenwood Press, 1980) is an another important work. Richard C. Crepeau, *Baseball: America's Diamond Mind, 1919–1941* (Orlando: University Presses of Florida, 1980), is useful although somewhat journalistic. Eliot Asinof's *Eight Men Out* (New York: Holt, Rinehart and Winston, 1963) is annoyingly undocumented, but it does provide the most detailed account of the Black Sox episode of 1919–20. The long-neglected Negro leagues are the subject of a number of recent books. Robert W. Peterson's *Only the Ball Was White* (Englewood Cliffs, N.J.: Prentice-Hall, 1970) lacks notes and bibliography but includes over one hundred pages of appendixes. Donn Rogosin's *Invisible Men* (New York: Atheneum, 1985) is another lively account without notes or bibliography. The drama of racial integration in baseball is splendidly recaptured in Jules Tygiel's *Baseball's Great Experiment* (New York: Oxford University Press, 1983). Rob Ruck's *Sandlot Seasons: Sport in Black Pittsburgh* (Urbana: University of Illinois Press, 1987) combines black and local sports history. There are numerous books devoted to seasons, teams, individual players, and—a tribute to the game's hold on the popular imagination—single games. Among them, Robert Creamer's *Babe* (New York: Simon and Schuster, 1974) and Marshall Smelser's *The Life That Ruth Built* (New York: Quadrangle Books, 1975) are among the most readable; both biographies are illustrated, and both lack documentation. Charles T. Alexander's *Ty Cobb* (New York: Oxford University Press, 1984) is a balanced work of scrupulous scholarship on a still controversial figure. Pat Jordan's autobiographical account of his brief minor-league career—*A False Spring* (New York: Dodd, Mead, 1974)—is a gem.

Baseball's plethora of statistics has attracted the economists, some of whom include economic history in their analyses. Paul M. Gregory's pioneering study, *The Baseball Player* (Washington, D.C.: Public Affairs Press, 1956), has been followed by Ralph Andreano's *No Joy in Mudville* (Cambridge, Mass.: Schenkman, 1965); Jesse W. Markham and Paul V. Teplitz, *Baseball Economics and Public Policy* (Lexington, Mass.: D. C. Heath, 1981); and James B. Dworkin, *Owners Versus Players: Baseball and Collective Bargaining* (Boston: Auburn House, 1981). Paul D. Staudohar's *The Sports Industry and Collective Bargaining* (Ithaca, N.Y.: Cornell University Press, 1986) also discusses football, basketball, and hockey.

Fans of other sports have to make do with much sparser fare. Professional historians have shown little interest in basketball, but Neil D. Isaacs, a professor of English with an informed passion for sports studies, has written *All the Moves: A History of College Basketball* (Philadelphia: J. B. Lippincott, 1975). Pete Axthelm's *The City Game* (New York: Harper's Magazine Press, 1970) tells the story of New York basketball. David Halberstam's *The Breaks of the Game* (New York: Alfred A. Knopf, 1981) is a detailed account of a season with the Portland Trail Blazers. Charles Rosen's *Scandals of '51* (New York: Holt, Rinehart and Winston, 1978) goes into the sorry story of bribery in intercollegiate basketball. There is no good biography of James Naismith; Berenice Larson Webb's *The Basketball Man* (Lawrence: University Press of Kansas, 1973) is poorly done. There is no adequate history of the National Basketball Association. David Wolf's *Foul! The Connie Hawkins Story* (New York: Holt, Rinehart and Winston, 1971) is excellent journalism. Of the many as-told-to autobiographies, Bill Russell's *Go Up for Glory* (New York: Coward-McCann, 1966) may still be the best.

The situation in football scholarship is also rather grim. There is no satisfactory history of the game. There is a shelf of books on Notre Dame's legendary coach, Knute Rockne; Michael R. Steele's *Knute Rockne* (Westport, Conn.: Greenwood Press, 1983) is both biography and bibliographical guide. Of the journalism I have read, Roy Blount's book on the Pittsburgh Steelers, *About Three Bricks Shy of a Load* (Boston: Little, Brown, 1974), deserves mention. Several of the best autobiographies have been written by alienated players angry about the treatment they received in college, the National Football League, or both. Of these books, the best is probably Gary Shaw's *Meat on the Hoof* (New York: St. Martin's Press, 1972), an attack on University of Texas football under Darrell Royal. Less critical, and better written, is Michael Oriard's *The End of Autumn* (Garden City, N.Y.: Doubleday, 1982). *The Courting of Marcus Dupree* (Garden City, N.Y.: Doubleday, 1983), by Willie Morris, is a minor classic that sets the chase after a high school football star in the context of Mississippi politics and race relations. Edwin H. Cady's *The Big Game* (Knoxville: University of Tennessee Press, 1978) is a lyrical speculation about the meaning of intercollegiate football. *The Nightmare Season* (New York: Random House, 1976), by Arnold J. Mandell, is a physician's grim story of drug abuse in NFL football.

While many fine studies of British soccer exist, the American version of the game waits for a qualified historian. There are scores of biographies and ghost-written autobiographies of hockey players; none of the ones I have read deserves mention.

Boxing, which has long been a favorite sport of novelists and poets, has recently begun to attract scholarly attention. Two sociologists, S. Kerson Weinberg and Henry Arond, beat the historians to the punch with a historical study of ethnicity in boxing: "The Occupational Culture of the Boxer," *American Journal of Sociology* 57 (1952): 460–69. Although limited to the nineteenth century and the bare-knuckles version of the sport, Elliott J. Gorn's *The Manly Art* (Ithaca, N.Y.: Cornell University Press, 1986) is a fine example of sports history as social and cultural history. Steven A. Riess, "In the Ring and Out: Professional Boxing in New York, 1896–1920" (in Spivey's above-mentioned *Sport in America,* pp. 95–128) is also excellent. Jack Johnson's autobiography, *Jack Johnson—in the Ring—and Out* (Chicago: National Sports Publishing, 1927) is well written but not always reliable. The best of the numerous biographies is Randy Roberts, *Papa Jack* (New York: Free Press, 1983). The public reaction to the black heavyweight champions is well documented in Al-Tony Gilmore's *Bad Nigger!* (Port Washington, N.Y.: Kennikat Press, 1975) and in Frederic Cople Jaher's "White America Views Jack Johnson, Joe Louis, and Muhammad Ali" (in Spivey's above-mentioned book, pp. 145–92). *Jack Dempsey* (Baton Rouge: Louisiana State University Press, 1979), by Randy Roberts, is, to the best of my knowledge, the only first-rate biography of a white champion. Of numerous books about Joe Louis and Muhammad Ali; the least unsatisfactory are probably *Joe Louis: My Life* (New York: Harcourt Brace Jovanovich, 1978), written with Edna and Art Rust, Jr.; and Muhammad Ali, *The Greatest: My Own Story* (New York: Random House, 1975), written with Richard Durham.

As for the most important of the "minor sports," historians seem to have abandoned the field to the journalists. Popular histories like Herbert Warren Wind's *The Story of American Golf* (New York: Simon and Schuster, 1956) and Will Grimsley's *Tennis* (Englewood Cliffs, N.J.: Prentice-Hall, 1971) are many. Angela Lumpkin's *Women's Tennis* (Troy, N.Y.: Whitson, 1981) is an informative documentary history. Popular biographies like Frank Deford's *Big Bill Tilden* (New York: Simon and Schuster, 1976) and Dick Miller's *Triumphant Journey: The Saga of Bobbie Jones* (New York: Holt, Rinehart and Winston, 1980) abound. When they write (or, perhaps more accurately, tell) their autobiographies, golfers and tennis players, like their counterparts in baseball and football, often form a team with a journalist. A few books deviate from the generally dismal norm: Robert T. Jones, Jr., and O. B. Keeler, *Down the Fairway* (New York: Minton, Balch, 1927); Don Budge and Frank Deford, *Don Budge* (New York: Viking, 1969); Arthur Ashe and Frank Deford, *Arthur Ashe* (Boston: Houghton Mifflin, 1975); Billie Jean King and Kim Chapin, *Billie Jean* (New York: Harper and Row, 1974), Martina Navratilova and George Vecsey, *Martina* (New York: Alfred A. Knopf, 1983).

Track and field has never been among the most popular American sports and has not attracted many historians. John Cumming's *Runners and Walkers* (Chicago: Henry Regnery, 1981) has neither a bibliography nor notes nor much in the way of interpretation. Robert W. Wheeler's *Jim Thorpe*, rev. ed. (Norman: University of Oklahoma Press, 1979) is an advance over its many predecessors. Meticulous research and a sense of the historical context make William Baker's *Jesse Owens* (New York: Free Press, 1986) a milestone. The most famous female athlete of her day, Mildred "Babe" Didrikson Zaharias, did an as-told-to autobiography with Harry Paxton, *This Life I've Led* (New York: A. C. Barnes, 1955); she is also the subject of one of the better works of journalism, *"Whatta-Gal": The Babe Didrikson Story*, by William Oscar Johnson and Nancy P. Williamson (Boston: Little, Brown, 1977). Although she was never a champion runner, Linda Huey's *A Running Start* (New York: Quadrangle Books, 1976) is full of insights into role conflicts and racial tension.

Swimmers, divers, and rowers, like track-and-field athletes, have their quadrennial moment in the sun when the Olympics roll around. The rest of the time they perform in the shadow of the major team sports. Their autobiographies are relatively few. Among the more interesting are Don Schollander and Duke Savage, *Deep Water* (New York: Crown, 1971); and Diana Nyad, *Other Shores* (New York: Random House, 1978). In the wake of the 1972 Olympics, Sherman Chavoor, the man who coached Mark Spitz and a number of other champions, teamed with Bill Davidson to write *The Fifty-Meter Jungle* (New York: Coward, McCann, Geoghegan, 1973). Rowing's 1984 Olympic trials attracted the attention of David Halberstam; *The Amateurs* (New York: William Morrow, 1985) is journalism of the highest order.

The Olympic Games are, of course, an international rather than an American event. There is no history of American involvement, but most of the general histories written by Americans emphasize American achievements. Dick Schaap's continually revised *Illustrated History of the Olympics* (published by Knopf) is lively and reasonably accurate. Ellery H. Clarke's *Reminiscences of an Athlete* (Boston: Houghton Mifflin, 1911) is a fascinating memoir by a Bostonian who won both the high jump and the long jump at the first Olympic Games. Allen Guttmann's *The Games Must Go On* (New York: Columbia University Press, 1984) is a biography of International Olympic Committee president Avery Brundage and a study of the politics of the games.

Although modern technology has transformed sports in many ways, John Betts is one of the few historians to discuss the matter in detail (in the above-mentioned *America's Sporting Heritage*). Among articles on the subject are Gary Allan Tobin's "The Bicycle Boom of the 1890's," *Journal of Popular Culture* 7 (Spring 1974): 838–49; Robert Knight Barney's "Astronauts, Aerostats, and Aerostation: Sport, Pastime and Adventure Ballooning in the American West," *Journal of the West* 21, no. 1 (January 1983): 11–29; and Judith Davidson's "Sport and Modern Technology," *Journal of Popular Culture* 18, no. 4 (Spring 1985): 145–57. Benjamin Rader's *In Its Own Image* (New York: Free Press, 1984) is a good study of television's impact on American sports.

On the topic of children's sports in the United States, Bernard Mergen's excellent *Play and Playthings* (Westport, Conn.: Greenwood Press, 1982) is both history and reference guide. The two standard works on the playground movement are Cary Goodman's *Choosing Sides* (New York: Schocken Books, 1979) and Dominick Cavallo's *Muscles and Morals* (Philadelphia: University of Pennsylvania Press, 1981). Martin Ralbovsky's *Destiny's Darlings* (New York: Hawthorne Books, 1974) is an excellent study of what happened to a team of Little League champions. Most of the research devoted to children's sports has been in the form of psychological and sociological essays. A good sample of this work appears in *Joy and Sad-*

ness in Children's Sports, ed. Rainer Martens (Champaign, Ill.: Human Kinetics, 1978), and in *Psychological Perspectives in Youth Sports*, ed. Frank Smoll and Ronald E. Smith (Washington, D.C.: Hemisphere Publishing, 1978).

Most books on intercollegiate athletics are either (a) upbeat institutional histories written for alumni rather than for students of history or (b) scathing criticisms by journalists who are appalled at the corruption of big-time college sports. George Lynn Cross's *Presidents Can't Punt: The OU [Oklahoma University] Football Tradition* (Norman: University of Oklahoma Press, 1977) is a better-than-average example of the former genre; Joseph Durso's *The Sports Factory* (New York: Quadrangle Books, 1975) is an example of the latter. To a rather extraordinary degree, scholars have limited themselves to essays rather than to monographs. Two good examples are Guy Lewis's "Theodore Roosevelt's Role in the 1905 Football Controversy," *Research Quarterly* 40 (December 1969): 717–24; and Ronald A. Smith's "Harvard and Columbia and a Reconsideration of the 1905–06 Football Crisis," *Journal of Sport History* 8, no. 3 (Winter 1981): 5–19. There is some attention to history in two recent collections devoted to intercollegiate athletics: James H. Frey, ed., *The Governance of Intercollegiate Athletics* (West Point, N.Y.: Leisure Press, 1982); and Donald Chu, Jeffrey O. Segrave, and Beverly J. Becker, eds., *Sport and Higher Education* (Champaign, Ill.: Human Kinetics, 1985).

Work done on the history of black sports is surveyed in David K. Wiggins, "Clio and the Black Athlete in America," *Quest* 32, no. 2 (1980): 217–25. Wiggins has also written a good article on a once-famous black jockey: "Isaac Murphy: Black Hero in 19th Century American Sport, 1861–1896," *Canadian Journal of History of Sport* 10, no. 1 (May 1979): 15–32. In addition to the above-mentioned books on black baseball players and boxers, there are a number of general studies of the black athlete, but few are histories. What little history we have is mostly shoddy. The exceptional book by Egon W. Steinkamp is, unfortunately, available only in German: *Sport und Rasse: Der schwarze Sportler in den USA* (Ahrensburg: Ingrid Czwalina, 1976). Aside from Steinkamp, the best historical source remains the entry on sports in *The American Negro Reference Book*, ed. by John P. Davis (Englewood Cliffs, N.J.: Prentice-Hall, 1966), pp. 775–825.

The history of ethnic sport in America has been woefully neglected. The story of the German immigrants and their gymnastics clubs is well told in Horst Ueberhorst's untranslated *Turner unterm Sternenbanner* (Munich: Heinz Moos, 1978). Part of the story appears in Robert Knight Barney's "German Forty-Eighters and Turnvereine in the United States during the Ante-Bellum Period," *Canadian Journal of History of Sport* 13, no. 2 (December 1982): 62–79. Gary Ross Mormino's "The Playing Fields of St. Louis: Italian Immigrants and Sports, 1925–1941," *Journal of Sport History* 9, no. 2 (Summer 1982): 5–19, is excellent. Gerald Redmond's *The Caledonian Games in Nineteenth-Century America* (Cranbury, N.J.: Associated University Presses, 1971) is another exception to the generalization.

There is no monograph history of women's sports in the United States (nor, to the best of my knowledge, is there one for any European country). Although most of the early general histories of American sports omitted women's sports entirely or limited their coverage to a few sentences, all of the more recent monographs include at least a chapter on the female athlete. There is also an excellent "Chronicle of Participation" by Ellen W. Gerber in Ellen W. Gerber et al., *The American Woman in Sport* (Reading, Mass.: Addison-Wesley, 1974), pp. 1–176. *Her Story in Sport: A Historical Anthology of Women in Sports*, ed. by Reet Howell (West Point, N.Y.: Leisure Press, 1982), contains forty-two short essays, some reprinted and some original, some excellent and some wretched. Three of the twelve essays in *From "Fair Sex" to Feminism: Sport and the Socialization of Women in the Industrial and Post-Industrial Eras*, ed. J. A. Mangan and Roberta J. Park (London: Frank Cass, 1987) are concerned with American sport; all three are excellent. There is a good deal of history in Stephanie L. Twin's edited anthology, *Out of the Bleachers* (New York: McGraw-Hill, 1979). For a first-rate introduction to the sociological and pyschological issues raised by women's sports, one should begin with *The American Woman in Sport* and with Mary A. Boutilier and Lucinda SanGiovanni, *The Sporting Woman* (Champaign, Ill.: Human Kinetics, 1983). Both of these books contain good bibliographies. Collections of essays on women's sports are a growth industry. Almost invariably the focus is upon legal, economic, sociological, and psychological factors, rather than upon the history of women's sports. Among the better collections are *Women and Sport*, ed. Dorothy V. Harris (College Park: Pennsylvania State University Press, 1972), *Women and Sport*, ed. Carole A. Oglesby (Philadelphia: Lea and Febiger, 1978), and *Women, Philosophy, and Sport*, ed. Betsy C. Postow (Metuchen, N.J.: Scarecrow Press, 1983).

As the attentive reader must have noticed, the study of history cannot be isolated from a wider concern for the social sciences. If the sheer quantity of published work is an indicator, then American and European sports studies (as opposed to sports journalism) have been dominated, until recently, by social scientists rather than by historians. For American sports, I have found the following works to be especially useful: John F. Rooney, Jr., *A Geography of American Sport* (Reading, Mass.: Addison-Wesley, 1974); Donald W. Ball and John W. Loy, eds., *Sport and Social Order* (Reading,

Mass.: Addison-Wesley, 1975); John W. Loy, Barry D. McPherson, and Gerald Kenyon, *Sport and Social Systems* (Reading, Mass.: Addison-Wesley, 1978); Guenther R. F. Lueschen and George H. Sage, eds., *Handbook of Social Science of Sport* (Champaign, Ill.: Stipes Publishing, 1981).

Historians who agree that literature is also an important part of social and cultural history will want to read the major studies of sports as a theme in American literature: Wiley Lee Umphlett, *The Sporting Myth and the American Experience* (Lewisburg, Penn.: Bucknell University Press, 1975); Robert J. Higgs, *Laurel and Thorn: The Athlete in American Literature* (Lexington: University Press of Kentucky, 1981); Christian K. Messenger, *Sport and the Spirit of Play in American Fiction: Hawthorne to Faulkner* (New York: Columbia University Press, 1981); Michael V. Oriard, *Dreaming of Heroes: American Sports Fiction, 1868–1980* (Chicago: Nelson-Hall, 1982); and Hans Lobmeyer, *Die Darstellung des Sports in der amerikanischen Erzaehlliteratur des 20. Jahrhunderts* (Ahrensburg: Czwalina, 1983). Of these five works I have found Messenger's the most helpful.

Index

Index

Index